# CANDOR U
## *Class in Session*

Jimmy Dean Roth

TATE PUBLISHING, LLC

# DEDICATION

Certainly I am indebted to all of those people in my life who have taught and mentored me through the years, both knowingly and unknowingly. Many of those people are central characters in the stories in this book. However, three men stand out in my life as having an overriding impact on who I am today, and it is to those three men that I dedicate this work.

My father, Lester Roth, was my first mentor and remained my most loyal supporter and continuing mentor until his death in 2001. He instilled in me both the requirement and the passion to be ultimately fair and honorable in all I do. When I have failed in those endeavors, it has not been due to the lack of proper training from him.

My advisor at Iowa State University in the late 60s, Dr. Leon Charity, was my second great mentor. He helped me navigate through the uncharted waters of higher education and higher manhood. Without his knowing, Dr. Charity set the future direction of my life in both vocation and family as he was ultimately responsible for setting the stage for my post college career and, more importantly, for my first encounter with the beautiful woman who later became my wife.

Finally, my most constant encourager in my early years at Cargill, Harvey Marxhausen, was my third significant mentor. Harvey became like my second father and his camaraderie, compassion, and coaching moved me forward as both a manager and a man. Harvey showed me more about how to be a builder of people than anyone else in the industrial environment. I continue to this day to try to be like him.

To Dad, Dr. Charity, and Harvey, I owe more than I can ever repay. Only to the extent that I can help others in the ways they helped me, can I even begin to balance the ledger with these three men.

# ACKNOWLEDGEMENTS

I certainly want to acknowledge my family and all of those other persons to whom I owe gratitude for their life long support of me. Additionally, as I evaluate the particular circumstances and efforts of writing this book, I do believe that there are specific other acknowledgments that deserve to be made.

First, I must acknowledge Cargill, Incorporated, the organization for whom I worked for well over 30 years. The majority of the stories in this book (and therefore the learning experiences) came from my experiences at Cargill. They (Cargill) provided the stage upon which a large part of my life has been played. Without question, they provided me the opportunity to learn every day. Whenever I had to answer "Nothing!" to the question "What have you learned from the people you encountered today?" it was not for lack of the opportunity.

Second, my sister Lavonne Mullet has been my most constant evaluator and critic during the writing of the book. Moreover, Lavonne has always been the most natural "writer" in the family. As much as anything, her writing skills and works encouraged me to "give it a try." She has not tired of my relentless leaning on her for advice and coaching as this work has progressed.

Third, my high school English and Language Arts instructor (and friend), Roger Williams, spent many hours in doing the initial editing and general critiquing of the first draft of the completed manuscript. More importantly, Roger and his wife, Doris, encouraged me not to sell myself short and to put forth the effort required to get my book published.

Finally, I must thank the good folks at Tate Publishing for accepting my work and giving me the chance to touch other lives with it. In addition, they are wonderful Christian people with whom to work, and they make the publishing process one of delight.

# TABLE OF CONTENTS

*A Reader's Guide*

# A Reader's Guide

*Candor U, Class in Session* can be read in any number of ways. It is not a chronology, but to some extent, the chapters do build one on another. It can be read traditionally from front cover to back cover.

Moreover, since it is a collection of stories, any one specific story can be read individually. Each chapter is a series of several stories, often of diverse subjects, but which share a common theme. Thus any one chapter can also be read individually and the book set back down until the next reading.

As noted in the Prologue, the book is devoted to promoting the critical personal and corporate characteristic of integrity (with its component characteristics of honesty, transparency, fairness, compassion, honor, and selflessness) as being critical to success in life. Additionally, the book is designed to show how the applications of these characteristics can be used to direct one well in the administration of life and living. Accordingly, *Candor U, Class in Session* is loosely organized in that fashion. About one half relates more directly to the noted personal characteristics, and the other half relates more to applications in such areas as communication, utilization of resources, and the seizing of opportunities.

Although each individual chapter may cut across a wide array of these characteristics and applications, each one does revolve around a central theme and focus. The following table categorizes the chapters by theme type, so the reader may also want to focus on all of the chapters of similar theme. This may be particularly worthwhile after the first reading when one chooses to go back and revisit a particular theme.

## Fairness, Compassion, Understanding Others, and Building Others Up:

## Forthrightness & Transparency:

## Integrity, Honesty, & Honor:

## Communication:

## Utilization of Talents & Resources:

## Seizing Opportunity:

## Summary:

Irrespective of how one chooses to read **Candor U, Class in Session**, the messages remain the same. True success in life comes about through commitment to integrity, compassion, fairness, and those characteristics that naturally follow. Candid action is both the classroom and the proving ground for that success.

# FOREWORD

Chances are that in the last day you have had more than one opportunity to add to your knowledge about yourself as a person: your interests, values, motives, needs, wants, understanding, wisdom and/or relationships with others. Did you take the opportunity to learn from your experiences, or were you so focused on the forest that you missed the trees, so focused on the trees that you missed the forest, or missed both? An associate of mine, a professional speaker, shares this insight with his audiences . . . "If you want to know more, you have to notice more."

In **Candor U, Class in Session**, Jim Roth shares scores of his life's experiences with others, what he "noticed" and the lessons he learned from them. Among his experiences, you will find common themes, which are a part of Jim's character. They define the way he has lived and continues to live his life. Jim shares with you how his lifelong commitments to integrity, fairness, and putting people first lead to success, which he defines as achieving happiness and internal peace.

Throughout his book, you will discover Jim's deep, lifelong commitments to his grassroots spiritual and religious values that have helped him build relationships, make better decisions, and, when necessary, correct his errors. Jim is as open with you about describing his mistakes as he is about describing his successes.

Just as important, Jim captures the lessons to be learned from "regular folks" who turn out to be "extraordinary people" who are simply working in ordinary jobs and facing typical work situations—the kind of situations that occur all around you each day. In story after story about the experiences of and with these work-a-day people, he proves that you can benefit handsomely by taking note of what others around you are contributing and experiencing. It is the learning that results from these encounters that is so often missed. In addition, what often appears to be a mundane lesson is actually preparation for a much more important challenge to come later. The range of personal and business experiences Jim describes is so broad that you cannot help from identifying with many of them and gaining the kind of insight that leads to personal growth.

As a management consultant, I gained as much professionally as I did personally from reading Jim's book. I am a better person for having read it.

Jim's everyday business experiences further confirm several important management principles from among those in which I believe deeply. I take no credit for developing many of the principles. I feel fortunate to have had them shared with me or to have discovered their use by successful managers and executives. In turn, I have shared the principles with hundreds of managers and executives. In particular, three of those principles surface time and again in Jim's book:

- Help others get what they want, and you will get what you want.
- Spectacular performance is typically preceded by unspectacular preparation.
- The most successful companies and relationships run on HOT - Honesty, Openness and Trust.

If the above sparks an interest, read on! All of this and more are what you will discover reading Jim's book. I know you will enjoy the journey through Jim's learning experiences and will be richer for having read about the lessons he learned from those who have touched his life.

**Dr. Larry D. Baker,** Internationally recognized speaker, consultant, author and publisher in Time Management, Strategic Planning Performance Improvement. www.DrLarryBaker.com 800–458–6468 Larry@DrLarryBaker.com

# PROLOGUE

People are motivated by many things. Certainly self-indulgent things such as power, position, possessions (including money), passion (sex), and prestige are among those things. Of course, self-giving things like people and principle (integrity) are a couple more. Obviously, people judge success on the basis of achieving their goals according to their motivations.

I have always held the character traits associated with *principle,* primarily integrity as well as the associated traits of honesty, forthrightness, compassion, selflessness, fairness, and honor to be the keys to leading a successful life. When a life based on principle and love for people is coupled with the willingness to fully utilize one's talents and put forth a full measure of effort, one can be assured of living a successful and satisfying life. Success and satisfaction are not necessarily measured in dollars and worldly acclaim, but rather in personal fulfillment. I think many of us aspire to that kind of success and satisfaction, but how does one make it happen?

I once chanced to work with a gentleman who liked to reference *The Big Black Book* at Harvard. He and I would occasionally have conflicts about the correct approach to a specific managerial issue. Most of the time, the issues of disagreement came on pragmatic matters. I was (and am) a cause and effect person, and I tend to look first to find the cause. He was much more of an idealist and tended to believe it was *what you knew* rather than *what you did* that drove success.

He would often attempt to defend his position with reference to the book noted above. At some point in our discussion he would recount in a certain broken pattern, "At least . . . that . . . is . . . what it says . . . in the. . . . . *Big, Black Book* . . . at Harvard!!"

I do not know if there really is a *Big Black Book* at Harvard or if the Harvard professors teach from such a reference if one does in fact exist. In all honesty, I do not think whether or not such a book existed (or exists) was the real point of the discussion. Reference to the book was more reference to a particular perspective on where to learn and therefore find answers. Many people tend to believe the best source of answers is *what the elite thinkers think.* I have always believed the most important source is *what the successful doers do!* Elite thinkers can probably be found on the campus of Harvard. However, I believe *successful doers* are far more apt to be found in the everyday activities around us.

Our church pastor, Rev. Steve Toews, told of a teacher in seminary whose wife was in the final stages of cancer. This teacher was teaching and preaching about death (the story of Lazarus in Chapter 11 of the Gospel of John) at the same time he was dealing with the imminent (and eventual) death of his wife. Pastor Steve had a close relationship with this teacher and noted that he learned much more about death by "living around" this man and observing his performance during this visitation of death than he did through the man's preaching and teaching about death. As with Pastor Steve in this example of "education" regarding death, the impact of exposure, demonstration, and experience in moving persons along to an understanding and "education" of the principle of integrity and how that impacts performance is powerful. There are few effective formal education channels for this type of learning.

I count myself fortunate in that I had parents and a number of teachers, bosses, friends, and other role models whose everyday performance displayed these traits and characteristics and encouraged me to acquire them through word and action as I "lived around and among them." For those not so fortunate, where does one go to gain this understanding? Where does the "living among them" happen?

It happens in all of those places in everyday life where just that happens; everyday life. Those places where the actions take place in candid* fashion without any knowledge or expectation of a teaching or learning experience. Where performance is not staged and the characters are in effect all "caught in the process of unbiased and unreserved behavior." Unbiased everyday activity is therefore a sort of "Candor University" and all of those places we find ourselves in everyday life form the campus of that university. *Candor U, Class in Session* is a collection of those experiences we encounter in everyday life. Experiences where things like pragmatism and integrity and love motivate us to action and sustain us as well as places where dogmatism and the absence of integrity lead to performance that ultimately ends in failure.

The professors and teachers in all of our everyday "Candor U" experiences are similarly all those common people who teach and demonstrate the value of the above noted characteristics in everyday life and activity, most often without any teaching attempt on their part.

No one ever graduates from Candor U. Some of us rack up more credits by accepting the challenge to take as many of the courses and educational experiences as an open mind can accept. Some courses are relatively short and can be quickly mastered and applied like all the hard work lessons in Chapter 8: "Why Stationed by the Plow." Others like the Doug Brooks teachings of Chapter 2: "Walk in My Shoes" are life long efforts where we probably never do achieve mastery.

All of us are teachers and experienced leaders at Candor U., whether we want to be or not. That should be very humbling to each of us. Just as Dr. Leon Charity shaped more of my life than he (or I) ever thought possible (Chapter 4: "Miss Leichty et al"), we can never be certain how much our own performance may impact the life of another person, perhaps someone we may not even know.

Not every day on the campus of Candor U. is filled with wine and roses, and not every learning experience there starts out or even ends in euphoria. Many times it is former classmates who return to ease the burden or share the pain and in doing so create a new or reinforce an existing learning experience as with Jim Salmons in Chapter 31: "Three Million Dollar Handshake."

Many of the Candor U. learning experiences "hit us like a ton of bricks" and are fully understood at the point of first exposure as experienced with Dr. Larry Baker (Chapter 10: "Magic Penny"). Other experiences must be allowed to gestate within one's being for some time (perhaps years) before the light of knowledge illuminates. The real lessons from Eddie (Chapter 29: "Turn Me Loose") and John (Chapter 32: "The Face in the Mirror") did not register for decades.

Many lessons are hard hitting and intended not only to educate, but also to make an immediate impact as with Jerry Mitchell in Chapter 28: "Short Skirts and High Heels." Other lessons are much softer in tone as the many learning experiences with Joe Culbreath in Chapter 12: "The Perfect '10'." Yet, as can be experienced, a softer tone does not necessarily negate a high level of impact.

Lessons may also help reverse the conventional. We normally tend to value others and ourselves by "what we do and accomplish" rather than by "who we are." My grandchildren are most concerned that

I "am grandpa," and they could care less what my resume says. As can be observed in Chapter 30: "Souls for Sale", compromising who we are in the name of what we wish to accomplish is not the formula for real and long term success.

Individually and collectively, the stories included in *Candor U, Class in Session* and all the learning experiences at your own Candor U can improve the quality of your life. We never outgrow our need to learn and the best environment to learn is where we can observe performance and be involved in activities, which are conducted with "unreserved, honest and sincere expression" (candor as defined by Webster).

Please allow the stories and the characters in the stories in *Candor U, Class in Session* show you how to lead a more satisfying, successful, enjoyable, and even entertaining life.

* Note: Many of us associate the word candid with the Candid Camera television shows. Unfortunately, the definition of candid has become skewed from that perspective and often is associated with hidden or surprise. Candid actually means sincerely honest and free of bias. The *candid* camera is simply catching people in the act of being honest.

# Chapter 1
# The Sell-Out

My future brother-in-law and I had just completed another Sunday afternoon adventure, watching our beloved Chicago Bears' football team. Perhaps with the exception of Chicago Cubs' baseball fans, few persons in the world have been so tested for perseverance, tolerance, and loyalty over the years as Bears' fans.

It was the early fall of 1968 and I was completing my senior year in engineering at Iowa State University in Ames, Iowa. My sister, Joyce, and her future husband Don Sandersfeld had traveled to Ames to visit me on that particular September afternoon. Little did I realize the impact their seemingly unpretentious visit would have on the rest of my life.

As we discussed the relative futility of being a Bears' fan, Don commented, "We should go see a Bears' game in person sometime. Maybe it's less painful that way!"

"That's a great idea," I commented, "but there are way too many other long-suffering fans like us, and the Bears always sell out in Chicago. However, the Minnesota Vikings (still a relatively new expansion team at that time) never sell out. Let's go to Minneapolis and watch the Bears when they play there."

Don and Joyce liked the idea. Finding out the Bears and Vikings were scheduled for the following Sunday, we made our plans. Although Don was concerned about getting tickets in such a tight time frame, I again assured him the Vikings never sold out and we could easily get tickets at the gate. So plans were set; I would contact Linda (a young lady attending the University of Iowa in Iowa City, whom I had occasionally dated) to see if she would like to go with me. That succeeding, Linda and I would meet Don and Joyce early Sunday morning at Joyce's apartment in Williamsburg, Iowa, and we would get an early start for Minneapolis. Linda liked the idea, and we were all set.

The following Sunday everything started off just as planned. We arrived at The Met (the old Metropolitan Stadium in Bloomington,

Minnesota where the Vikings played) at 11:00 A.M. for the 1:30 P.M. kickoff. That was before the days of tailgate parties, so we were about the only car in the lot.

"Let's go get our tickets and then find something to eat," was my suggestion.

That's when the wheels started to come off our plan. We made a full lap around the stadium looking for an open ticket window with no success. Finally finding an attendant, we asked what time the ticket windows opened. His response caused our hearts to sink, "Oh, they won't be opening today, this game is sold out!"

While no one made any comments to me, I'm sure to this day three people were thinking that my lunch entree (crow pie) had just been served. "What do we do now?" Don queried.

"We need to learn the art of getting scalped, and do it quickly!" I responded. And that we did.

For the next two and one half hours we ran from bus to bus in the charter bus area, to the scalp area at the gate, to the buses, to the Thunderbird Motel, to the buses, and back to the scalp area. We rushed off to wherever someone mentioned spare tickets may exist. We had 20 dollar bills (ticket price was $5.00 per seat) stuck in our pockets, our ears, between our fingers, wherever and whatever the "professional scalpees" told us to do to attract the attention of the scalpers with tickets.

Our actions were so incredibly overt, I remain amazed yet today that if scalping is illegal or even unwanted there is probably nothing on earth that could be more easily seen and identified. One can only surmise the purpose is to get all the tickets to an event sold, and if there are entrepreneurs who choose to "invest" in extra tickets in the hope of later profit, then hey, we operate in a capitalist society!

At about 1:20 P.M. we were just about ready to admit defeat (a tough task for me) when we were approached by a young boy. He asked if we were looking for tickets. Were we looking for tickets! Gosh, is a football oblong? Why do we have these $20 bills hanging from all parts of our bodies and apparel? Gathering myself, I responded, "Yes, we are. Do you have any?"

The boy showed us two tickets he had. We negotiated price for a short period of time and settled on $15 for the two tickets (without question well below the market). It was obvious this kid did not understand the market demand for his product, and he was certainly no relation to the two young boys we would encounter only a few minutes later. We consummated the deal and walked off with the two coveted tickets.

We debated among ourselves how we could get 4 people in on two tickets. This debate covered both the ethical and the physically possible. Being relatively naïve, we got by the ethical question fairly quickly reasoning we would have been more than happy to buy two more tickets if the system would have let us. Unfortunately, ethics sometimes get reduced to expediency. With the ethical question thus handled, we moved to the physically possible and decided two of us could go in and one return with both tickets and bring another in and then repeat the step again or for two of us to go through and then pass the tickets back through the chain link fence to the other two. Both of these plans potentially failing (We had trouble believing the masses had not figured this out long before, and conversely the ruling class had not seen the actions of the proletariat and taken sufficient steps to thwart them.), our backup plan was Linda and I would go in for the first half and come back out at half-time and give the tickets to Don and Joyce. I had won the coin toss with Don to gain the right to go in first as we both assumed that midway through the third quarter the gates would be opened and "the first half couple" could go back in.

With both primary and backup plans in place, Linda and I walked through the gate. As we passed the ticket taker, Linda inquired about returning to the car to get a blanket (a thinly disguised question to find out the procedure for exit and re-entry). The ticket taker told us to go down to the press gate to exit. There they would punch a specific character in her ticket that they would then check for on re-entry and then punch a second character in the ticket to confirm reentry. Alas, the ruling class had developed just the thwarting plan we had feared.

After passing through the gate, we sadly walked over to the fence area where Don and Joyce were waiting and informed them of the bad news. About that time a young boy (I would guess his age at 11 or 12) walked up to me and asked, "Are you trying to figure out a way to get your friends into the stadium?"

Assuming he was in the same boat and hoping to learn something from someone who obviously appeared to be knowledgeable and savvy, I turned to him and said, "Yes, but there is not any way to do it!"

"Oh, yes there is!" he replied. "When you exit the stadium through the press gate, they punch a T in your ticket. I have a friend who can carve that T in to look just like the official punch mark. For two bucks a ticket I'll get him to do that. Then you just hand the tickets through the fence to your friends and they can go down to the press gate and walk right in."

I was a bit skeptical so I offered him $1.50 per ticket payable upon entry of Don and Joyce. The young man called out, "Hey, Harvey, I got a guy here who will pay us three bucks for two tickets. Do we want to take it?"

At that point another young man also about 11 or 12 (Harvey, I presume) stepped out from behind a column and grunted, "Sure, we'll do that." I handed the two tickets to the first young man who took them to Harvey. Harvey walked down the ramp until the ledge was about waist high then took out his razor and began to carve. In a few seconds he returned and handed me the tickets, now complete with a much coveted exit T. I walked over to the fence and handed them through to a puzzled Don and Joyce with the instructions to just go down to the press gate and enter.

Harvey, his front man, Linda and I walked down to the press gate. As we walked down, Harvey began to talk to us about his enterprise. He said this was the first game they had worked at the Met that had been sold out early and they were having a fairly decent day this Sunday as there was a relatively large and willing group of customers. However, what he was really looking forward to was a couple of weeks down the road when the Green Bay Packers came to town. "That game has already been sold out for weeks," he said. "We are going to make a killing!!!"

About that time Don and Joyce came through the press gate just as promised. I paid Harvey the $3.00 as I promised, and we each went our own way happy (at least we were happy). I have no idea where Harvey and his salesman friend are today, but I would be highly surprised if they are not multi-millionaires somewhere. I often joke with people that the Mall of America that now occupies the site of the old Met is likely owned by Harvey and his friend. Perhaps it is no joke!

At the young age of 11 or 12 and without the aid of Deming or

Crosby or Tom Peters or a host of other business "gurus," it appeared Harvey and his friend already had it pretty well figured out. Find a customer need, plan a sound marketing strategy, produce a quality product, and guarantee performance.

I often wonder today where has all of the common sense and natural savvy for those things gone. We often so cloud the issue with the thinking and techniques forwarded by various consulting gurus, we loose both the ability and the creativity to move to quick action to capture the opportunity of the minute (of even sometimes of the decade).

That September day in 1968 was a fun and memorable day. Don and I had the opportunity to see a couple of our heroes, Dick Butkus and Gayle Sayers. Obviously Joyce and Linda had that same opportunity, although they probably do not remember the day in the same light as Don and I. To this day I get a kick out of recounting that story. My children love to hear it and my wife tolerates it. She reasons while I'm telling it, I'm not telling one about one of my other shenanigans about how to beat the system and/or the establishment. She apparently assumes (or hopes) certain traits are learned and not inherited. She hopes to spare our children from the temptation to follow in their father's high school and college age footsteps.

For all of the events of that day, I had no idea of what a profound effect that day would have on the rest of my life. Once I was back in Ames, Iowa and had recounted the story to all of my friends, I dismissed it from my mind. However, it came back vividly a few weeks later as I was checking out the College of Engineering recruiter's schedule for the following week. Listed as one of the companies coming to campus was Cargill Incorporated, a Minneapolis based multi-national agricultural marketing and processing company.

I had virtually no knowledge of who this company was and likely might have passed right by them, but I was quickly drawn to their Minneapolis base. Remembering the fun I had at the Bears' game with the Vikings in Minneapolis, I immediately signed up on the interview sheet, reasoning I could likely get by the campus interview and secure a trip to Minneapolis. I further reasoned I could likely schedule that largely at my convenience and therefore pick a Monday following another Viking football game. The final piece of this puzzle would be I would fly to Minneapolis on Sunday morning, attend the Viking game, and then complete the Cargill corporate interview on Monday. This time, however, I would order my ticket in advance.

Not too surprising to me, that is just the way things panned out. Perhaps I should have been alert of things to come as I was thoroughly impressed with the two Cargill managers who interviewed me on the ISU campus, including Hershel Austin who was one of the facility operating managers. Only a short time later, "Hersh" would be my first mentor as I spent most of the first week of my career at Cargill with him at the soybean processing facility he managed at Port Cargill, just outside of Minneapolis. At any rate, when I received my invitation to come to Minneapolis for further interviews, I went right to the NFL schedule. The Vikings played the Los Angeles Rams on December 1, so I responded to Cargill I would like to schedule my visit to their offices on Monday, December 2.

They confirmed December 2 would be fine and suggested I plan to arrive in Minneapolis sometime on Sunday. Alas, my plan was working to perfection. I immediately sent for a ticket to the December 1 game. My gut told me to purchase two extra tickets (only a ten dollar investment) and scalp them when I got to the game. However, my financial manager (my wallet) reminded me that I was a college student and that what limited resources I had were best invested in books and tuition, so I dismissed my gut from the decision making process.

December 1 arrived and I winged my way to Minneapolis early in the morning. I had never flown before, so I enjoyed that experience even though it was on a Braniff flight. In years to come, Braniff would fall from my favor and I would refuse to fly with them, but for this day, they provided me with one more new life experience. It was a nice sunny flight as we were flying above the clouds. However, as we came down through the clouds in Minneapolis, it was a cold snowy day.

As I rode in the taxi from the airport to the Met, I was happy I had not followed my gut and purchased those extra tickets. The taxi pulled up to within about 30 feet of the gate into the stadium. I paid the $2 cab fare and took the short walk to the gate. To my amazement and chagrin, in that short walk, I was approached by 4 people who asked if I had extra tickets for sale. What a missed opportunity! I learned one of life's lessons and that was: "Always keep your gut in the decision making process!"

The Rams proceeded to disassemble the Vikings 31 - 3. I was a big football fan, but not particularly a fan of either the Vikings or the Rams. As such, the final score did not really matter. Once again I had a good time (even in the snow). I returned to the airport, picked up my suitcase, and took the downtown limousine to the North Star Inn where I had been instructed to stay.

The details of the events of the next day are not critically important other than to say the people to whom I talked that day, E.H. Gustafson, Dick Fulmer, Bob Woodward, Ray Pound, and Pete McVay were some of the most impressive and forthright people with whom I have had the pleasure of speaking. A couple of the secretaries, Betty Gill and Gen Kulusa helped get me from place to place efficiently and without worry. Further, Cargill was a food company (one of my preferences) and although rather large (for the times), it appeared the divisions and plants operated quite autonomously.

I certainly had a take away message from the events of the day! Cargill was the kind of company and these were the kind of people for whom I wanted to work! What had started out for me as a ball game ticket—and maybe a bit of a throw away interview—had turned into what I hoped could possibly be a long-term relationship. I went from being the party in control of this journey to being the party who was vulnerable. I certainly wanted a job offer.

A few days after my Minneapolis journey, I did receive an employment offer from Cargill to work in their soybean processing division. A few days later, I received a handwritten letter from Pete McVay, one of the top ranking Cargill officers with whom I had spoken. Mr. McVay indicated he enjoyed visiting with me, I was the kind of person Cargill was seeking, he felt Cargill was the type of company with which I could be happy, and he sincerely hoped I would give Cargill serious consideration.

I knew at the time Mr. McVay was a very influential person in the organization, but it was not until later I understood just how influential he really was. To this day, I mark it as an honor I received that hand written note. I also mark it unfortunate Cargill or any company in the pursuit of and realization of its goals of growth becomes so large it is impossible for persons of Pete's stature to still maintain human touch with the new college recruits like the Jim Roths of 1968.

I had a number of additional on-campus interviews and corporate visits that fall and early winter. I even had one in Chicago. It was after the football season though!!!! Cargill had become the standard bearer and each of the other organizations from which I had job offers was compared to Cargill. Even though I had higher salary offers from other companies, in my heart, I knew I would eventually settle on Cargill. After a follow-up visit to the Cargill operations in Cedar Rapids, Iowa (where I was told I would most likely be assigned), I ended any further interviewing activities and informed the people at Cargill I would like to accept their offer.

Although I had ups and downs in the Cargill organization as you will see as you traverse the up coming chapters of this book, I have never regretted that original decision.

It is unfortunate that as a company grows in size it becomes much more difficult to create and maintain many of the people centered management philosophies (and activities) that so impressed me on my recruiting visit in 1968. It is even more unfortunate size creates (or at least fosters) a hierarchy that often rewards political correctness more than performance. Finally, it is unfortunate size makes it increasingly more difficult to allow specific operations to function autonomously and yet still be able to "draw the circle" around the entire organization when seeking that position that is in the best total interest of the organization.

While Cargill and many other large organizations have hugely successful track records, it is in precisely the areas just noted that I think Cargill (and many other mega-companies) often fall short. I think there are important lessons that could be learned. Interestingly, I think this is where the small organizations have a significant opportunity to outmuscle the big guys for the very reasons above noted. However, I think they also afford the big guys the same opportunity to out muscle each other if they are willing to take an introspective look at themselves. That having been said, I continue to fear many of the mega organizations have become so infatuated with their own size and magnitude that they have become in many respects a religion worshipping themselves.

# Chapter 2
# Walk in My Shoes

We have all heard many variations of the timeless concept, walk in my shoes. We all basically understand the concept: *become me for a little while and you will see why I respond like I do.* Obviously, it is impossible to become someone else and most of the time it is also impossible to walk in another's shoes literally and often even difficult to do it figuratively. Even so, I certainly always subscribed to the theory, and I thought I understood how to make it work.

However, I was wrong. In 1978, when I became the General Superintendent of the corn processing plant in Memphis Tennessee, I also became the recipient of a daily series of great lessons. These lessons were on how important it is to be able to understand the shoes in which the other person is standing. My mill superintendent in Memphis, Doug Brooks, gave me those daily lessons at no charge other than perhaps to my pride.

Doug was a black man who was a Memphis native. We were both about the same age (very early 30s at that time). Doug was one of the premier managers on our team, and we quickly became both close associates and good friends. That I was the boss and Doug the subordinate never came into play, we simply worked together as associates. While I think for the most part it was that way with all of the Memphis team, Doug and I had a special relationship.

The Memphis work force was made up principally of relatively young black men who were Memphis natives. I have always prided myself in seeing the person and not the color, sex, or age of the people with whom I work. I treated all of the Memphis people as equals as I truly believe God gives us all one unit of worth in His sight and that is how He expects us to view and treat each other.

The lessons I noted above began after I had been at the Memphis operation for only a few months. Doug came into my office one day and began, "Jim, you treat all these guys very well, but you are not hearing what they are saying to you. I think you are listening, but your ears are tuned to Midwest, well-educated, rural, white, upper middle class wavelengths. Most of these guys are speaking to you in southern, poorly or modestly educated at best, very urban, black, mostly mid to lower class wavelengths. You may hear their words, but you automatically put them through a filter that is in the context of your background. That often changes the meaning and intent of the message significantly."

I usually have a response (just ask my wife), but I was left numbed. I had not considered I might be unconsciously altering the intended messages simply because of my point of reference. Doug went on to explain when I talked, the exact same thing was happening in the opposite direction. I had an intended message, but it was delivered in one wavelength and received in another.

Doug proceeded to give me a number of examples that staggered me. "You have never spent a night in jail! You have likely never carried a knife or gun as a means of protection! You have likely never missed a meal. You have likely never struggled with schoolwork and wondered what the use of it was. You have never . . . ," and the list went on. Then Doug started in on the *you haves.* "You have always had a car to get you where you wanted to go, you have always had fresh air to breath, you have always had access to good educational systems, you have always had sufficient money, you have always known where home was, you have always. . . . . . . ." and this list went on.

Doug's point was not that I had it so much easier than all the other people at the Memphis plant (although it became obvious I had). His point was because our life experiences for whatever reason had been so different, our perspectives on like issues could be and most likely would be vastly different. We spoke, heard, and understood from the reference frame of our own personal experiences.

Now I was not going to live in inner city Memphis for a time, nor were each of the guys in the plant going to go to Iowa and ride a tractor around a farm for a few days. Doug was no more able to make himself white than I was to make myself black. Yet Doug had enough of both cultures in him to bridge at least part of the gap. More importantly, he was an extremely bright individual who understood he had some particular interpretive gifts. He was a daily mentor and tutor to me during my two-year stint in Memphis.

Doug also mentored and tutored the people in the plant. He would tell me how he would talk to them just as he had spoken to me, "Hey guys, Jim is speaking from his background as a highly educated white Midwestern farm boy and you guys are hearing his message like it came from a black inner city dude. Listen up; here is what he means. . . ." Interestingly, after you are coached long enough, you begin to catch on to how to frame your message in the wavelength of your listeners as well as remove your own wavelength filters from your listening mechanisms.

Unfortunately in most of life's circumstances we do not have a Doug Brooks at every turn to inform us of existing differences of background and then coach us through the integration of our differing points of reference. It falls to us to make ourselves aware of what shoes the other person is standing in and moreover what paths those shoes have worn in the sands of time. It is only then that we can tune to the proper wavelength. While I believe that is the most difficult part of the task, we cannot stop there. We must then make the effort to turn our dial (minds) to that frequency and turn up the volume.

For the past twenty-five plus years, I have attempted to put Doug's mentoring into practice and determine and understand the frame of reference of the people with whom I am interacting. Sometimes that is easy and sometimes it is impossible. Idle social chatting is not something I particularly like, nor is it something at which I am proficient. Yet, whenever I am "exchanging pleasantries" or engaging in social discourse with a new acquaintance or associate, I try to determine something about the person's background and who they are. I think many people recognize the value in that and do the same thing.

However, the part that is often overlooked is the flip side. In that conversation, whenever an opportunity presents itself, I attempt to plug my own background and who I am into the discussion. Tuning my frequency to the new wavelengths will result in a much higher level in my understanding. However, giving the other party the resources to tune their frequency improves the opportunity for mutual understanding and positive relationship building.

As you read these stories, my intent is that you will understand the lessons involved and may possibly be able to put some of them to work for you. The more you understand of me and about me, the more likely this is to happen. Therefore, it is in both of our interests to give you at least some modest background into my person and make-up.

I have certainly been shaped by my parents and the conditions of my upbringing. My religion and educational processes have also contributed to who I am. Although we are pretty well cast by the time we get married, a certain amount of tweaking is effected by our spouses and without exception, our children expand our horizons. With that as the basis, I will in the next few chapters attempt to briefly put you in my shoes.

Recognizing there may be random readers of these writings, I cannot predict the perspective a given reader will bring to this interaction. In that case I think it is always best to speak in a common language. Obviously I am writing this in English so that is at least one commonality that must exist between the reader and me.

Beyond the common dialect, the most common language I know is laughter (it is the same in all dialects). I remember when our daughter Renee was only four and we were hosting a family from Holland. They had a little girl who was about Renee's age, but spoke only Dutch and of course, Renee spoke only English. After dinner the two little girls just sat around looking blank for a little while. Then my wife and the mother of the little girl from Holland talked the girls into going upstairs to Renee's bedroom to play with whatever they may find. Within a few minutes, the most incredible sound came from that room. It was the sound of two little girls laughing. That laughter went on for the remainder of the evening. I am convinced no one that night had a better time than Renee and "her guest." They both found the common language and used it to communicate the entire evening.

When possible, I will always try to find the humor in a situation. If we are willing to laugh at ourselves, we will always find humor is an integral part of our actions and is sprinkled liberally through all of our daily activities. Nothing relieves tension like laughter. I do not think the healing effects of laughter happened by default in God's creation of us.

Beyond the universal language of laughter, people are more apt to enjoy listening and will better understand and remember information if it is in story form. Life is a series of stories. Some are short and some are not. Whenever one reminisces about life's experiences, the format of the recollections is almost always in story form. Further, if one thinks about all of the good presenters they have experienced in their life (teach-ers, preachers, friends, associates etc.), I would submit they all had (or have) one thing in common. They use lots of actual life occurrences, examples, and stories, AND they are all **good storytellers**.

Most people (even a high percentage of professing Christians) remember only bits and pieces of Jesus' Sermon on the Mount as found in chapters 5, 6, and 7 of the Gospel of Matthew, and yet this is unargu-ably the greatest sermon of all time. Yet many people (even many non-professing Christians) understand and remember many of the parables told by Jesus (like the wise man and foolish man building their houses respectively on the rock and sand or the prodigal son leaving home and returning or the good Samaritan to name a few). Jesus' ministry is recorded much more as stories (parables) than as sermons.

Although Jesus had a 33 year life on earth and His ministry was in large part His example in life; His "traditional" ministry lasted only three years. To be remembered for generations, Jesus had to make a very dramatic impact in those three years. It doesn't seem strange to me His message was so often delivered as a story (both in action and through speech). Nor does it seem strange Jesus spent 30 years living among the people and literally walking in their shoes (sandals) before He began His teaching and preaching to them. Ten years of "walking in their shoes" for each year of teaching!! We should take a lesson!

Interestingly, the Bible has a wealth of things to teach us about life, communications, and even good business sense without regard to the real theme of being a story of a chosen people of God. I realize there is always danger in making reference to the Bible or stories in the Bible, as certain people shut their minds down at the mention of any-thing Biblical. That notwithstanding, the Bible and religion have played a vital part in shaping me, and I have detailed that in the chapter titled "The Best Seller." Irrespective of your religious perspective or lack thereof, I encourage you to read that chapter.

Transparent, honest, and understandable communications are critical to building relationships. Understanding each other's back-grounds and perspectives, if not critical or imperative, is at the very least immensely helpful in achieving that kind of communication. If we can indeed "walk in another person's shoes," we will have moved ourselves well down the road to a greater appreciation for that person as well as a greater opportunity for mutual understanding. Both of these make for a better life for both of us.

# CHAPTER 3
# Love, Chocolate Milk & Turkeys

A couple of years prior to my birth in 1947, my parents, Lester and Grace Roth, began raising turkeys on an 80-acre farm near Wayland, Iowa. That statement encapsulates four critical elements that have shaped my being; my parents, raising turkeys, farming and specifically that farm, and Wayland, Iowa.

My father graduated from the eighth grade and like his two older brothers and one older sister (three more brothers and two more sisters followed) went to work on his parent's farm. While he did not have the opportunity to go on to high school, much less college, he was and remained until his death in 2001 one of the smartest people I know. My dad's example was critical in showing me learning is a function of your desire and work and not necessarily a function of classroom time. His example also taught me intelligence comes as much from experience and savvy as it does from a lecture.

My mother was the only girl in a family that included 5 brothers (three older and two younger). She graduated from high school near the top of her class. She had a very high capacity to learn and, until semi incapacitated by Parkinson's disease and a stroke while in her 80s, her memory was incredible. Genes from Mom and Dad made me a very intelligent person, and in fact, one of Cargill's top officers once described me to a Cargill manager with whom I was working as "IQ wise, one of the smartest guys in Cargill." The same gene pool created my two highly intelligent sisters. Joyce is two years older and Lavonne, whom I desperately wanted to be a boy, is five years younger.

I comment on our intelligence not to boast, but for two very important reasons. First, it is a part of who I am and my perspective is certainly impacted by my IQ. More importantly, I do believe we are a product of both our heredity and our environment. Mom provided us with very good memories, and we inherited a fairly high capacity to learn from both Mom and Dad. While heredity puts us in a relatively high population percentile, it certainly does not put us in elite territory. We were also fortunate enough to have a learning environment from which we got an extra boost. We had a dad who had to educate himself at the higher levels. Dad taught us how to learn independently and that is something our education systems do a poor job of teaching. We were in fact made smarter by the fact Dad had only an eighth grade formal education, but rose to college level intellect through self education.

I grew up in a very disciplined environment. Dad and Mom were the authorities. They loved us dearly and believed in both compassionate and tough love. We had rules and boundaries and consequences for deviation. I had my fair share of engagements with the "paddle" during my formative years and remain today convinced all of my "spankings" were deserved, except one. To this day, my sisters and I still often joke about that one.

School was also an exercise in discipline. In the fifties and early sixties, the teachers were the authorities in schools. Most of the kindergarten teachers today are superior in style to my kindergarten teacher, who was like a drill sergeant. Certainly many other teachers today are also superior to the old models. I know of at least two who are, my sister, Joyce and my daughter, Renee. However, the learning model and atmosphere today are often not the same, and I would not trade my education experiences for equal ones today.

From grade 1 through grade 6 I attended Flowers, a small one room country school in rural Wayland, Iowa where grades 1 through 8 all survived and thrived in one room. I should probably also not diminish the role this likely played in fostering my ability for independent learning as is detailed further in Chapter 4.

I have an almost uncanny ability to focus my attention and blank out all surrounding distractions. My wife finds this to be most comforting when I am driving and most frustrating when I am engaged in something and she is trying to speak to me. Actually she isn't trying to speak to me; she IS speaking to me. What she is trying to do is get me to hear. I am sure I honed this skill in the one room school where there was always one "class" going on at the front of the room with one grade or 12.5% of the school involved in that "class." The other 87.5% of us were a few feet away at our desks studying.

By the time I landed in high school in Wayland (and later in

WACO, a consolidated district), I had figured out I was smarter than some of my teachers. I challenged the authority when I knew it to be wrong. I had an analytical mind and had become an excellent problem analyzer and problem solver. I also discovered I had a knack for figuring out how to get around the system.

I used this "knack" to accomplish "worthwhile" things the establishment (teachers and administrators) in their infinite wisdom would not otherwise allow. I was not anti-establishment, I was only against establishment policies or programs that were dogmatic or totalitarian and did not come with adequate supporting reason. I was a natural and innovative leader (student council rep, class president, athletic team co-captain, high honor roll scholar, etc.). I occasionally used these traits and my positions to create what the administration often viewed as minor insurrections. I always viewed them as justifiable means to a proper end.

Many of these "insurrections" are the stories my kids love to hear. My wife, on the other hand, worries about their detrimental effect on young minds. As you will see in the events that unfold in my work life, this skill or perhaps predilection to this type of action can serve one very well and also can create big problems. It is often as simple as whether the establishment values performance and results more highly than it values its own pride and desire or need to control.

My philosophy is like the coaches response to a player who takes a big chance that is not necessarily in the game plan. Your gut is often better than the designed plan so go ahead and react to your gut. But, if you do, your gut had better be right! In my career if I've deviated and been wrong, then I expect the whip to crack. BUT, if I have deviated and been right and another party receives and accepts the benefit of my action, then I deserve the credit for my actions. I don't expect to be hammered because I strayed from convention or plan. Unfortunately, it often does not happen that way.

My kid's favorite story (and one my wife would prefer they not hear) was the chocolate milk escapade. We always had good basketball teams in high school and filled the gymnasium to capacity for every home game. We knew we were a key revenue generator for the school sports programs, so we did not think it out of line to retreat to the cafeteria after practice and down a few cartons of chocolate milk from the lunchroom cooler.

We had done this for months when the school suddenly removed the standard open access cooler and installed one that required the payment of one penny to secure an 8-ounce carton of milk. This was one of those machines where the cartons were placed in rows with just the top seam extending through the slot at the top of the row. To remove an individual carton, you slid it over to a special jaw-opening device that was triggered by the insertion of a coin (in our case a penny).

The penny cost was not the problem. The problem was ball players don't generally carry their wallets in their jocks or basketball shorts and thus, we did not have ready access to pennies following practice. We offered to pay lump sums or keep a record or whatever, but the administration would not waiver. The penny-eating machine was in place to stay. If we didn't have pennies after practice, tough luck! So while some players tried to figure out how to get supplies of pennies to the lunchroom after practice and others simply lamented our bad luck, I always stayed busy studying the machine and the resources available around the lunchroom.

After some period of analysis, my eyes focused on a box of straws. Of course, that was the key! I got a straw and went to the machine. There was enough of the top seam of the box protruding for me to open it slightly. I then inserted the straw, and presto, I had my chocolate milk. Several of the players watched in awe as this process unfolded. Most of them thought the process was over when I had emptied the carton. "No, No," I explained. "That leaves all the evidence, and the powers that be will simply lock the machine or remove it altogether. Now I need to remove the empty carton."

Before I had emptied the carton I had decided even in the static mode, the penny- activated jaws would provide a slightly larger opening. This opening was large enough to first get my fingers in to collapse the empty carton and then get the collapsed carton turned up on edge. With the carton collapsed and on edge I could work it out through the jaw opening and properly dispose of it in the wastebasket. Bingo! The process was complete.

For weeks the team enjoyed the fruits of my labor. The word soon got around I had beaten the system. Virtually every night at practice our coach would ask me how I was able to get around the penny issue on the chocolate milk. I would act rather shocked at the question and he would say, "Hey, look, I know you have figured out a way to get milk out of that machine without a penny. I don't care that you're doing it. I just can't figure out what process you're using to get it done and I'm curious." We continued drinking, the coach continued asking, and I continued looking shocked. The season ended, and as far as I know, our coach never did figure out how we did it. Perhaps I should send him a copy of this chapter!

Obviously, one of the issues my wife raises with this action is a case can be made we were "stealing" the milk. One would have to be pretty narrow-minded to not allow for that interpretation and I would not do the same thing today for that very reason. That notwithstanding and given the price of 1 cent per carton, we probably didn't drink $3 or $4 worth of milk the entire season, and we would have happily given the school those 3 or 4 bucks.

Our problems with the penny issue were first, it had been a past practice benefit that had been somewhat arbitrarily taken away and second was the mechanism of the charge. We didn't mind the charge, but let us pay a buck and then work off a hundred cartons of milk. As earlier noted, the problem was that it was not an easy task to get pennies through the practice session and into the lunchroom, and that in effect caused us to loose our after practice refreshment. We interpreted this to be a backdoor method on the part of the school administrators to eliminate a perk without actually confronting us and saying, "Hey, we're denying you this benefit."

It is still kind of fun for me to recall this caper. I suppose in many respects because it takes me back to a fun time in my life. However, I also always try to learn something about how others may react based on how I react. Certainly in my life I have tried not to be arbitrary in doing things that impact others. In both home and work environments, I try not to eliminate perks that have come to be counted on (even though one may have every right to do that). I especially try not to backdoor anything. If something is being changed, do it so everyone understands, explain the change and listen to alternatives.

When I wasn't in school or playing football, basketball, or baseball, I was helping Dad in farm work of one type or another. My mother was a superb worker and had always been an integral part of the farming operations with Dad. Mom did not, however, particularly enjoy farm work and was delighted when I turned out to be a boy, figuring Dad now had a farmhand and she would soon no longer have to fill that role.

Mom was much more oriented to housekeeping, yard keeping, gardening, nursing, and cooking. She has been described more than once as one of the best cooks people have encountered. My wife commented early in our courtship after her first visit to our home, "Your mom is really going to make life tough on some girl who winds up marrying you!" I don't know if she was making idol chat or thinking ahead it might be her. At any rate, we ate very well, and we did so at least three times a day. Even during the busy times of the year, Mom would bring meals and snacks to us in the fields. Simple foods always tasted better sitting in itchy stubble in the shade of a tractor or wagon.

Dad began the training process with me even before I can remember. He took me with him most of the places he went. He began making me a little farmer by the time I was three years old. The tractors we had then were mere garden tractors by today's huge iron standards. The good side of that was Dad was able to put me on the little Ford (about 15 or 16 horsepower) even before I was in Kindergarten. He didn't put me on and turn me loose at that age. However, for jobs that required moving a wagon or cart slowly (like taking up range turkey fence) he could put me on the tractor in the lowest gear and at the slowest speed. I could steer it and stop it as he directed. I have a love for tractors that remains to this day. There is nothing I would rather do than work the ground. Today, I have a whole shed full of tractors I enjoy using to that end.

A big part of the farming operation was raising turkeys. I should point out this was one component of the farming operations Mom did not get a pass on. Until I was in my teens, she continued to be the principal manager in the turkey brooder house (arrival of 1 day old "chicks" up to 7 week old birds that were then moved to range or later to the pole barn). Turkeys helped Mom and Dad gain a certain amount of financial independence. They were the principal industry that paid my way through college, so I do owe a lot to them. Today, we often have flocks of wild turkeys that inhabit our farm. There is something nostalgic about seeing the splendor of those great birds even in the wild today.

While I see splendor today, back from as early as I can remember until I left for college at age 18, turkeys principally meant one thing to me, WORK, and lots of it. Dad was a believer in MBO (Management By Objective) long before the acronym was ever printed in a textbook or muttered from the mouth of a business consultant. Dad laid out the work for me, trained me long enough for a person of reasonable intelligence to understand the "how to do" of a job and told me what the expected result was to be. He then often went off to do something else if it was a one-person job. Most importantly, he expected me to get the job done and get it done correctly. If I didn't, there would be a "coaching" session. The turkey dust bothered Dad, so from a relatively early age, I was given the principal responsibility for managing the turkeys (particularly after they were moved out of the brooder house and into the pole barn).

One of the hated jobs I had was bedding the pole barn when the surface got wet or manure laden. The pole barn was an 8000 square foot building that housed 2500 turkeys at a time (peanuts by today's mega standards but large at that time). Dad would drive the truck through the barn while I threw off the 20 or so bales of straw that would be used for bedding. Then Dad would be off to do something else and I would be left to shake out straw bales over the 8000 square feet of space with turkeys running all around and gobbling up a storm.

Bedding the pole barn was hard work and there was no easy way to do it. However, there were three key rewards to getting done. 1) Not having to shake out more straw was the pragmatic reward. 2) Dad virtually always complimented me on a job well done. 3) The environment always looked so nice with 2500 bronze/blackish turkeys with vivid red heads strolling around on wonderfully bright yellow straw.

When not working with the turkeys we owned, I would use our brooder house (during idle time) to brood turkeys for other people or businesses on a contract basis. My sister, Joyce, would help me do this and I'm sure she grew as a person from these experiences as well. In addition, when time allowed, Dad also allowed me to work for a local business that was a large turkey producer as well as a feed manufacturer. Normally this work was early in the morning (2:30 to 6:30 A.M.) or late at night. It usually involved loading and moving turkeys, cleaning the houses (barns), or "debeaking" small turkeys (removing a small amount of the upper beak to prevent cannibalistic like activities).

What I gained from all of this was obviously an understanding of both hard work and responsibility. More importantly, I learned the *absolute joy of accomplishment* and the pragmatic realization that positive things are usually the result of hard work and intelligent effort. Results aren't always profits as sometimes the economics work against you, but there will virtually always be tangible growth or evidence of one's efforts. While Dad taught me page after page of the lessons of life, the one thing I hold most dear is that joy of accomplishment. I try to instill that in my children and in every person with whom I have the privilege of working. I can only hope I am able to do it with some measure of the skill my father possessed.

I do not wish to suggest my parents were only about work. They were not. We did all kinds of things together as a family and Mom and Dad were our biggest supporters in athletic, musical (my sisters only - my music talents got lost at birth) and scholastic endeavors. But other than religion and family, both Mom and Dad believed work came first. You did your work, and then you went on to other activities. In fact, work made possible most, if not all, of the other activities.

There are also ways to go about one's work. For both Mom and Dad the way was one of honor. You were honest in all of your dealings. Dad was once described as being "too honest for his own good." During a deposition, I was once described by a lawyer as "so honest I was boring." I'm sure that description pleased Dad far more than had that lawyer described me as "being a most cunning, persuasively twisted and interesting character." Unfortunately, the world today measures by some different standards, but I remain thankful I was raised in the old-fashioned way.

Beyond being simply honest, Dad and Mom believed in being fair. I know my father inherited that trait from his parents. The golden rule says to do unto others as you would have them do unto you. This is so simple a test and yet is failed millions of times a day throughout the world. Why is it so difficult to say, "Now how would I like to be treated in this circumstance?"

I think one of the operating principles I have inherited that is the most difficult for the world to understand is: "Be fair in all things even when the laws and rules of man do not require it." This is also an operating tenet that has not always stood me in good stead with my supervisors in my business career. No matter what is said, business often finds if very difficult to pass up the opportunity for profit or advantage when faced with a choice between absolute fairness and what the laws of man allow. Dad was most certainly one of my supervisors who did not ever have a problem with the concept of absolute fairness. He not only expected it, he demanded it, and in fact, he taught it.

I have spoken more about my dad than about my mother. My mother was a wonderful person who had a significant impact on my life, and I do not wish to belittle her accomplishments in the least. I could tell stories about her impact as well. However, for hours and days and years, I worked along side of my dad. He taught, he coached, and he led. He unarguably had the greatest impact of anyone in my life.

# CHAPTER 4
# Miss Leichty et al

I have long subscribed to the idea that in large part teachers really only make a key difference in the *scholastic or knowledge* education of a person in the fringe areas. I believe it is much the same with coaching as well as supervision and management. That is not to say any of those positions or people are not important. Indeed they are. However, I believe the key is not as much in knowledge transfer as it is in motivation to learn, play, or work.

Like most people, I have been through a number of teachers and coaches in my life. I have also been through a number of supervisors and managers, but later chapters will deal with them. I remember all of my teachers and coaches and can still name most of them. All of them made some impression on me, but only a very few really impacted my life.

Impact means that five years down the road there remains some life movement that would not have existed without the given impact. I often use this definition with my children (or even co-workers) who are distraught over some particular occurrence or circumstance. I ask them if this will have an impact on the state of their life tomorrow, one week, one year, or five years from now. Obviously the shorter that time, the less the real impact is. It is amazing how few things we fret over have a half-life much longer than a few hours. So like I said, few of my teachers really had an impact.

Oh sure, my kindergarten teacher was tough on us little kids. My first grade teacher embarrassed me by having to lead my stubborn pony away from the country schoolhouse. Our sixth grade teacher was really smart, but she was so "out-manned" that we took advantage of her and didn't allow her great intellect to impact our learning as we could have. Our seventh grade math teacher was a knockout before we all learned to appreciate that characteristic in a woman. My seventh grade geography teacher treated me to a chocolate-malt for correctly identifying, placing on a map, and spelling the names of all of the African countries and their capitals. Aside from the chocolate malt, that didn't do much for me in life! Today, I think all except Egypt and South Africa have different names. My basketball coach (of chocolate milk fame) didn't kick me out of practice one night when he should have and did kick me out one night when he shouldn't have. Certainly, I can recall and list something interesting about most of my teachers, but you get the idea: Impressions, but not really Impact.

Miss Leichty, on the other hand, was the first of my teachers to cross the line from impression to impact. Interestingly, Rachel Leichty is my first cousin although she is about twelve years my senior. Forgive me Rachel if I have made you older than you really are. Miss Leichty (in any school context she is still Miss Leichty to me) was my teacher for three years in grades three, four, and five. She also taught grades one, two, six, seven, and eight in those same years and all in the same room.

One-room schoolteachers are in a class by themselves in my book. They had to be sort of super human. Imagine having to prepare and deliver math lessons, reading lessons, spelling lessons, social study lessons, and science lessons not once, but TIMES eight. In addition they had to teach art and music, supervise recess and lunchtime, do the janitorial duties, and even shovel coal into the furnace. I know that was in the mid fifties, but I think the pay for all of that was not much more than about $200/month (much less than a buck an hour considering the time they spent).

Miss Leichty didn't just teach us, she made us learn! She was a kind and compassionate person, but she was also very much a no-nonsense person. There was an acceptable code of behavior, and we were expected to obey it. If we didn't, then there were consequences. Such a novel concept; there are consequences associated with your behavior!!! I say novel by today's standards. There was nothing especially novel about that in the mid 50s. There was especially nothing novel about that for me. That was a message I had been living under for my entire life. School under Miss Leichty was an extension of home.

I think just the concept of the one room school dictated that to be anywhere near effective, a teacher had to motivate the student to learn very much independently. With twenty plus students and 40 to 50 independent lessons to plan and conduct, there just wasn't much time for a lot of one-on-one assistance sessions. On the other hand, I assume the case could be made with only two, three, or four students in each grade; every ten to fifteen minute class session was pretty close to one-on-one.

As I reflect on this, perhaps the old one room country school automatically forced all the most critical components of learning on us. Real world life is very much like the old one room school experience, brief very personal teaching (instruction) and then independent study and learning (analysis and task action) in a somewhat disruptive (many other activities happening simultaneously) environment. Of course the difference between Miss Leichty's classes and the real world was we were encouraged by a teacher who had as her primary objective to turn out good kids who had developed a capacity to learn. Real world objectives are often get what you can get from whom you can get it before they get it from you!

Incidentally, Rachel Leichty did not limit her commitment to helping others to those first few years at the one room Flowers schoolhouse. For most of her life she has been involved in teaching, and for many years she has been involved in working with Indians on reservations in Arizona. Rachel Leichty's life may not likely be viewed as very rich by the standards most people unfortunately employ today. However, when one critically evaluates her life, she has touched more people in a positive way than most of us could ever dream of. I count it a privilege to have been touched by her.

The old one room country school lasted only one year after Miss Leichty left. Then we fell victim to the mass move to consolidation. After the 1958–59 school year, Flowers was closed and we were bused to Wayland (actually, we rode the bus to Wayland which was the only place to ride the bus to). I wasn't particularly displeased with this turn of events as I was in seventh grade and would get to play competitive junior high basketball. My homeroom teacher, Mrs. Curly, was a beautiful young woman who also taught math and science! What a waste, if we could only have had her a few years later when our levels of $C_{19}H_{28}O_2$ were higher.

By the time eighth grade rolled around, Mrs. Curly had left and was replaced by Lyle Bowers. Lyle Bowers had been a teacher for many years, but had left teaching for a while to work as a plumber. Interestingly, while I had (and continue to have in memory) the greatest respect for Lyle Bowers, I have trouble thinking of him as Mr. Bowers. He was always Lyle Bowers when he was a plumber, and I have always continued to think of him as Lyle Bowers or just Lyle.

One of the really unique things about having Lyle Bowers for my teacher in eighth grade in 1960–61 was he had also been my father's eighth grade teacher in a one-room country school in 1928–29. Thirty-two years later I would have the same experiences as my father. I doubt if that scenario is repeated many times today or even then.

Lyle Bowers was very different from Rachel Leichty and yet they were very much alike. He was not a man who possessed a vast amount of earthly resources, yet he was a very rich person. He had a huge interest in developing us both academically and as worthwhile human beings. He was a scientist who believed for every action there was a reaction and that included the behavioral sciences (behavior had consequences, both good and bad).

Two learning experiences with Lyle Bowers stand out as epitomizing what he was all about. Early in the year, we were given an algebra problem in our math books. In those days, no one was exposed to algebra prior to high school. The book stated if we could solve the problem we were superior eighth grade students. I devised a method of solving the problem by trial and error (as did one other student). In class, Lyle Bowers showed us how to solve it algebraically.

A few days later as I walked into his classroom, there was a set of numbers on the chalkboard with no instructions or story line. As I sat there waiting for class to begin, I noticed the numbers were similar in nature to the earlier "superior eighth grader problem." I decided Lyle was going to present a story line similar to the earlier problem and then have us use the numbers he had written on the board as the known data and solve the problem algebraically. Assuming that to be the case, I solved the problem in my head as I waited for the bell to initiate the start of class.

When class began, my prediction was right and we were given the predicted story line and challenged to solve the problem. I got up and walked up to Lyle Bower's desk and quietly told him what I had done. He told me to write my answer on a piece of paper on his desk. I did. He smiled and told me I was right. What sticks out most about that experience was Lyle was as excited about my learning as was I. Student success was Lyle's success. He shared my effort with all the other classes, not to pump me up (although that was a side benefit) nor as much to challenge the others, but to encourage the others. Lyle Bowers was an encourager. He fully understood you can pull a rope, but you cannot push it (unless it is frozen). Lyle also knew how to freeze the rope.

That brings us to my second defining experience with Lyle Bowers. Three or four of us had been having our sport in between class sessions one day. I don't recall the exact circumstances, but I think it was as innocent as gently placing Peavine (one of the guys in class) butt first in the waste paper basket. One of the other teachers did not find this to be as humorous as we did and demanded that Lyle Bowers (also the acting Jr. High Principal) take action.

Lyle rounded us all up and marched us into the coatroom for privacy. He then explained while our actions were certainly not particularly malicious, they could be lodged in the category of juvenile. He also explained his position as enforcer and the attendant responsibilities with that position. He did not give us any BS about how the butt warming he was about to give us would hurt him more than us. He proceeded to give each of us a couple of good whacks with some fashion of a paddle he had in his possession. We then all talked and laughed together. The laughter was not in contempt of anybody. The laughter was the summation of the discipline.

Lyle cared every bit as much about us and was as much our friend as he had been ten minutes earlier. We all understood fully not to do "juvenile" things again, and we didn't. We all exited the disciplinary session with our sights set ahead on the rest of the activities of the day (and year). Maybe if we had more people like Lyle Bowers, teachers would still be able to discipline (up to and including spanking) students today. And maybe if we had more people like Lyle Bowers, students would be more apt to behave in acceptable manners (and enjoy it).

Like Lyle Bowers, I have tried to be an encourager of others. I often fail and resort to enforcer and try to freeze the rope when it should be left limber and pulled. I have also tried to exact discipline as Lyle did, without condemnation and with a sense of closure on the action and movement to the next step. Most of us are doing well if we can terminate discipline on a neutral basis. My goal, however, remains "the Lyle Bower's approach" where the person receiving the discipline actually walks away happy (or at least satisfied) with the process.

High school brought another new set of teachers and coaches and again there are a number of people in that group who conjure up various memories. As noted earlier, I could name them all and tell interesting stories about each. However, I had what I could term a high level relationship with only two. One was the high school principal my senior year, Mr. Boekleman, who had earlier been my math teacher as a freshman. During my senior year I worked closely with Mr. Boekleman as I was the senior class president, and, as noted, he was the principal.

The second, Roger Williams, was my senior English/literature teacher and accepted the challenge of trying to create in me a literary connoisseur. I really did get a kick out of *The Canterbury Tales,* especially the miller's and reeve's tales, but I still have not completed the book *Absalom, Absalom* by William Faulkner that he assigned me. Mr. Williams was also the senior class sponsor, and again, as I was the class president, he and I worked closely together on class activities and became good friends. I probably should not discount Mr. Williams' role in my life as today I do consider myself to possess excellent communication skills in writing, and he at least deserves some credit for helping develop that skill in me. Maybe even some responsibility for the writing of this book!!

High school did provide me with my first significant life experience of reverse (or negative) impact. Our football coach had become somewhat of a legend in the community, and we all viewed him almost as a pseudo-god. He had made our small school a football powerhouse—that is what coaches are supposed to do I guess.

However, some of my experiences with him left me wondering if "legendary" was the correct description, and his god-like image faded before me. In my eyes, he was as poor at dispensing discipline as Lyle Bowers was good. Coach was much more the traditional crack the whip guy, and when he was done, you knew he was the authority, you were the subject, you had just been hammered, and you better darn well not forget it in the near future! He always seemed to be less concerned with whether he had taught you anything that would be beneficial to you in life during the disciplinary process, but most concerned that you change behavior, even if out of fear rather than understanding.

However, the most lasting impression (and impact) I have from Coach occurred early in my freshman year during football practice. Our school was fairly small so a number of us freshman were pitted each day in practice against the varsity team. Needless to say, we got summarily pounded in each practice session.

One practice session I rushed toward the ball carrier and arrived second. Another defensive player, Sid, had arrived first and had his arms around the quarterback's waist. However, the quarterback was so strong that as he spun around to get away, he simply swung Sid around with his feet straight out and into me. I felt an unbelievably sharp pain in my left leg. As I walked back to the defensive huddle, Dave (one of the toughest guys on the team) looked at me and said, "What happened to your leg?" I looked down and my entire leg and shoe were soaked in blood from just below the knee.

I went over to Coach and said, "I think I need something for my leg." He called the trainer and told him to put a band-aid on it. He then turned to me and said, "We'll make a man out of you some day!" Talk about impact!!! What had happened was Sid's spike had knocked a hole in my left leg about 3/4 inch round and 1/2 inch deep. When I got home from practice my sock was soaked in blood. The next morning my bed was soaked in blood. My leg continued to hurt like the dickens. Later when I finally did go to the doctor, I had infection in my leg. Today, I still have a very distinct 1/2 inch diameter scar on my left leg. I wonder if all of that qualifies me as a man now.

In addition to the fact I have a scar that has lasted well over 40 years (qualifying as impact since it has lasted well beyond the 5 year qualifying time) Coach's impact has been for me to try as best I can to NOT be like him. I try to qualify someone as a man or woman based on the integrity of their being and not on some macho action or particular physical image. In particular, when I coach young people in athletic endeavors (which I love to do), I want them to have fun and view their coach as a compassionate person interested in their growth, not just their performance. Most of all, I try not to be a person of reverse impact. I want people to be able to follow my example directly, not learn what NOT to do by observing me.

College follows high school and Dr. Howard Johnson and his wife Pat became the closest thing to an extra set of parents I had experienced. Only Ray and Janiece Freeman (a later chapter) became more parent-like than Howard and Pat. Howard and Pat reached out to a number of students in the department and made their home as accessible to us as it was to their children. We transcended the visitor status to virtual household members. I assume I fell heir to this exemplary treatment by virtue of the fact I was the department student branch club president and Howard was the sponsor. For whatever reason, those of us fortunate enough to be able to take advantage of the Johnson's hospitality profited handsomely. From Howard and Pat, I learned the value of graciously opening one's home and life to others as well as the ability to bridge generations with such simple effort as a meal and a genuine interest in another's well-being.

Notwithstanding Howard and Pat Johnson, the greatest impact any teacher or instructor had on my future was registered by one Dr. Leon F. Charity. Dr. Charity was the head of the Electrical Power and Processing Division of Agricultural Engineering. I had originally registered at ISU in that area, but before enrolling (or ever meeting Dr. Charity) I had switched to electrical engineering. After one term in electrical engineering, I knew it was too theoretically oriented for me, and I transferred to a technology area that seemed more practical and earthy.

Nevertheless, my love of agriculture still remained. I was working for my Uncle Edwin (Roth) during breaks. We did a lot of farm electrical work I found to be fun. Thumbing through the course books and thinking some of the Ag Engineering courses dealing with farm electrification systems looked interesting, I went to the department to see if I could take some of these courses "on the side." I was directed to Dr. Charity who took one look at my transcript and entrance test scores and said, "What are you doing in a technology curriculum? You belong in engineering." He proceeded to make his case and talked me back into the Ag Engineering program.

Dr. Charity was not only one of my instructors, he was my advisor, he was my mentor, he was my conscience, he was my employment agent, and he was my most vocal and active supporter. In addition, Leon and Maxine Charity made me a welcome visitor in their home. Through Dr. Charity's efforts, I became an agricultural engineer. I became involved in many extracurricular activities within the ISU department and the four state regional area. More importantly, Dr. Charity steered me to become a member of the Alpha Zeta service and scholastic honorary society, and I later met my wife through my association with this group. Finally, I had meaningful and profitable summer employment, and I was a sought after commodity upon graduation.

Dr. Charity contracted Parkinson's disease at too young an age and died long before he had lived the full length of life's measure. I was able to visit with him a number of times on returning to ISU prior to his death. Before some of the visits, I was cautioned by some of the other department people how difficult it was to understand him and communicate with him as his disease commanded more of a grip on him. Yet even in my last conversations, I was able to understand him fully and we had great discussions. Perhaps God grants us a special measure of ability in those really special times.

Without Dr. Leon F. Charity, Jim Roth would certainly lead a very different life today. Would I have different values? I think not, but I would still be a very different person since my wife, children and vocation have certainly continued to shape who I am. Without Dr. Charity, I would never have met my wife nor would I have wound up working for Cargill, so history would certainly be different for me. From Leon Charity I have learned many things, but the most important is to never take your relationship with another person lightly. The ultimate influence you may have could totally change or dramatically affect that person's entire life.

It is very interesting to note that among other things, Rachel Leichty, Lyle Bowers, Howard and Pat Johnson, and Leon Charity all had something in common. They all earned my respect and they all gained my friendship. They did this by being well-grounded in principle, by being fair and consistent in all they did, by being a friend, and by having my interests occupy a position equal to those of their own. I count it as one of my life's great gifts from God to have been put into position to receive the impact and enjoy the friendship of each of these people in my life.

# CHAPTER 5
# The Best Seller

Month after month, new books land on the best seller lists around the world. Generally these books survive for a few weeks or maybe months. They then disappear from these lists and from their pre-eminent position at the front of bookstores. The books get relegated to the less prominent "category or subject matter" shelves of the bookstores, and if lucky may survive there for a few more months or maybe a few years. Often, these books have little to offer readers and survive or thrive largely because of the fame or notoriety of the author.

There is, however, one book that refuses to live and die this relatively short life cycle. Of course, that book is the Bible. The Bible has stood the test of time for thousands of years. Many people have proclaimed the author (God) to be dead, only to find He is not only alive, but well. Others have dismissed Him and His Writings as irrelevant and out of touch with today. All of that notwithstanding, the Bible continues year after year to remain at the top of the bestseller lists.

I will allow a good many Bibles that are purchased (thereby keeping it at the top of the list) are not frequently read and probably seldom read from cover to cover. Without question, anyone who reads a book as my wife (last chapter first) will put the Bible back down in bewilderment. The Revelations are difficult even for the most learned of Bible scholars. What is my point then for including a chapter in this book on the Bible?

I am trying to help the reader "walk in my shoes" to understand from where I am coming and be able to understand what I say by understanding my reference frame. The Bible and religion have played key parts in my life and have had an IMPACT on me, who I am, and how I act. While the Bible and religion may be very closely related, they are very different things and may also not be related at all. There are certainly religions in the world that do not have the Bible as a base and do not believe in it. I will focus my discussion primarily on the Bible as opposed to religion.

I was exposed to the Bible as soon as I was able to read. In Sunday School and Bible School we learned verses from the Bible, beginning at very young ages. We even had a Bible verse day at the old one room country school. On Fridays, we would each learn a Bible verse and recite it right after the Pledge of Allegiance, so we learned for ourselves and from others. I think it is safe to assume the American Civil Liberties Union never heard of Flowers School.

My wife and children remain impressed today at the number of verses I can quote from memory. I need to hasten to note quoting verses does not make one's life exemplary in any way. That only happens by the living out of what the verses say. Knowing what the verses say and mean may give one a leg up on how one is supposed to act and live, but God has given us free will in how we act. So, final action is still up to us.

My particular religion (both personal and corporate) is based on the Bible and includes both the Old and New Testaments. My personal interpretation places more emphasis on the Old Testament than does the interpretation set forth by my corporate religion, which happens to be Mennonite. A lot of what I have to say about the Bible deals with the Bible as it relates to the Will of God for our lives and the codes of ethics set up by God to guide our lives. However, to me the unique thing about the Bible is even if you choose to believe God is dead (or never was alive) and the Bible is no more than a chronicle of Jewish history, written by a collection of mere mortals, the Bible would still be an incredibly fascinating book.

Several years ago, my wife and I taught an eighth grade Sunday School class. We chose not to use any of the reference material provided by the church (that wouldn't surprise many of my business associates). We decided rather to take the one-year period and go through the entire Bible. Our purpose was to try to get these kids to see the Bible as an interesting collection of short stories that combine to make one big story.

The first day of class, we had a little quiz. We had made up a questionnaire that said at the top, "The Bible is:" Following this were about twenty different statements that were to be answered true or false. These statements included things like "an R-rated story, a business guide, a history of Jews, a guide to health management, the history of Jesus, a songbook, a counseling guide of popular adages, and so forth. It should be obvious to anyone familiar with the Bible, the answer to each of these is true (yes, even the R-rating). The Bible is all of these and much more.

Of course, virtually all of the students would respond (as would most of the general populous) by noting things like a history of Jesus and a few others were true, but most of the others were false. We would simply collect all of the papers and save them until the end of the year when we would pass them back out to each of the students. They would then understand all of the statements were true, and if we had done our job well, they would no longer fear or dread the Bible. They would rather look upon it as an interesting book of stories as well as a resource and a tool for living.

That is precisely my reference frame on the Bible; it is a resource and a tool for living. If all societies and world governments had only one page for their constitution, bill of rights, laws and regulations, congressional record and every other government document, and if that one page were common among all, and if all societies abided by the laws of that one page, and finally, if that one common page was the twentieth chapter of Exodus, I would submit that we would all be living today in much greater peace and harmony. Exodus 20 is the chapter that contains the Ten Commandments.

The Old Testament is a history of the *National* People of God (the Israelites). Moreover, the Old Testament is explicit in its discussion of the proper kinds of human behavior and accountability and responsibility for behavioral activity. I believe very firmly there are specific codes of behavior that are proper and need to be followed. I also believe there are both personal and corporate penalties for failure to adhere to correct behavior. God allows us free will to make choices, but He cautions us that we have responsibilities and that there are consequences to making improper or foolish choices. I do not believe in the concept that since God gives everyone the freedom to choose, He doesn't care about our choices nor should it matter what we do or what anyone else does or how that behavior impacts society.

The New Testament is the early history of the *Spiritual* People of

God (all who believe in Christ). The New Testament is based on Christ's redemption of us and our requirement of agape love. I believe we all have one unit of worth in Christ and we are both commanded and commissioned to love and have compassion on all others. I also continue to believe we are all still required to live according to God's specific code of behavior. However, what I am afraid is lost in some contemporary religions is Jesus' statement He "is not come to destroy the law, but that the law should be fulfilled." I do not believe Jesus' commandment of love reduces our requirement to continue to behave according to God's laws regarding human behavior.

That is the extent of my religious philosophy and preaching. My purpose was not and is not to proselytize or call to salvation. However, if you are not there, you may want to give it serious consideration! My purpose was rather to define my religious frame of reference. I am not, however, done talking about the Bible as it affects my point of view.

As noted earlier, apart from all religious aspects of God's law and redemption, the Bible is a great reference book. This also extends to the perspective of people in business and industry. The only allowance you have to make (accept) is the secular activities described are true (you can even discount the miracles and supernatural events and feats). Any study of how masses of people react when faced with a variety of circumstances and oppressions, as the Jews have been throughout history, is a valuable tool in evaluating how people will react today. History does in fact repeat itself and people today have the same lusts for money, power, sex, and fame as in Biblical times.

Beyond the simple historical and mass reaction lessons to be learned, let me name just a few specific business and relationship principals that were set forth in the Bible long before being espoused by business leaders and consultants of the current day.

In Exodus, when Moses was trying to judge all the people, the scriptures say he was getting worn down by the constant barrage of issues brought to him by all of the people. In addition, the people were getting disgusted with the length of wait for judgment. Moses' father-in-law suggested he delegate the work and in effect set up a court system similar to what we have today with Moses essentially having to act only as the Supreme Court or as a business hierarchy today with Moses as the CEO. All issues would be dealt with by "judges of 10." Difficult issues would be passed up to the next level of "judges of 50." Even more difficult issues went to "judges of 100" and so on. Not only has the concept remained sound for 3500 years, even the numbers square pretty well with present day thinking. Generally 10 to 25 employees per supervisor are considered ideal. We do not like to see student to teacher ratios in the classroom above 20 and so on.

We generally credit Solomon with being one of the wisest men (or women) in history. His writings in the Proverbs are daily lessons in down to earth common sense action. He possessed savvy and God-like wisdom in resolving difficult issues (Read I Kings 3: 16–18). Moreover, beyond his simple wisdom (or maybe because of it) Solomon and his Jewish nation became fabulously wealthy by promoting international trade. Pundits would point to cheap labor as the source of his wealth. I must allow most of Solomon's laborers were conscripted.

However, wealth was not Solomon's only preoccupation with international trade. He had accepted the commission to build the temple, and a number of the raw materials could not be accessed in his native land. He had to have foreign trade to expand the range of goods and services available. However, what is most fascinating about Solomon's incredible mastery of international trade is the way he built relationships with the leaders of foreign nations. Others before Solomon had forged alliances, but none had demonstrated Solomon's ability or foresight to build relationships.

While it is likely easier to find good business and commerce examples in the Old Testament by nature of it's more elaborate recounting of history for thousands of years, the New Testament is also replete with both examples and teachings that can be put to profitable use in both personal and business endeavors.

Jesus used various examples of business acumen in his parables. The parable of the vine growers in Mark and the parable of the talents in Luke certainly detail how "managers" are (or should be) treated according to the value or treachery of their actions. While Jesus was likening these to elements of His Kingdom (The Kingdom of Heaven), there should be no mistake that Jesus understood the concepts of the business environment.

The golden rule espoused by Jesus and His followers is probably the most important element of relationship based buying, selling, operating, and cooperating in business today. This is dealt with in much more detail in the chapter on relationships (Chapter 31: "Three Million Dollar Handshake"). Suffice it to say here, in my humble opinion, a thorough understanding of Jesus' teachings about how to relate to other people would go further toward helping persons establish worthwhile business relationships today than many of the highly educated MBAs and high powered business consultants they have in their employ.

My life is subject to all of the frailties that exist in human nature just as everyone else. However, the impact of religion and the Bible in my life has been and continues to be the establishment and maintenance of the ultimate standard of behavior. Where the laws of man may (and often do) allow and permit unfair behavior, the higher standard of God's law mandates a different course of action.

# CHAPTER 6
# Heroes

All of us have had heroes throughout our lives. In particular, I remember Hank Aaron was probably my biggest hero as a boy. Certainly most of my heroes in my early years had some relationship to sports. Bill Russell, Warren Spahn, Rick Casares and even a local sprint car racer named Freddie Lambach were persons at whom I looked with respect and a certain amount of adoration.

Most of us tend to associate heroes with someone who holds a position higher than we do and where that position is one to which we either aspire or hold in high respect or reverence. Among other definitions, Webster also defines a hero as "a person admired for his/her qualities or a person who is a central figure in an event." My focus in this chapter revolves around these definitions.

You may recall from previous chapters relating to persons who shaped my life that it is my belief most of our "shaping" is done by the time we get to early adulthood. By that time in life, too much of the foundational make-up has been cast and achieved too high a level of curing to be reshaped. We act very much like concrete that takes its shape early in its life and then continues to increase in strength with age. Make no mistake, we continue to be impacted by others, but our foundational make-up is pretty well cast.

That having been said, this is a chapter about my "adult life" heroes and how they have affected and shaped my life and perhaps even my foundational makeup. Those heroes who meet Webster's definition as noted above include my wife of more than 30 years, Billie Christine (Chris) and our four children; Renee Annette, Derek James, Ryan Thomas, and Brandon Kyle. I certainly admire them for their qualities, and without question, they have been (and are) central figures in an event (my life). They are the real animating effect in my life. It is because of them and for them I live each day of my life.

On a very cold Saturday morning in December of 1968, I went outside of my mobile home in Marvin's Mobile Manor at 409 South Duff in Ames, Iowa to start my car. It refused to start. One of the honor fraternities of which I was a member, Alpha Zeta, was giving a Christmas party for a group of young children at a day care center on that afternoon. Alpha Zeta was an all male organization, and we were coupled that day with an all female honor organization. As I walked back into the mobile home, I remember deciding I would just have to miss helping with the party. I did not see this as having any lasting impact on my life.

Shortly after noon, I decided to go out and give the ole 65 Chevy— the Rothmobile as it was later named—one more try. Just as I was about to give up, it started. I let it warm up a bit, and off I went to the Iowa State University Memorial Union where we were to meet. As I walked into the meeting room, I noted a table with three young women and an empty chair. I proceeded to make my way across the room and asked if I may join these young women. They were okay with that arrangement, so I took a seat. Little did I realize that in the next few moments I would make the acquaintance of a young woman with whom I would share the rest of my life.

Within a short period of time, we were all instructed to find our way across town to the day care center. It was suggested that persons without cars (most of the females in those days) should find rides with someone who had a car (most of the males then as now). I asked the three girls at the table with me if they would like a ride, and they all readily accepted. I did note the young woman who had caught my fancy found her way to the front seat with me.

We proceeded to the day care center where I had a wonderful afternoon playing with young four and five-year-old kids. My wife recalls she watched this performance in adoration and concluded I would make a great dad. Whether at that exact time she considered I may be a great dad to *her* children is debatable. Nevertheless, I made an impression on her with at least one part of my foundational makeup she knew she would not have to change.

Many of the events of that day remain indelibly etched in the minds of both my wife and me, including the incomprehensible (at least by today's standards) ending to our day care episode. All of the parents had picked up their youngsters except for one. A young boy with whom I had played much of the day had not been picked up yet and the day care provider staff wanted to go home. I had made particular friends with this young boy. The three young women who had ridden with me and I offered to take him home.

We did not have his address, but he told us he could show us where he lived in Ames, a town of about 25,000. The day care staff was more than happy to oblige and sent him with us. Today that would likely result in loss of license, loss of job, and probably a lawsuit. While this may speak for more intelligent day care providers today; it probably is as much an indictment on our moral decay and often well-founded fear of trusting anyone.

In any event, we were able to get into the vicinity of this young lad's home, but he could not point out the exact house. In the meantime his mother had arrived at the day care center to find no one, and most importantly her child, there. Without apparent panic she drove toward her home. As we continued to circle the area, we ultimately spotted a car with a woman who appeared to be seeking something. Hoping for the best, we hailed her over and asked if she might be looking for a small boy. It was a neat reunion although certainly not one of uncontrolled emotion. Incredibly the mother thanked us for our thoughtfulness and our attempt to be helpful. Perhaps the entire day was prearranged by a Higher Being to bring and keep Chris and me in sufficient company to ignite a fire.

In any event, a fire of sufficient strength was ignited to keep me interested through an exasperating attempt to find Chris' campus phone number and address. She had introduced herself as Chris Findley, and I looked through every campus list I could find for a Chris Findley only to come up empty. Only by going through my prior year's yearbook and looking through all the girls' residence pictures for her face did I happen across the clue. She was listed under her given name of Billie. How was I to know her name was Billie Christine?! Once past this hurdle, I could find her campus address and phone number. A short time later I asked her to one of the campus dances and the rest became history.

Amazingly Chris and I had and have many key things in common. We shared a common religion type, Protestant, although she a United Methodist and me a Mennonite. More importantly we shared a common perspective of the key role of religion in life. We were both farm kids who continued to love the farm and rural life. We were both hard workers, but we understood the need to play (and we did teach each other some different ways to play). We both love children and find great pleasure and satisfaction in teaching, coaching, and playing with them.

I do believe the thing that separated our relationship from most others and perhaps has been the most enduring bond is that our first preference is to work. We are not workaholics who tend to have a limited focus on working toward a specific target. Rather, we just enjoy work of many different types. This character in Chris complements mine and has been both a reward and a continuing challenge. We actually found great joy and fun in building several houses with Chris doing electrical, finish carpentry, mason tending, landscaping, and insulation work along with the standard painting and interior decorating. The feminists would love her, and I am sure some of you are left wondering what I did in this whole process!

Obviously, I was attracted to Chris for her inner beauty. Yet, as Dr. Ellen Kreidman notes in her books *Light His Fire* and *Light Her Fire*, women are mental and men are physical. No discussion of my wife would be complete without a comment on her physical attributes. At the time of our meeting, she was a coed of average attractiveness, becoming, but not stunning. I guess I would largely categorize her that way yet today. However, she became very cognizant of many of the particular things I found attractive and alluring in the opposite sex and worked hard to cultivate those things in herself. Much like hard work levels a playing field in terms of talent, Chris leveled the playing field in terms of appearance and made herself stunning in my eyes. I'm sure those same feminists who would find her house-building prowess "right on," would find her apparent capitulation to my desires "abhorrent."

Often when we would go out to parties, I would compliment her on being the prettiest girl there. I did not ever do this when a certain young lady associate named Penny happened to be at the same event, which lent great credence to my proclamations. Chris knew that I, and many other Cargill guys, found Penny to be quite stunning. I do remember a particular mid 70s evening when we, along with another couple, went to Jerry Kramer's Left Guard restaurant and club in Minneapolis. At one point the two girls went to the powder room and came back giggling. It seemed Chris had been "hit on" by two different gentlemen during that short trek. While Chris found it to be somewhat amusing, I found it to be an unbiased and objective confirmation of my own feelings.

As I was recently looking back over pictures of her during that time frame, 1970s and well into the 80s when she would have been in her 20s and 30s, I was again struck by how pretty she was and how easy it would have been for me to find her the prettiest girl of the lot. I am not discounting her continuing attractiveness, but with age comes an inability of any of us to objectively compete at the top of the class. Nevertheless, while she may no longer always be the prettiest girl at the party, I am still always thrilled I am the guy who gets to take her home.

Not too long after we were married in May of 1970, Chris informed me she had been to the doctor and she was pregnant. This was a complete surprise to me as we had not planned to have children for at least a couple of years—until we got our feet on the ground financially. While surprised, neither of us was necessarily unhappy about it. As the day approached I continued to plan the things I would do with my new son. My son would be my son as well as the younger brother I didn't have.

Finally, the time came on early morning, April 9, 1971. Chris woke me and said we needed to get to the hospital. We lived in Memphis, Tennessee at that time, so the trip to Methodist Hospital in mid-town took about twenty minutes. To this day, Chris reminds me of my insistence on obeying all traffic laws while her contractions were getting closer. As we arrived at the hospital (a baby delivering machine with large nurseries on two different floors), Chris was whisked away from me. I was sent to one of two large waiting rooms adjacent to the nurseries.

As father after father was brought the news and family after family marched to the viewing glass to see the new arrival and comment on how cute he or she was, I continued to wait alone as both of our families were in Iowa. Finally I was called to the phone where the doctor told me I had a little girl and he would be down to talk with me in a few minutes. I sat in stunned disbelief, a girl!!

In just a couple of minutes, the doctor came to speak with me to tell me everyone was okay. He gave me a little card and told me if I went to the second floor nursery and held it up to the window, they would show me my daughter, who we had earlier agreed would be named Renee Annette. I followed his instruction, and a nurse held up the reddest looking ugly creature I had ever seen. How could this be my daughter? I finally nodded in acknowledgment and retreated to the waiting room where I dutifully placed all the phone calls a new dad is supposed to make. I then went back and sat down in the waiting room until I could go in to see Chris who had been anaesthetized for the delivery.

As I sat there and listened to another long dissertation of beauty as another family went up to view their new addition, I decided I had to have a look at what a "regular beautiful baby" looked like. I got up and went to see. To my amazement and delight this creature was even uglier than Renee. I soon realized a key fact: All babies come out red and wet and kind of ugly looking when measured against normal. Only later did I realize a second more subjective, but far more important point; considering the marvel of creation and birth, there is nothing more beautiful than that red and wet living-breathing extension of you and your family.

I went back to the upstairs nursery to see my daughter with this new perspective. To my amazement, the wet, red, ugly baby with the delivery induced misshaped head was no longer there. Instead was the cutest little girl I had ever seen. She was no longer beet red, her face was round and she had the fullest head of dark hair in the nursery. I fell in love and immediately thanked God for giving me (and us) this beautiful little *girl.* Note: Although I am (and was) unquestionably prejudiced in my opinion of Renee's beauty, she spent an inordinate amount of time in the front row of the nursery babies during her four day stay. Nursery workers are always anxious to advertise their wares to the people passing by, and Renee was a real eye-catcher.

Renee has continued to be a hero to me throughout her life and we have had all types of great relationships together, including her basketball career as both player and coach. She is very much like me in that she can do anything and she is willing to take on about anything or anybody. I could count literally hundreds of "heroic" experiences in the past 30 plus years Renee has given me, including the indescribable feeling of walking her down the aisle at her wedding. However, none of these compare to what she accomplished simply with her birth. She made me understand what new life is about and she made me the proudest dad in the world at a time when I had no idea what fatherhood would bring. I have always counted my blessings that she was a girl. God just knows what to give us and when!!

When Chris became pregnant in 1975 with our second child, Derek James, I was elated. Interestingly, not once in the pregnancy did I give consideration to wanting a boy. While I think I really had no preference, Renee had so completely won me over that if I were to have had to make a choice, it would likely have been a girl.

When we went to the hospital on that day in February of 1976, I stayed with Chris through the pre delivery activities. I then pulled the biggest blunder and act of inconsiderateness one could imagine. Unlike Memphis in 1971 where I had no choice but to wait in a father's lounge, in Cedar Rapids, Iowa in 1976, I had the opportunity (and I should add the duty) to accompany Chris into the delivery room. Not knowing if I could handle all of the biology of the birth, of which women have no choice (not to mention the pain), I opted to wait outside.

How I could have passed the opportunity to be with the woman I loved at one of the most significant times in our lives remains beyond me? Moreover, how I could have passed on the opportunity to be present at life's greatest event is just as puzzling. Apparently cowardice has the capacity to remove all sanity from us. To this day if God would grant me the chance to go back and do any one thing over in my entire life, it would be to be present at the birth of Derek.

When I was given the news I had a son, there was a strange sensation that went through me. Even though Renee had created in me the knowledge little girls can steal and hold their daddy's heart, I think there is something internal to a man about having a son. I again stood in disbelief–although this time of a much more reflective nature.

While Renee had more of my characteristics and Derek had more of Chris's, he was my little boy and we played together at length. One of his first words was "tractor" and he and I have shared a love of tractors, implements, and farming all of his life. It was this love more than anything else that encouraged me to find ways to get back into some type of farming enterprise in the early 80s. Derek began to reach that age where young people can find satisfaction and life long learning experiences through all sorts of agricultural and farming activities and experiences.

This process began with expansion of our Iowa farming operation and Derek accompanying me on trips from Kansas to Iowa where we continually changed radio channels to hear the Oakridge Boys singing "Elvira" as many times as we could. These trips were wonderful reminders to me of trips with my father when I was Derek's age. From the Iowa operation we spawned a small operation in Kansas, relocated that to Illinois and grew it much bigger, and then relocated it back to Kansas and again grew it much bigger. Certainly our return to farming has had a significant impact on our adult and family experience. Note: Renee has also always been a farm girl and I do not want to take anything away from her contributions.

Derek used the farm as a springboard and took his love of agriculture to impressive heights in his youth. You will read more about this in Chapter 8: "Why Stationed by the Plow?" As I noted in an earlier chapter, I always loved working with my father on the farm and now I had an opportunity to enjoy that relationship from the other side of the age spectrum. I continue to enjoy that with Ryan and Brandon, but Derek was special, perhaps because he was first. Further, in our sharing, I found so much of my own childhood with my father.

One of the things that makes Derek more like my wife is he enjoys engaging people, and he is a super salesman. At some point in his life, Derek will become a primary player in Chapter 24. I hope I can be in position to share in that experience. He is also an accomplished auctioneer and "Colonel" (as auctioneers are called) Derek with his Stetson hat, commanding voice, and engaging personality is both impressive and entertaining.

In 1982 soon after we had moved to Kansas, following our second mission in Memphis, Chris and I discussed increasing our family size again and agreed that at 34 and 35 respectively, we were not too old. Chris checked with the doctor who told her there should be no particular health problems, but he feared she may have trouble getting pregnant. To his amazement, a couple of months later she was back in his office to confirm pregnancy.

The birth of our third child was scheduled for Wednesday, February 16 since Chris's doctor wanted to go skiing the following weekend. This time I was going to be in the room with Chris during the birthing process. No man can do that and not appreciate what a woman goes through to bring life into the world. The fact that women endure pregnancy and childbirth with such an inner joy, as witnessed by the "glow" of pregnant women, has to be a gift from God.

When the baby arrived, the doctor announced that it was another boy, this time Ryan Thomas. Then suddenly all the nurses and the doctor began scurrying around with little Ryan. A short while later, I was handed a little bundle all wrapped up in a blanket and allowed to carry this little bundle to Chris's room. I cannot describe the thrill I had.

Our euphoric joy was tempered a short time later when we learned from the doctor that when Ryan emerged, he had the umbilical cord wrapped around his neck and had been choking. He emerged not the "red color" that had so bothered me with Renee, but rather with a blue color. He had registered three on the scale of ten in terms of color and the medical people were concerned as to whether permanent damage had been done by a lack of oxygen to the brain. Twelve years after Renee had been born, I discovered how thankful one should be for a "red" baby.

Fortunately we could soon recognize no damage had been done to Ryan, and we had one more opportunity for thanksgiving. Ryan was soon wowing adults with his mathematical wizardry. At a very young age, he could do more math in his head than a lot of people could do with a calculator. Renee's friends in particular (12+ years his senior) got a big charge out of giving him math problems and marveling at how quickly he could solve them.

Mathematical genius notwithstanding, Ryan essentially came out of the womb with a ball in his hand. While both Renee and Derek were good athletes, they achieved most of it with intelligence and hard work. Ryan was more the natural athlete although he too utilizes intelligence and the hard work ethic. For many years, Ryan has been the central focus of family support at his athletic competitions. The contingent of supporters that accompany Ryan to his ball games is large.

Virtually all of our family is there and we all often have to "jump through hoops" to get there. In addition to feeling good about everyone supporting Ryan, as I look over the group, I continually recognize my immortality is in this group all around me. I thank Ryan for setting up the platform for that continual reassurance.

Beyond athletics and math, Ryan is so much like me it sometimes scares me. Knowing some of my background capers, I think it also scares Chris. Watching Ryan grow up is somewhat deja vu for me. It gives me the chance as an adult to watch what my life was like as a young man and in many ways see that played out before me.

By the mid 80s, Chris and I had lived in three states (Tennessee, Iowa, and Kansas) and had a child in each. When we moved to Illinois in 1987, I don't know if that fact played on us or if we simply missed having a little one again. Given I was 40 and Chris was 39 at the time we did debate whether trying for another child was a good idea or not. We finally determined we would try and allow God and nature to make the decision.

On a Saturday morning in March of 1988 as we awoke, Chris handed me a small gift-wrapped package and said happy birthday (my birthday is March 8). I innocently opened the box and there was a picture of a baby. What an exciting birthday gift that was!!

Several months later, Chris was planning a trip to St. Louis in the early morning to take sheep to market when she woke me in the middle of the night and announced she would not be going to St. Louis, but rather to the hospital in Springfield. This was about a month early so we weren't particularly prepared. One car was out of fuel and I experienced radiator problems with the other. Nevertheless, we did get to Springfield in time, and late in the morning of October 18, Brandon Kyle was born.

Once everything had settled down and Brandon was in the room with Chris, I returned to work. Soon after I had returned to work and proudly told everyone of my new son, I received a call from Chris that Brandon had breathing trouble and had been taken to intensive care. I returned to the hospital to find my son hooked up to all sorts of monitors and oxygen apparatus. Over the next few days, Brandon would be stuck and probed and constantly administered to. Each time I would see them come to stick his foot and know how he would cry, I just wanted to change places with him, so the pain could be on me and not him.

God again granted our petitions, and in a few days Brandon's lungs had cleared and we were allowed to bring him home from the hospital. Just as there is something special in the first child, I think there is something special in a child of older age. It is kind of like you are getting something you had thought was out of your reach. It is special and you are mature enough to be fully able to recognize it as such. I can understand the Old Testament's Jacob (later named Israel) who was so reluctant to let the son of his old age, Benjamin, travel to Egypt with his older brothers. I have been able to work through the process of "leaving the nest" with all of our other children. I think it will be the most difficult with Brandon.

Brandon was (and still is) fortunate in that he had (has) two mothers; Chris and Renee. It is really neat to see how he has returned the favor to Renee as he is now uncle, playmate, mentor, and protector to Renee's and her husband, Jon's children, Titus, Kayla, and Madison. In addition, Brandon is one of Benjamin and Lucas' favorite people as well. Benjamin and Lucas are our other grandsons and the sons of Derek and his wife Kris. If Ryan is like me in his approach to the establishment, I like to think Brandon is like me in his approach to children.

Brandon is very much his own person, and while our other children are independent as a result of their demeanor, Brandon is independent as a result of both demeanor and often necessity. Brandon is very much the most spontaneous person in our family, and I am trying to learn some of that art from him. He is an avid reader in a family that historically has read very little.

Brandon looks at today and this minute as today and this minute, rather than as some point on a time continuum. I am also trying to learn at least a piece of that art from him. Just as I have enjoyed watching Ryan grow up to see what I experienced, I am enjoying watching Brandon grow up to see what I missed.

Hank Aaron may have hit 755 home runs in his career, Bill Russell may have been the best defensive basketball player of all time, and Freddie Lambach's sprint car driving may have caught my fancy as a lad, but my real lifelong heroes are Chris, Renee, Derek, Ryan, and Brandon.

# Chapter 7
# Can You Speak the Language

When I started work for Cargill on Monday morning, the second of June in 1969, I reported to Minneapolis with the expectation of spending four weeks there and then being assigned to the West Side Soybean plant in Cedar Rapids, Iowa. I remember only two things about my first day on the job.

First, as soon as I had been introduced to everyone in the office, Gus assigned me to go check out of the $35 a night swank North Star Inn where Cargill had put me up when I arrived on Saturday night. He then assigned me to go to the Curtis Hotel and check into an $8 a night room. The Curtis was an old hotel a few blocks away that had been relegated by the sands of time to mostly a boarding house. My room in the Curtis was about one third the size of the one at the North Star and was right next to the elevator. Cargill made an instant point of conveying the message it was an organization that kept a close eye on operating costs. As a farm boy with largely conservative roots, that was not a new paradigm for me, and I was not bothered by the room in the Curtis. To this day, I believe it is of primary importance to be a low cost producer, and I have always believed it was and is incumbent on all employees to be judicious in their use of company funds.

The second thing that remains indelibly etched in my mind from that first day was the discussion with Gus when he informed me that following my four to five week Minneapolis training stint, I would be going to the soybean plant in Memphis, Tennessee. This was the top performing plant in the Cargill soybean group, and Gus told me they wanted me to go be a part of that team. While I was certainly honored to be assigned to the top plant, I had been expecting to be in Cedar Rapids, Iowa. In Cedar Rapids I would be close to home and the farm as well as to Iowa State University, where my soon to be fiancée, Chris, was in her senior year. Memphis! A few second thoughts raced through my mind.

When I arrived in Memphis just after the July fourth holiday, I was greeted by a string of seventeen straight days when the temperature climbed to over 100 degrees with a wringing humidity that turned every aspect of the soybean plant into something between a sauna and an inferno. Nevertheless, Memphis had a great operating management team led by Fred Brosius, arguably the best plant superintendent in the Company at the time, and a good crew of operating people in the plant.

Before my arrival in Memphis, I had never been any further south than St. Louis. I thought the only language barrier between North and South was "you guys" vs. "you-awl" and the only semantics problem one was likely to encounter was knowing when the word was "all" meaning everything in total versus when the word was "awwll" meaning the lubricating material you put in your car engine crankcase. My education was about to begin!

I also knew Memphis had a large black population. That fact did not trouble me as I had always prided myself in looking at the person and not the color. In the North, most of the blacks I had encountered (including Dr. Graham, the best technical educator I had at ISU) had only one thing different from the rest of us, black skin. They spoke like we did and generally lived their lives in the same manner as we did.

What I discovered when I arrived in Memphis was the white people spoke one language and the black people spoke another language. In addition, there was a technical language that was associated with the operation that was also very specific. To my total dismay, I didn't understand much of any of these. To be sure, I came closer to understanding the white language, but even that was no small challenge.

What I am referencing here are the actual words. The Doug Brooks concept discussed in Chapter 2 of understanding the person behind the words was still a light-year away. I was just trying to figure out whether someone was asking a question, making a statement, or telling me where to go! I was afraid to say yes or no. I'm equally certain the guys (there were no gals at the plant in those days) in Memphis wondered what kind of dialect I spoke since after "hello" the next most used phrase of mine was "I'm sorry, could you say that again?"

Tommy (Tommy in the South would have been either Tom or Thomas in the North) was one of the operators and became a friend of mine. One evening as I walked into the lunchroom where Tommy was taking a break, he looked up at me and said, "Hey, how about a coke? I'll buy."

"Sure," I replied, "thanks."

Whereupon Tommy looked at me with a somewhat puzzled look then commented, "Okay, what kind do you want?"

"Coke is fine," I noted.

"Yeah, what kind do you want?" queried Tommy again.

"Coke is Okay," I said. This exchange went on for a couple of more rounds with me becoming more and more puzzled and Tommy becoming more and more exasperated. Finally, not willing to proceed with what he perceived as a dumb conversation going nowhere, Tommy burst out, "Look, I offered to buy you a coke and you said okay. Now for the past five minutes I've been trying to get you to tell me what kind of coke do you want! Do you want a strawberry coke or do you want a root beer coke or do you want a 7-up coke or do you want a Coca-Cola coke?"

That last phase finally struck home, a Coca-Cola coke. If it would have been a written conversation, I might have noted Tommy's coke was not capitalized and mine was. To Tommy and to the rest of Southerners, coke was synonymous with our Northern terms, pop or soda. To me Coke was a proper name meaning the flagship product of the Coca-Cola Company. Recognizing this difference I smiled and said, "A Coca-Cola coke would be just fine." Then I proceeded to engage Tommy in a discussion about the relative meaning of the terms pop, soda, and coke. We enjoyed a good laugh over it, and then for the remainder of my stay in Memphis, Tommy and I continued to pimp each other about pop or coke flavors.

I also remember one of the black meal loaders, Marcel, engaging me one night near one of the meal bins and asking me for something. His words were so foreign to me that I had no earthly idea what he was asking for. Cautious not to acknowledge something that was wrong or dangerous, I continued to ask him to repeat what he had said. Finally, a second Marcel, another black man, walked over to come to my rescue. Unfortunately, Marcel II's dialect was absolutely no different than Marcel I's. Now I had two guys trying to get me to understand what they thought was perfectly clear, and yet, I was as foggy as a London morning on what they were saying.

Finally, Marcel II began to do a kind of crossbred pantomime/charade/point to other objects. Eventually, I understood they needed a claw hammer. Can you believe it? Something as simple as a claw hammer and we couldn't get the connection made. As time went on and I learned more about the operation, I was more able to narrow down the choices and thereby increase my chances of understanding simply by recognizing the discussion was likely geared to something in the operation. Marcel had needed to install a grain door. This is a paper door with metal straps that is nailed in the doorway of a boxcar prior to loading. Had I recognized that, I might have gotten to the claw hammer a lot quicker.

Finally, as part of an industrial complex, I now ran into nomenclature that was as unknown as a foreign language. One of the principal maintenance tools was a channel-lok. I had no idea what a channel-lok referred to. I had used what we had called a "crooked nose pliers" on the farm for years, but we didn't ever know its real name was channel-lok. What for years had been pulleys (and still were when I returned to the farm to work with Dad) all of a sudden became sheaves. In addition, lots of things I had never seen before had names I had never heard before.

How does one overcome these obstacles? Hard work! I did work very hard to understand the words. The old adage "a picture is worth a thousand words" became very real to me. I was eventually able to "master" all of the languages principally by the application of this adage. Remember Marcel had finally made me understand his request for a claw hammer by actions and objects. I made use of all types of pictures and objects. I had an entire room full of vendor catalogs in my apartment and review of these made it easy to associate technical names with objects.

I did lots of pointing in verbal discussions both as statements and as questions. Since I was always pretty good at drawing and sketching, I became more focused on drawing pictures as I talked. Some people today think I cannot talk without a pencil and paper (particularly on technical issues). Actually, this trait is not so much limited to technical issues, but rather to issues that are not indigenously familiar to either the listener or me. Drawing became my backup to straight verbal conversation. Unquestionably one cannot draw or even sketch as fast as one can talk or listen. Accordingly, drawing slows down the processing for both speaker and listener and perhaps this is as important as the pictorial depiction itself. Certainly, when understanding is the desired end point, pictures are hard to beat.

With time (and work), I came to understand the dialects, and I could both speak the languages and understand them without any crutches. As years went by, this ability proved to be both valuable and enjoyable.

After I left Memphis, I was assigned to Cedar Rapids East (CRE). This was a great facility and will be discussed in various other chapters. For now, center stage goes to Bill Matson, the general manager at CRE. Bill was a top-notch person who was cut in the traditional Cargill conservative manager mold and was initially a bit suspicious of my political leanings, since I had just come from Memphis, Tennessee. Because we were never guys to pass up the opportunity to have some fun, my boss, Uli Sander and I played along with Bill's fears and concerns. We allowed (and baited) him to think I was just a little bit prejudiced and a lot red-necked. Uli's wife, Marianna, was very liberal politically so our charade extended to social encounters where we made great sport of my "ultra-conservatism and red-neck nature " as well.

Eventually, Uli left for another Cargill location, and I was promoted to plant superintendent reporting directly to Bill. Bill and I developed a good working relationship with Bill continuing to work quietly to shape my political leaning more toward "the Cargill way" which was predictably fairly conservative and relatively non-confrontational. Then one day, the managers and superintendents of all the plants were instructed to make arrangements at their own convenience to go to Memphis and observe the plant security systems that had been installed there.

I could hardly wait. I looked forward to this journey as a farm cat looks forward to winter when all the field mice work their way toward the farmstead buildings. I would get to see some old friends in Memphis and I was going to have some fun with Bill. When we arrived at the Memphis airport, I took the lead. Walking out to the taxi area, I spotted a large black woman taxi driver. This lady looked to me like she probably spoke "Memphis black" and had a "thrill-a-minute" driving pattern. I would not be disappointed on either count.

I walked over to her and asked if she could take us to President's Island, which was the location of the plant and about a 20-minute cab ride. She nodded and Bill and I climbed in. I immediately initiated a conversation with her and she obliged. For twenty minutes she and I conversed like old buddies about everything and anything. Poor Bill could only understand my half of the conversation and I purposely picked topics that could not be easily followed without understanding both sides. In addition, this all happened as we wove in and out of traffic with the cab driver continually looking back at me, conversing and the two of us laughing frequently. I think it was the "longest" ride Bill ever had.

When we arrived at the plant, Bill scrambled out of the cab. I think he was half angry with me and half thankful I was with him. I immediately ran into Vaughnsy, a short black man who had been on one of my crews in earlier years. Vaughnsy came right up to me, put his arm around me and said in his native dialect, "Jim, I've really missed you. Are you coming back to be with us?" Then he looked at Bill who was obviously somewhat stunned by this show of affection and said in language Bill could understand, "Jim's like my brother."

I looked at Vaughnsy and said very clearly, "Come on Vaughnsy, anybody can see there is not any way we can be brothers. Look how different we are." Bill was starting to squirm as he was sure I was about to create an incident with a racial remark. "Look at us Vaughnsy," I went on. "You're way too short to pass for my brother!" Vaughnsy threw back his head in laughter and slapped me on the back a couple of times.

I really believe it was at that precise minute Bill understood I was not a racist, not a red-neck, not a bigot, and not a Wallace activist. Rather I was just a guy who had figured out how to look past the color, look past the socio-economic status, master the language barrier and create lasting friendships with people with whom my only apparent commonality was that we worked together. Interestingly, from that point on, my relationship with Bill continued to move from one of mutual respect to one of mutual friendship.

As the years went by, I continued using the picture, object, and association techniques to speak the languages of the different businesses, industries and localities I was assigned to. In addition, it proved highly valuable when I gave a group of Russians a tour of the corn processing operations in Cedar Rapids. The Russians were corn millers, so they understood some of the process. Although they had an interpreter with them, she understood very few of the technical terms I used and had trouble converting my English words to words that the Russian delegation could understand. Once again, lots of picture drawing, animation, and object association turned an otherwise frustrating effort into one of positive delight.

Experiences like that of the Russians notwithstanding however, not until I became involved in the development, construction and commissioning of a pork processing facility in Taiwan in the early 90s did the task of understanding the language take on the same kind of monumental proportion as it had back in Memphis in the summer of 1969.

In early 1990 I was given the assignment of being the principal Cargill USA manager in charge of developing the Taiwan pork facility. The facility was to be built by Cartai, a joint venture company between Cargill and Taiwan Sugar Corporation. Cartai had a 20-year history of business activity in Taiwan. Excel, my employer and a USA subsidiary of Cargill, was to manage the technical components of the project. My qualifications for doing this work included a fairly impressive list of USA construction and operating experiences in pork and related industries. However, other than one short journey to Europe and one to Honduras, I had no foreign experience. Without question, I could speak the language of the business. Without question, I once again could NOT speak, write, or understand the language of the region.

What I would soon discover were the challenges of Memphis in 1969 were dwarfed by the challenges of Taiwan/Republic of China in 1990. Interestingly, the Chinese alphabet actually mirrors my theories on pictures and objects. However, since the Chinese alphabet is several thousand years old, it is likely this is merely coincidental and not a result of any collaboration between them and me. The Chinese written language is based on pictures and/or graphical depictions of the meaning of each specific word. For example, woman is depicted by a stick figure that is obviously pregnant.

To my way of thinking, this makes a tremendous amount of sense. As I have maintained, how better to convey understanding than to draw a picture. The problem comes in time and numbers. The English language is made up of several thousand words that are depicted in written form by some combination of 26 letters or characters. On the other hand, the Chinese language consists of some 40,000 words, each of which is depicted in written form by some unique combination of lines.

We can recognize all the words in the English language as some simple combination of some of the 26 letters. This is true whether we know what the word means or not. However, I am told even very educated Chinese people will at most recognize "only" about 10,000 Chinese words in written form. Further, over the years, in an attempt to "speed up" written communication, the Chinese have "reduced" many of the pictures to more simple lines and strokes. Of course, the further away from the "real picture" one gets, the more one must memorize the characters and connect to the word rather than understand the word because of the characters.

Other than a few words of cursory interest, I did not try to understand any of the Chinese written language. I did, however, have the firm intent to learn and understand at least some of the spoken language. I soon found out the spoken language is as difficult as the written language. In the USA, we generally use inflection in our speech to convey our feelings. While people may utilize inflection to understand our intent, the actual meaning of a word does not change if we speak it softly or forcefully. However, the Chinese spoken language includes five different inflections in speech. The very same pronunciation may have five distinct and usually very different meanings depending on the inflection. Even if you get the word right, you have only a 20 percent chance of conveying the right meaning.

On my first visit, I asked one of the expatriate American managers at Cartai about learning Chinese. He cautioned me not to. He said Cargill instructions were to conduct all business in English. The Chinese recognize few foreigners will speak their language so many of them are willing and able to conduct business in English. Since the Chinese are willing to play on our turf, we should accept the home field advantage and not confuse the issue by trying to learn and use their language. Although history seemed to tell me differently, I assumed others knew far better than I, so I did just as I was instructed.

However, let me give a word of caution. There is little home field advantage if you are playing by rules that are written in language you do not understand. The home field advantage is further diminished if the scoreboard is keeping time and recording the score in characters you do not understand. Finally, the home field advantage virtually disappears when the other team has your playbook memorized and you do not even know how to keep track of which players they have in the game. Most importantly, the game looses a lot of its luster, no matter where it is played, when it is virtually impossible to get beyond the game itself and become personal friends with the other players since the only interaction can be on game day and on the playing ("business") field.

How different would be a return trip to Taiwan with a Bill Matson type associate, like my return trip to Memphis with Bill. There would be no embrace and no friendly interchange with a "Vaughnsy type" comrade. The cab driver would very likely not be a black woman. Nevertheless, once again, my associate would understand only my half of any conversation I would have with the cab driver. Unfortunately, so would I.

# CHAPTER 8:
# Why Stationed by the Plow

When our oldest son, Derek, entered high school he enrolled in a vocational agriculture class and became involved in the FFA (Future Farmers of America) organization that is often a part of these programs. Six officers and an advisor make up the administrative team in each of the FFA chapters. At the start of each formal meeting, the advisor and all of the officers stand behind their chairs for the call to order. On the table in front of each of these persons is a specific symbol; an open hand, an American flag, a bust of George Washington, an ear of corn, an owl, a plow, and a rising sun.

As the meeting begins, the President asks the Vice President if all officers are present. The Vice President responds he will call the roll, whereupon he proceeds to call out each office individually beginning with the Sentinel. That officer responds he/she is "present, stationed here by the . . . (whatever his/her symbol is)." The Vice President then asks, "Why stationed by the . . . (reference to the symbol)?" The particular officer then responds with the correlation between the symbol at his station and his particular job function. In the Sentinel's case, he responds he is stationed by the hand because he welcomes people at the door and extends the hand of friendship to them. This process continues through all of the officers below the Vice President level and then to the Advisor.

After the Advisor completes his discussion on why he is stationed next to the owl, he asks the Vice President why he is stationed next to the plow. The Vice President proceeds to explain *The plow is a symbol of labor and tillage of the soil. Without labor, neither wisdom nor knowledge can accomplish much . . . etc.* The first time I heard that and every time since, I am moved by it. It says so succinctly what I have firmly believed all of my life.

Derek, in fact became the Vice President of both his local chapter as well as the regional chapter. I never tired of hearing him repeat those words, nor could I have been more proud of what they meant to him. FFA was very good to Derek. His accomplishments included a top 4 finish in forage production in the entire United States and a subsequent trip to Europe with some 40 other FFA members. That trip was earned by Derek on the basis of his performance, performance that had as its foundation, labor and hard work. Derek's accomplishments were a direct result of his application of being "stationed by the plow."

Our second son, Ryan, was later a part of the FFA programs and made the same application of those principals of work and labor. I take the liberty to substitute the word "work" for the word "labor." Although in many instances "work" and "labor" are synonymous, that is not always the case. Interestingly, one of Ryan's coaches once told the team how he lamented the invention of the big round baler.

[*Note for city folks:* Big round balers bale up about 1600 to 1800 pounds of hay in one bundle that is then transported by tractor to storage and ultimate feeding. Prior to this, and when I was a boy, hay was baled in small square bales of about 75 pounds each. These bales then had to be "manhandled" (quite often by teenage boys) at least three times between baling and ultimate feeding. No matter how you sliced this process, it was hard labor and hard work.]

The point the coach was trying to make was that today's kids often don't have the opportunity to learn about hard work through hard labor as we did since mechanical means now remove a lot of the hard labor component. It can still be hard work using a big round baler. In our part of Kansas, most of this is done between the hours of 10:30 P.M. and 5:30 A.M. The take-home message here though is there is nothing that better teaches the concept and value of *hard work* than *hard labor.*

Being of that general persuasion, I'm sure there were times in my career when others with whom I worked thought I expected and perhaps demanded too much. One person who did not and who in fact has driven me by his own relentless effort is Dick Robinson. Dick is a 6 foot 2 inch, 240 pound ex-marine MP with the penmanship of an English teacher. When we (Cargill) took over the pork processing operation in Beardstown in the mid 80s, Dick was my maintenance manager. We became close friends at that time and have remained so ever since. It does not get too tough for Dick, nor is there any job he will not tackle.

In fact, Dick and Dan Schnitker are the two hardest working guys with whom I have had the privilege of working.

Dick is also the embodiment of the concept that hard labor is the father of the hard work ethic. There is virtually nothing Dick cannot do with his hands. He is obviously skilled in all facets of equipment maintenance by nature of his position. Moreover, he is a skilled heavy equipment operator, a superb welder (his one-of-a-kind stainless steel belt buckles have graced the midsections of men and women in all regions of the country); he is a skilled concrete finisher, an accomplished cook, and I could go on. The point is, in general, he can handle just about any job that requires the use of one's hands, save perhaps medical surgeries. In addition to all of that, Dick is a professional bass fisherman on the pro circuits, and he tackles fishing with the same intensity he does any other project.

I have long subscribed to the notion you need never worry about being unemployed if you can do things with your hands. When we were commissioning the plant in Taiwan, Dick was there for several weeks helping us get the plant up and running. Although Dick spoke no more Chinese than any of the rest of us (which was next to none), he had an uncanny ability to teach and train the Chinese maintenance group with whom he was working. Dick did not do this with eloquent speech or sophisticated training manuals. He did it with his *hands.* The Chinese maintenance people simply watched in absolute awe as this giant of an American in both stature and ability performed all of the maintenance functions with skill and determination.

Now if you are not aware, the Chinese are the greatest copiers in the world. $39 Rolex watches and other "knockoffs" can be found on virtually any street in Taiwan if you know how to get into the back room of certain stores. At the plant, the goal of the Chinese maintenance people was to copy or emulate what they saw Dick Robinson do. You could not design a more effective training program. Dick and a couple of other good hands people were certainly the most effective of all of us in training the Taiwanese nationals in the plant operating functions.

I bring the example of Dick into my work philosophy discussion because he is the absolute apotheosis of the work concepts I hold to and preach. Check the story of "Dick Robinson and the Taiwan Mafia" in the "More Stories" section at the end of the book for another side of him. Back to my point, as I have said and as Dick has demonstrated, hard labor breeds the hard work ethic.

My thesis is that any labor you do with your hands will generate an immediate and observable result. Consider Dick cooking steaks, welding intricate stainless steel pieces into a beautiful belt buckle, moving earth with heavy equipment, repairing a piece of equipment, finishing concrete, or even reeling in a big bass. Each one of those creates an immediate gratification and an enriching sense of accomplishment. The satisfaction elicited from that experience drives one to put that kind of effort into every type of work one does, both mental as well as physical.

Lyle Bowers, one of my eighth grade teachers and a man who I admired immensely, was a prime example of a hard worker in the teaching profession. You may recall Lyle from meeting him earlier in Chapter 4. Lyle worked hard to provide a learning experience for us. He was not satisfied to only teach; he worked very hard to insure that we learned. Our learning is what gave Lyle his sense of accomplishment.

In case you are wondering where or how Lyle Bowers learned about hard work or if he was ever involved in any type of physical labor or working with his hands, consider this. My Uncle Edwin Roth recounts the details of the following story regarding Lyle. In the late 1930s, Lyle spent a summer digging a well by hand. Even on the surface this would seem to qualify him as having done some very heavy manual labor. In this case, however, the story goes well beyond the surface, 90 feet below the surface in fact. The well he dug by hand was 90 feet deep.

As told by Uncle Edwin, who incidentally also helped me understand the work ethic and reward structure—I worked part time for him in his electrical contracting company during my high school and college years—Lyle was hired by a local farmer to dig a well for him. Lyle dug down a few feet and then fashioned a tripod over the top of this "well hole" to lower a bucket into the well hole via a horse drawn rope through a pulley at the top of the tripod. Inside the hole, Lyle would fill the bucket and his assistant would lead the horse to pull the bucket up out of the hole and then dump the material outside and lower the bucket back down. As Lyle moved down he shored up the hole, which I am told was about 4 foot in diameter, with curved wood pieces like barrel staves to keep it from caving in.

When Lyle had completed the digging at about 90 feet, he cleaned the hole then screened and bricked the bottom. Then, as he worked his way back out of the hole, he cased the sides of the well hole in brick. As he moved his platform upward, he would remove the bottom level of "staves" and replace them with bricks and mortar until he reached the top. Once there he had completed the job, and the fruit of his labor was a fully cased (bricked) 90-foot deep water well. Obviously, I was not around at the time, but I am told this was about a summer's project for Lyle and his assistant.

I have to muse at the thought of Lyle giving his classes the mind-bending question of the frog that fell into the 20 foot deep well and began to climb out. The frog advanced 5 feet up the wall each day, but slid back down 4 feet each night. On what day did the frog finally get out of the well? [*Note:* If you said the 16th day you are right.] I would venture to say there probably has not been another math teacher in America this century who could give that example with the same sense of experience and "been there/done that" as Lyle Bowers!! Is it strange that Lyle Bowers took his job as a teacher so seriously, put himself so completely into it, and worked so tirelessly at it? Not hardly!

I could not get back to some form of farming operation quick enough as our children began to grow. I wanted them to get involved in that kind of physical labor. Farm labor is work for which the results of effort are sudden and sure. Once that has been ingrained, the concept of effort and associated reward is in place and one can extrapolate to a variety of work types, like teaching and coaching as our daughter has done. Even though the results may not always be as sudden and sure, they can still be confidently predicted.

Working hard to effect substantial and worthwhile results is something in which one can take great satisfaction. Such work becomes not only a way of life, but more importantly the source of pride, accomplishment, and satisfaction. These provide a joy in living and often a reason for living that I fear is lacking in many people's lives today. I am confident the Lyle Bower(s) and Dick Robinson(s) of the world measure life against a standard of fullness. For them, the glass is always at least partially full, never partly empty.

I do not mean to suggest everyone must be a skilled welder or be involved in some farming operations or dig a 90-foot deep well to understand hard work themselves and moreover to be able to teach their children about labor and develop and instill in them a positive hard work ethic. However, I do suggest the more anyone, and particularly young children, can be made to use their hands—mow the yard, shovel snow, bake cookies or cakes, do any number of woodworking or craft type projects, etc.—the more likely will be the chance they will be able to associate results with effort, performance with work, and satisfaction with accomplishment.

I have always tried to instill the spirit of hard work and the associated sense of accomplishment in the people with whom I work. I do this selfishly because I know they will perform better and more productively if I can instill this in them. This will obviously make my operation better and make me in turn more successful personally. However, my selfish motives (while present) pale in comparison to my real purpose for working so hard to instill these spirits in my co-workers. The real reason is I know how good it is to go home at night feeling that wonderful sense of accomplishment. I want all of my friends and associates to be able to share that same feeling.

I liken this mission to my efforts when I coach little league baseball. I think I am a fairly good hitting instructor and I work very hard to get the kids to hit the ball. Obviously, if kids can hit the ball, we will likely win a lot of games. I like to win, but once again, that is of secondary importance. What is of primary importance is I know what it feels like to connect with the ball, see it rip off the end of the bat, and then ultimately stand on second base with a double, or third base with a triple, or even touch home plate after a home run. Talk about sudden and sure results! Nothing seizes the moment like that for a kid. It will keep him or her coming back to play day after day. And that sense of accomplishment will inevitably transfer to a host of other situations in those young lives.

Beyond the kids, the results for me, the old man coaching these kids, are often just as sudden and sure. The satisfaction and shear joy of looking out from the dugout or the coaching box to that kid standing on second or third base and seeing a smile that is as broad as Texas warms my heart and reinforces for me the timeless nature of the joy of accomplishment.

My little league discussion leads me very naturally into my final point on hard work. Hard work is not something you do at work. It is something *you do at life!* It takes hard work to be a successful little league coach, measured not by Ws & Ls, but by how much the kids develop and enjoy the experience. If you wish to be a good weekend golfer and enjoy that sense of accomplishment at beating par (no matter what par is for you), you will have to work at it. If you wish your yard to be well manicured, you will have to work at that. Houses do not paint themselves, nor do gardens pull their own weeds.

How many people go on diets or try to quit smoking or initiate exercise programs only to fail? I can speak to diets and exercise from experience, and I surmise smoking cessation is just as tough. Each one of these extremely commendable undertakings comes replete with a huge dose of difficult and often unpleasant requirements. To stay the course on any of them demands hard work. Unfortunately, the results while sure are not usually sudden. People who are not inclined toward a hard work ethic and who can only appreciate immediate gratification are doomed even before they start.

Without diminishing the impact of the examples just enumerated, of all the places where your work ethic affects your personal life, no place else is the impact so great or the stakes so high as in marriage and raising a family. It is quite easy to fall in love as evidenced by the fact that millions of people do it, and many do it numerous times. It is quite another issue to stay in love year after year. Long-term meaningful love takes a lot of very hard work. And true to form, the accomplishment of effecting a long-term loving relationship carries with it a bountiful share of joy and satisfaction.

Creating children is also like falling in love. For most couples, it is very easy to do. Certainly, having children (the birthing process) starts to be a lot harder work for a woman. At least that is my perspective as a man. Raising children is then where the real work comes in for both parents. Unfortunately, too many parents today are either unequipped for that process or unwilling to take the process on in full measure.

My opinion is that generally both of these are a result of an insufficient work ethic. In the case of not being properly equipped; the successful parent goes out and gets equipped and that takes a lot of work. In the case of not being willing to take the task on full bore; it is usually a simple matter of a parent not having enough of a work ethic to accept the challenge and put forth the additional effort to insure that his/her off-spring are loved and supported. Like effecting and demonstrating real love for a mate, effecting and demonstrating real love for a child also demands a prodigious amount of hard work. It also results in a plethora of joy and satisfaction.

No matter what one's professional walk in life and no matter the length and breadth of one's personal life and experiences; one cannot have any greater opportunity for success and happiness than to have been, for at least some part of his or her life, *"stationed by the plow."*

# Chapter 9
# What Makes the World Go Round

Old conventional wisdom says it is love that makes the world go round. That may be the case in idealistic and romantic circles. As a pragmatist, I tend to be a little less romantic and therefore, look to alternate power sources as the impetus for a spinning world. While doing so, I do not wish to downplay the value or impact of love. Indeed, I expect my wife will read this chapter too, so I certainly do not want to create any conditions for my world to stop spinning.

While I may seem a little capricious in my selection of the motive source, my machine design instructor back at Iowa State University was not. Dr. M was a retired naval officer who returned to the teaching profession much to the chagrin of many of us who wound up in his classes. If you took ME 316, 317, or 318, Machine Design I, II, or III, you did wind up in his class as he *was* machine design at Iowa State in those days. It was not that Dr. M was not intelligent or knowledgeable in his field. He was both of those. What bothered us most about Dr. M was his philosophy, "The world revolves on right answers!!!" No room for love, romanticism, or idealism, just right answers!!

Now to college students, exams are tools instructors use to test your understanding of the general concepts of both the subject matter and more importantly, test taking. *Certainly,* they are not supposed to test your ability to get to the right answer or even whether you actually *understand* the details. If you understand the general concepts or if you can create a perception on the part of the instructor that you possess that understanding, then your test scores will be okay no matter how badly you butcher the real solution.

Partial credit has been the salvation of virtually every college engineering student from the beginning of time. Set the problem up in some reasonable fashion, shove some numbers into the equations, slam down an answer and go on to another question that you *might really* know how to solve. Most instructors give a cursory look and award from 7 to 9 points (of a possible 10) for "knowing how to set up the problem."

Not Dr. M! As he reminded us day after day, "The world revolves on right answers! If you design a bridge and do everything right but incorrectly do the math and are off by a factor of 10 (which was pretty easy to do with the slide rules we used before they were replaced by electronic calculators and later computers), the bridge will fail. Vehicles and people will be plunged into the icy waters of the river. In your criminal neglect and civil liability lawsuits, do you think your lawyers will be able to get you 9 points for setting it up right?"

We did have to admit he had a point. Dr. M was doing us a service we failed to appreciate. He was preparing us for passage from academia to the real world. Unfortunately, many people are not able to make that transition successfully. In most instances that is a direct result of their inability to understand and lay claim to the philosophy espoused by Dr. M.

The world does revolve on right answers. Consider the space program. Scientists and astrologers must be able to predict exactly what position the various space bodies will be in at precise times before scheduling a space craft to go into orbit. Being off by a few minutes is not cause for reduced credit; it is cause for absolute catastrophe. If I am the astronaut, I certainly want Dr. M's philosophy pasted all over the walls, desks, and minds of the engineers and scientists at NASA.

While failure in the general business and industrial world may not always have the kind of dramatic and cataclysmic results as failure in space flight, it nevertheless always results in adverse consequences. Right answers are every bit as much the fuel that powers progress and success in the industrial environment as in the space program.

There is one clarification I think should go without saying, but in today's politically charged atmosphere I do think must be pointed out. When Dr. M referred to right answers, he was referring to scientifically correct results. In today's environment, "right" often means politically correct or socially correct or emotionally correct and a host of other "correctnesses." I will not dispute the fact that a person's career may be enhanced by being politically correct as is discussed in later chapters. I will also not dispute that a person's social standing within given groups may be secured by taking socially or emotionally correct positions. However, the natural world obeys all of the scientific laws of nature and machines and process operations are based on application of those laws.

I will also not dispute the subjective nature of certain elements in business and industry like sales and advertising, etc. However, in all those business disciplines where real value is added to raw materials via machines and processes and so forth or where numerical functions are utilized as in banking, finances, accounting and information technology, the laws of nature are alive, well, and not compromised. Scientifically correct answers are necessary or the process grinds to a halt.

Native intelligence is a good attribute to have to be able to arrive at right answers. It is not an absolute requirement, however, nor does its presence insure right answers will be forthcoming as some of the following examples prove. Finding scientifically correct answers is not difficult, but the process is comprehensive. It does demand several disciplines and certain abilities.

The first part of the process is to properly define the problem. The right answer to the wrong problem is still probably the wrong answer to the right problem. Amazingly, for many people this is a most difficult assignment. In the early 70s, we installed a new DT (desolventizer toaster) in the Cedar Rapids East soybean plant. This unit was manufactured by Morehead Machine and was supposed to be the class of the industry. We had no end of trouble with this unit and found one workmanship problem after another.

As we corrected these problems, particularly some of the more significant ones, the unit began to perform properly. The difficulty was that in solvent extraction, you get one chance a year to do normal maintenance, including the introduction of cutting and welding. During the rest of the year, even the tools used for day to day adjustments needed to be brass coated to avoid sparks, and worker's clothing needed to be natural fabric to avoid static electricity. The bottom line is there are not easy opportunities to recover from poor installations, poor workmanship, or poor equipment in the extraction plant.

You can imagine the chagrin of our management team, Jeff Stanley, Bob Foote, Virgil Tharp and me, a year later when we were to install a new stripper condenser in the extraction plant and our instructions were that we would purchase that unit from Morehead Machine. The unit arrived, and we were set to install it on our annual shutdown.

We had contracted with McVay Construction Co to do the installation. As they started the installation, they discovered a problem they brought to our attention. The mounting feet were welded on the condenser upside down. Still vividly remembering our past experience with Morehead, we did not find this surprising and simply told McVay's people to cut off the feet, turn them over, and weld them back on.

As the installation continued, McVay's people informed us the vapor inlet was two feet above the centerline instead of two feet below centerline. The inlet and outlet water lines were on the bottom of the unit instead of the top. The vapor outlet at the top was four inches instead of the two that was specified and the condensate outlet at the bottom was two inches instead of four inches as it was supposed to be. As each of these were called to our attention, we cursed Morehead, lamented the fact we had been forced to use their equipment, and then ultimately instructed the McVay people to make the necessary alterations to accommodate Morehead's mistakes.

When we started the plant back up, as one might expect, the stripper condenser did not work well at all. The new larger condenser did not do as good a job as the old smaller unit had. On a daily basis, we railed at the incredibly lousy workmanship of Morehead and concluded the internal baffles were likely as messed up as all the external components had been.

One day about eight months after this installation, our plant clerk, Ron Dirks, went out to the extraction plant to get one of his daily inventory numbers. Ron had no technical background at all. On this particular day, however, as he walked by the stripper condenser, one particular thing caught his attention. He hurried back to the office where Jeff, Virgil, Bob, and I were having a production scheduling meeting.

Ron burst into the room and excitedly interrupted our discussions. "Boy!" he exclaimed, "I can see now why you guys complain so much about Morehead. You know the workmanship on that stripper condenser is so bad, I noticed today the nameplate is even on upside down." The four of us looked at each other in stunned silence. Without anyone saying a word, we each grabbed our hard hats and hurried off toward extraction. Poor Ron stood there in disbelief. What he thought he had discovered as the epitome of shoddy workmanship had not even elicited a comment, much less a congratulatory remark.

What Ron had not realized was he had unwittingly arrived at the right answer to the original question raised by McVay's guys when they informed us the feet were on upside down. McVay's people had simply rigged the wrong end of the condenser when they hooked onto it with the crane to lift it into place. As the crane lowered it down, the feet were obviously upside down—the entire unit was upside down. However, we were so pre-occupied by past experience blindness, we instantly moved our thought process to lousy workmanship instead of identifying and defining the real problem. Interestingly, every other problem encountered should have been as obvious to us as the nameplate, but a colored and perhaps closed mind nullifies even the highest IQs.

On the next welding shutdown, we had McVay's crew come back in and turn the condenser back over to the correct position with the nameplate and everything else now in the correct orientation. As one might predict, that part of our operation smoothed out, and we had no further problems with the stripper condenser.

Once the problem is properly defined, the breadth of the problem can be determined. That brings us to the next element; the discipline and ability to break the problem down into simple components. Most of us have heard that complex problems are just a combination of several simple problems. The best way then to solve the complex problem is to break it down to the simple problems and solve each of them individually.

In the early 80s, we installed an automated box storage and retrieval system at our beef facility in Dodge City, Kansas. This was a unique system and was at the cutting edge of technology at the time. We hired a firm out of the California Silicon Valley to do all of the computerized software work for this system. The principals and technicians in this company were essentially all Ph.D. types. The company in total probably boasted as high an IQ as any company in America. The system we installed was a very complex system and these guys were used to dealing with complex systems.

Their specialty was solving complex system problems in their native form; that is as complex system problems. They were not in the business of solving simple problems. As a result, these people gave us a complex operating system we could not support internally. As complex problems arose, they solved them in the complex state. However, we did not have the ability to understand the complex documentation. Moreover, when simple problems came up, they could not solve them in simple form so they aggregated them into complex problems and then solved the complex problems. Again, we were left out in the cold. We learned to work with simple people who we could understand.

Once a problem is properly defined and its breadth determined, information and data gathering abilities are called into play. [*Note:* This information is often required for problem definition and breadth determination as well as for solution evaluation.] Data gathering is one of the most difficult tasks for many people and is often particularly perplexing for people transitioning from academic environments to real world conditions.

In school, most of the time all of the data needed to solve a problem is given and usually no other extraneous data is included. I took Newtonian physics in my first semester of college. I had not yet learned how to manage college course work, so I struggled through most of the semester and had a very weak C going into the final exam. Recognizing I needed a good score on the final exam and by now realizing that *all the necessary data and only that data* would be presented on the exam, I simply memorized every formula in the book. On each problem on the final exam, I looked at all the data given. If the problem described acceleration, distance and time, I pulled the formula from the back of my mind that included a, x and t (acceleration, distance and time) and plugged the data into that formula. I aced the final and got a solid B in the course. If the instructor had introduced just one extraneous data element into each problem, I would have absolutely gone down in flames.

Unfortunately in the real world, the "needed" information and data are not neatly packaged at the end of the problem description. There is not even a guarantee that it exists. If it does, it is somewhere out there mixed in with a boatload of other information and data. The needed information is likely not inextricable, but it is also not readily apparent.

In the mid 70s, one of the people who worked for me at the Cedar Rapids Corn Plant was Mike Eddy. Mike was affable and a very popular guy who everybody liked. He had worked his way up from the ranks. Mike was knowledgeable about the operations, but technical problem solving was not one of his particularly strong suits. One day one of our employees, Leo, sustained an injury in Mike's area. Leo had been climbing a ladder up to the platform of the scalper dust collector when he slipped and bruised his leg on one of the ladder rungs. As was our procedure and requirement, Mike investigated the accident and reported back to me. Mike's assessment of the root cause of the problem was Leo had been in too much of a hurry. The corrective action to prevent further occurrences was that Leo had been told not to hurry.

I quizzed Mike as to the thoroughness of his analysis and whether he had in fact gathered all of the available and pertinent information on the occurrence. Mike assured me he had. When I pressed the issue further, Mike commented he had secured all of the information that was "available." Available to Mike was very much like the neatly packaged scholastic data we discussed earlier.

Mike had never been taught how to "dig and ferret out" data from an environment that did not proclaim it as either useful or useless. I told Mike I would work with him to see if we could not unearth more relevant information. Mike was hardly enthusiastic about my intervention, and a couple of the other supervisors, Virgil and Paul, made great sport of chiding him almost mercilessly about "getting to work so closely" with the boss.

As we dug deeper, Mike and I found lots of information that was extraneous to this particular incident. We also found some extremely valuable information. We discovered Leo was climbing the ladder to unplug the dust collector on the corn scalper. He had come across the bottom of the steep house through standing water. There was considerable dust in the scalper area and the combination of water on Leo's shoes and dust on the ladder rungs made a slick condition. The ladder rungs did not have any anti-slip grips on them. Leo was carrying a broom handle up the ladder with him to unplug the dust collector.

From all of this, Mike concluded we should work on housekeeping to prevent the water and dust. I agreed and we did. He further concluded we should put anti-slip grips on the ladder rungs. I also agreed with this and we did it too. Finally, Mike concluded we should put a broom handle or some other "unplugging" device permanently on the dust collector platform so that when it needed to be unplugged, a tool would be readily available. I did not agree with this, and we did not do it!

At this point, I queried Mike as to how often we should expect the dust collector to plug. "The operators tell me it does it all the time and has done so for years," Mike replied. I continued my interrogation by asking Mike why our efforts shouldn't be directed toward resolving the problem with the collector plugging. Mike sheepishly agreed.

He and I returned to the area and studied the installation of the dust collector discharge where the plugging occurred. Almost immediately, the source of the problem jumped out at us. The spout (tube) that connected the dust collector discharge to the take away point was at about a 45 degree angle. Dust does not like to fall down such a shallow angle, so it would just sit there and collect until it plugged the spout and then continue to back up until it plugged the collector. Once it plugged the collector, dust collection in the room halted and the incidence of dust lying on things in the room (like ladder rungs) proliferated.

Mike and I decided if we installed a short conveyor to move the point of take-away directly under the dust collector discharge, the spout would not have a reason to plug. That is what we did. Talk about striking a blow for liberty! We solved a personnel safety problem. We solved an operating headache as for years it had been almost a daily job to unplug the collector. We solved a major housekeeping problem inasmuch as when the dust collector stayed running, the dust stayed collected where it was supposed to be. And Mike was a hero with his people as he had solved a chronic problem. He even had a last laugh on Virgil and Paul. I must confess the last laugh was a short-term thing as the two of them had a penchant for finding things to chide Mike about. Mike also continued to have a penchant for creating opportunities to be chided.

This chapter has been focused primarily on finding the right answer. Obviously, the right answer simply written down or proclaimed verbally does little to move the world forward. It is the fuel that powers forward progress, but implementation is the engine that burns that fuel and actually brings about that forward progress. Implementation is such a key element of any successful endeavor that the next chapter is devoted to a discussion of it. I'm sure implicit in Dr. M's premise that *"the world revolves on right answers"* was that those right answers, once determined, are in fact implemented.

# CHAPTER 10
# Magic Penny

My wife and I have frequently taught toddler and pre-school Sunday School classes. Those are always my favorite hours of the week. The unbridled enthusiasm and simplistic innocence of these most precious of God's creations make the teaching experience one of sheer joy.

In one such setting, the first component of the class was to gather together with several of the other very young classes for singing. There are a number of songs that are really great and that the children enjoyed singing. One of their favorites was Magic Penny. This is a song comparing love to the magic penny. As the song goes, it says,

*Love is something if you give it away, give it away, give it away*
*Love is something if you give it away, you end up having more*
*It's just like a magic penny, hold it tight and you won't have any*
*Lend it, spend it, and you'll have so many, they'll roll all*
*over the floor*

While I certainly subscribe to the idea of getting more love in return if you give a lot of love away, I am a little more pragmatic about believing in a magic penny. My wife and I often muse as to the likely political leaning of the songwriter. We're relatively sure it was someone of a much more liberal persuasion than are we.

That having been said, I am continually amazed at the number of highly educated persons in the business environment who believe there are magic pennies out there. These people spend big chunks of time looking for these magic pennies, gold egg laying geese, silver bullets, and a host of other voodoo magic. Of greater concern, however, is that these people also commit the time and talent of subordinates to this same senseless chase.

These people all seem to have one thing in common. They believe success is principally a function of what you know. Specifically, they seek some form of magical proprietary knowledge hidden from the competition. They never seem to acknowledge that success may have a relationship to how well you do *anything and everything.* A competitor who is doing better than they are always "knows" something they don't. Again it seems no thought is given to the fact that perhaps the competitor knows no special secret. The competitor may be doing the very same thing they are doing, the competitor is just doing it a lot better!!!

You may recall the discussion of right answers at the end of Chapter 9: "What Makes the World Go Round." Right answers only make the world go around if they get properly implemented. You must put the right answers into practice. Implementation means you execute the work processes efficiently and effectively according to the plans in order to bring to fruition the results that you predicted. That being done, the world continues to spin.

While implementation may seem simple, it is in fact the most difficult of all of the management components to achieve. Operations and businesses that are successful achievers are often viewed by others as "knowing something special." The fact is they do know something special!! They know how to successfully implement a plan. They can execute.

Sports are great parallels to business and make superior analyses tools. All football teams have access to the same technologies as the others. The fields are level and there are an equal number of players on the field from both teams. Both teams play under the exact same rules. No team can "know" something the other team does not at least have open access to understand. Why then do some teams absolutely dominate others? It is usually because one team has the ability to execute their game plan. There are likely also some differences in talent levels.

Certainly, talent also plays an integral role in successful execution of the work processes (implementation) in the business and industrial environment. There are also a number of other components to successful execution like leadership, integrity of purpose, effort, communication, training, more effort, coordination, follow through, and even more effort. Finally, there is also a component of knowledge that is not "special," but rather the result of more effort in ferreting it out, understanding its value to the process, and then putting it to proper use.

When we entered the pork business via the plant in Beardstown, Illinois, we were pitted against some very formidable competition from companies who had been in the business for several years. We viewed our principal competitor as IBP. IBP had been in the pork business only a few years, but had already demonstrated an ability to set the standard for the industry.

Those of us in the local management of the Beardstown facility had histories of success in implementing operational plans through sound business principles. We had done this by addressing employee needs, environment, health and safety issues, loss control, low cost operating platforms, holistic management approaches, customer focus, and so forth. We recognized we may "bleed" in the short-term, but sticking to those efforts which had fostered past successes would be the best assurance of long-term success in this new venture.

As a result of certain start up issues, not the least of which was buying our way into the market, we did bleed profusely at the outset. Unable to focus on long-term health in the face of short-term losses, some of our leaders began an aggressive push to locate the magic pennies. Each week we were chasing another silver bullet. Changing conditions such as special makes, further processes, and specification changes came our way as frequently as the tide rises and falls. All of these were tabbed as the reason others were able to make money in the business and we were not. Don Quixote, himself, would have been proud of many of our efforts.

None of these efforts stopped the bleeding. The bleeding slowed as we stopped chasing these dream solutions and continued to focus our efforts on doing all the things we already knew how to do and doing them a little better every day.

Successful organizations have one thing in common, they can move to action and execute. These are the two most critical elements of implementation. If one assumes we all generally have access to similar technologies, similar materials, and similar people (just as a sports team does), then the only real separating difference is how we use those resources. Implementation is just that, putting the available resources into action effectively. There is nothing magic about it.

One of the people who has been an inspiration to me in moving to action and executing a plan is Jim Hutson, a good friend of mine from Beardstown, Illinois. Jim is not a highly educated man. In fact by most of the world's standards, Jim would be considered a relatively uneducated man. Yet there are few people who I have encountered who can execute their plans as well as Jim Hutson. Jim's vocation is heavy equipment operation, and no one can make dozers, graders, loaders, and other earth moving equipment perform any better than Jim.

However, it is Jim's avocation that sets him apart from the crowd. Jim likes to pull antique tractors. If you are not into antique tractor pulling, let me give you just a little background. These machines are anywhere from 40 to 70 years old or older. At the time of their original birth, they may have sported horsepower ratings of 10 to perhaps 60 or 70 horsepower. When these tractors enter the ring to pull today, they may have horsepower ratings that approach 300 horsepower.

What is amazing is there are very strict rules on the alterations that can be made to the original tractor. Generally speaking, the original engine block for a given series of tractors must be maintained. These engines are bored as large as possible and stroked as long as possible to get increased cubic inch displacement. Then they are tweaked in dozens of other ways to make them venerable powerhouses. Jim is a master at this and his current model, a 1939 International Harvester W40, generates some 250 plus horsepower.

Much like winning and succeeding in business involves the ability to bring a number of resources and components into concert toward one purpose, antique tractor pulling is the same. Creating a powerhouse engine is just the beginning. Raw power, power transmission, weight distribution, speed, and management of track condition must all be properly handled to take home the first place trophy. Jim does all of that, including taking home the first place trophy much of the time.

Most of the old tractors were built using a lot of iron. That is great in terms of wear and tear and reliability. It is likely why many of these old tractors are still around in the first place. Much of this iron is, however, a liability when pulling in competition. Since most tractor pulls break into classes at each 500 pounds, one of the keys is getting as much power per unit weight as possible. Further, one can continue to add weights to move up in classes and Jim may pull in as many as 4 weight classes at a given meet, and win them all. Few other pullers can manage their weight and weight to power ratio well enough to do this. Finally, getting the old original weight down allows a puller to re-apply portable weights in just the right positions to optimize the weight and power distribution.

Jim is unequaled in reducing original weight. He replaces old radiator components made out of cast iron with aluminum components he builds himself out of old road signs. The reconstructed "Jim Hutson" radiators look identical to the original at a fraction of the weight. He removes the original flywheels and cuts them in half. Balance is critical on flywheels so this is no small task. Jim tinkers with frames, wheels, tires, gear trains, and all sorts of other items to optimize the weight reduction objective.

With power and weight managed, Jim turns to speed. The key to moving a tractor through the full length of the pull is usually not power, but rather traction. Too much power and too little speed will result in spin out. Too much speed can result in power out early. The secret is to have the right speed ranges to be able to start out and get up to full speed immediately so that the tires are clawing and the momentum of the tractor is forward. Again, few people are better able to set up tractor speeds and then manage speeds on the track during the pull than Jim.

Finally, after Jim puts all of this package together, he meticulously paints and details his tractor so it looks like it came off of the showroom floor. While Jim does an excellent job with the appearance of his tractor, appearance does not win pulls nor does it particularly set him apart from the competition. Most of the pullers have made their tractors look like new. That is one of the fun things about attending a pull. It is like a step back in time 40 or 50 years where all these old tractors look like they just came off the showroom floor.

Jim Hutson regularly wins pulls because he effectively manages all his resources and executes his plan from each element of the tractor design and re-building to the management of all of the capabilities of his tractor on the track. Jim probably doesn't know any secrets that are not known to the rest of the pullers. He will not score at the top in any standardized IQ tests. There is no magic in any of his pulls down the track. On the other hand, few will score higher than Jim in indigenous intelligence for which there are no tests. No one will work any harder than Jim. No one will be any better with his or her hands than Jim. No one will be any more meticulous in the details. No one will be any more intense in their drive and desire to win. Others probably come to the track hoping for some *magic* to dethrone Jim, but Jim relies on the things just noted to keep adding trophies to his collection.

Another old friend of mine who can make things happen is Warren Hingst. I first met Warren in 1980 when I came to the beef business with Excel. Warren has a lot of indigenous intelligence and also scores high on the standardized IQ tests. Warren had done a variety of things in his life, but all of them seemed to center in some fashion or another around building and construction.

For the past 20 some years, Warren was one of the premier "on-site" construction, building, and project superintendents in the business. What made Warren particularly effective over the past decades was his ability to "create solutions." Many of us could coordinate the equipment vendors, installation contractors, governmental regulators, and whomever or whatever else was needed to move a project from the design stage to the physical facility phase.

Warren could do that as well, but he also added another dimension. Warren had the uncanny ability to "fill in the gap" whenever some key component (design, person, thing, or system) was missing. Most of us focused on other third party groups to come to our rescue in that event and some of us were pretty good at ferreting out those other third parties (relationships help do that).

On the other hand, Warren resorted to three specific "resources." First, Warren had his own collection of various and sundry pieces of material and equipment stored in warehouses around the area. Most of us had no earthly idea where any of Warren's "junk" could ever be used. Second, Warren had his own cadre of people to go to when unusual custom "things" needed to be made. Finally, Warren was the Rube Goldberg of non-conventional design and used that effectively.

When things were missing either during a project or at the end (i.e. the project was complete with all components in place, but the system did not work as expected), Warren called on these resources and skills to "make it happen." Warren would take what resources were available and fill the gap. Not only would Warren succeed in filling in the gap, he would invariably create some new system of value. That prototype would soon find its way into the mainstream design at the remainder of our operations. Rescue work of Warren's often became base work in the next project.

I am made to think of Warren Hingst when I watch the movie *Apollo 13*. When the Apollo crew had to come up with a new filter out of only the materials that were available in the space ship, the people on the ground at Ground Control in Houston were assigned to figure out a way to build that filter. They were given only the materials that were available in the space ship. I immediately think if I am one of the astronauts in that case, I certainly hope Warren Hingst or someone just like him is on the ground working on that filter. I have no doubt but that Warren could have come up with a filter that would have worked (as did the ground crew in Houston).

Guys like Jim Hutson and Warren Hingst are the real implementers, and we can all learn a great deal from them. They recognize the conventional and use it to their advantage. They are not, however, bound by the conventional and can use the non-conventional to their equal advantage. Finally, they possess indigenous qualities that are not learned in a classroom, but rather in the schools of hard work and hard knocks. They learn from their own experience as well as that of others. Most importantly, they recognize that "for it to happen" they have to do something "to make it happen." They do not wait for anything to happen by magic.

Jim and Warren notwithstanding, the person who has most impressed me with his ability to "make it happen" with the tools he possesses is Dr. Larry Baker. In the 70s, I attended a management seminar in New York City. Why I choose to go to New York City for any seminar is still a mystery to me. Nevertheless, I did attend. This was a time management seminar that was conducted by Dr. Merrill Douglas, an associate of Dr. Baker. As this two-day session unfolded, I found it to be one of the most beneficial professional learning experiences I had encountered. I took the teachings and examples back to work and found them to be of a great deal of help in planning my activities and making the right things happen.

A few years later, after I had transferred to Excel as a vice president, I encountered numerous instances in the plants where I felt the management teams were not utilizing time and talent as efficiently as possible. Remembering my experience at the time management seminar several years earlier, I decided to set up an "in-house" seminar for the plant managers and engineers. After contacting a couple of the other

VPs to get their support, I contacted Dr. Douglass' group to see if we could contract with him to conduct the seminar. I was told he would not be available, but his business partner Dr. Larry Baker would be. Although I was quite disappointed, I reluctantly agreed to accept Dr. Baker and proceeded to get the arrangements put in place.

A few days before the seminar, I was informed Dr. Baker's wife would be traveling with him and we would be responsible for her travel expenses as well. In addition, we were to have the $2500 seminar fee available to give to Dr. Baker at the beginning of the first session. I became more disenchanted with these conditions, but I had gone so far down the road, I really didn't think we could turn back. I accepted these conditions and proceeded to get a check cut for the $2500 so I would have it in my hand at the start of the first session.

On the appointed date, I arrived at the meeting room several minutes early to be sure all arrangements were in order. Dr. Baker and his wife were at the front of the room setting up. They were a very handsome-looking couple who appeared to be in their early to mid 40s. I walked to the front of the room and introduced myself to them. We exchanged a number of pleasantries and I handed Dr. Baker the check. He immediately handed it to his wife. We proceeded to talk at length about some of the peculiarities of our business and some of the things I hoped Dr. Baker could fold into his subject matter.

As it approached time to begin, I made my way back to my chair. As I walked back, my mind was much more at ease. I was quite impressed with Dr. Baker's demeanor and obvious control and grasp of the task at hand. I had made a decent choice in accepting him in lieu of Dr. Douglass.

As I settled back into my chair, Dr. Baker began by making a few introductory comments about how pleased he was to be there and how he looked forward to a productive two-day session. He then began a short discussion about general limitations we have. What a dynamic ploy I thought. He is starting right out on this, and he will deftly move us to thinking about the limitations of time in our schedules. What a brilliant approach!

Dr. Baker did not follow that line of discussion, however. "Many of us have limitations that seem to others to be difficult or impossible to manage or live with," he noted. "The truth is often those limitations are workable and simply take a little more effort on the part of all of us to manage our way through. I have one of those limitations that may seem to some of you to limit our ability to have a normal teaching and learning experience. I hope you will not let that affect you, since I do not let it affect me. You see, I am BLIND."

The room became deathly silent. You could have knocked me off of my chair with a feather. I was dumbfounded. How could I have interacted with this man for 15 minutes or better and not even had a clue I was conversing with a blind man? That interaction probably gave me a huge advantage over the rest of the participants as I fully knew that other than loss of eyesight, there was not anything different about this man. One did not need to act differently toward him or probably not toward any other person who happened to be blind. I certainly hadn't and I didn't even know it.

After we all gathered ourselves, Dr. Baker explained he had suffered a very high temperature at the age of 25 that had left him without sight. He then proceeded to conduct a seminar that was not only superior in content, but also superior in delivery. He would move from point to point at the front of the room with comfort. He would write down a point on the flip chart then move across the room then come back and write down another point on the flip chart. Interestingly, he was so adept at leading the class most of us were fully focused on the point he had made on the flip chart and not the shear amazement at how he traveled across the room then back and still knew where to place point 2 under point 1.

In those first couple of hours, Dr. Baker went from being a blind man to a man who happened to have lost his eyesight. In fact he had opened the eyes of some of us to our own blindness. At the first break, I hurried back up to Dr. Baker. I don't recall anything I had to say in this conversation other than we quickly established a friendship. His wife asked me if there were any shops nearby since Larry did not need her for the next few hours. I told her of several of the types she asked about. Since most of them were several blocks away, I suggested she take my Toyota pickup and use it for the day. She did, and I was thrilled. That evening we had a group dinner and although we invited the Bakers, they asked to be excused to spend the evening alone. I suggested a good restaurant and gave them back the keys to my Toyota.

The next day, when I came into the meeting room, I said good morning and handed over the Toyota keys to Mrs. Baker for the day. The second day passed as rapidly as the first. Larry Baker did a marvelous job in that two-day session to help us improve our time management. He did way more than that, however. He taught many of us acceptance of persons we would otherwise have held at a distance. He taught many of us that disabilities, even severe ones, don't necessarily *disable*. And he impressed on all of us that "making it happen" was a function of work, effort, talent, and desire, and that it did not need to be limited as a result of any physical conditions.

In that two-day period, I gained a tremendous respect for Dr. Baker the seminar leader, and Larry, the person. More importantly, I learned some of the most valuable lessons in my life (and not just about managing my time) from one of the best instructors I ever encountered. In addition, I felt very blessed that I had made two new friends in Dr. and Mrs. Baker. For several years we exchanged greetings at Christmas time, and then as so often happens in our mobile society we lost contact. Unfortunately we tend to live life at such a fast pace that when we loose contact, we do not make the effort to immediately reconnect. I didn't, and the years that passed before I eventually made that reconnection were certainly my loss.

Perhaps it was magic that allowed Larry Baker to "see" without his eyes. I think not! God gives some of us all the "normal" resources including sight. We then often wait around for God to use those resources within us, almost like we are waiting for some magic from God. I think God gave Larry Baker the gift of utilizing each resource he had to its absolute fullest extent. Larry Baker didn't wait around to see if God was going to do anymore. He accepted that gift *and the hard work that went with it* and made more of his God given abilities than most of us even dream about, let alone achieve.

Larry Baker is an extraordinary person! Larry Baker touched me and impacted my life in a way no ordinary person could have.

# CHAPTER 11
# I'll Take Two

When I started into the engineering curriculum at Iowa State University in 1965, one of the standard issues was a slide rule. Electronic calculators and later computers have made the slide rule as obsolete as the buggy whip. Nevertheless in the "old days" slide rules were an essential tool for performing all mathematical calculations beyond simple addition and subtraction.

The story goes of the new engineering student in those days, who upon receiving his schedule, proceeded to the college bookstore to purchase his books and supplies. After filling his cart with all the essential books and supplies, he proceeded to the check out line. The cashier rang up item after item and book after book until she had emptied the cart. With books for calculus, chemistry, and graphics, along with the standard freshman English book, the student was obviously enrolled in freshman engineering. Recognizing this and not having rung up the normal Post Versalog 23-scale slide rule, the cashier politely asked, "You are obviously enrolled in engineering, and yet you have not purchased a slide rule. Do you already have one?"

The new student looked puzzled and replied, "No, I don't already have one. What is it for?"

To this the cashier replied with all the details of the things a slide rule can do and ended by saying, "If you're going to be an engineer, you absolutely must have a slide rule. *It will do half of your work for you!*"

The new engineering student thought about this for just a minute as he did the math in his mind. "Hey great," he replied with a big smile, "I'll take **two**!"

I don't know if this actually happened or if it is just a good story. However, it certainly could have happened just that way. To this day, I marvel at the number of instances where people actually believe they can put together enough technology to do all of their work for them.

This concept becomes even more pervasive with the advent and explosive usage of computers. We have become a society that worships the computer related technologies. We have come to believe we can in fact line up enough computer hardware and software to do ALL of our work for us.

What is just as amazing is the bewilderment of people who wonder how we existed without computers. In 1969 when I entered the workforce, cars were manufactured, ore was mined, steel was forged, agricultural products were produced and turned into food and fiber products, leather was tanned, shoes were made, and every other product manufactured on the face of the earth came to market with no or precious little help from computers. How did we do it?

Without question, the quantity of information we had available to use in those days pales in comparison to that available today. However, with information at a premium, we had to be selective. The key was we identified the information that was essential to our operations. We then trained ourselves in how to gather and make use of that information. Beyond that, when cc. meant just that, carbon copy, we were very selective in who all we distributed information to. Using carbon paper to make multiple copies while typing was not easy. Today, with a half dozen clicks of the mouse, we can make information available to literally millions of people.

I am not anti-technology nor specifically anti-computer. On the contrary, I am a strong supporter and user. I simply believe we must use them to enhance our own intelligence and efforts. Further, we cannot rely on them to be some panacea that indigenously does all our work and solves all our problems.

The first really unique piece of technology I was exposed to was in 1971 when we installed a Crown extractor in the soybean processing plant in Cedar Rapids, Iowa. Solvent extractors had to have a choked feed to them in order to maintain a product seal and keep explosive vapors from escaping into the room and other parts of the plant. Historically we had done that with plug screws. The Crown did it with a Geiger tube receiver and nuclear device on opposite sides of the feed hopper. As the feed level decreased in the hopper, more gamma rays hit the Geiger tube, and the electronic signals developed from that slowed the extractor drive down preserving the seal. Conversely, as the feed level increased, the reverse happened and the drive sped up to prevent an over feed plug.

While this worked very well, it was cutting edge technology and not readily understood by most of the workers. However, while the nuclear physics and electronics were not understood, the mechanical concepts of matching extractor speeds to hopper levels were. When the technology failed, as it did several times before we finally got it fully wrung out, the operators simply bypassed the nuclear device and stationed a person at the feed area to manually control the speed based on visual observation of the level. I remember Harold, one of the maintenance men, inherited that job on several occasions. Harold's eyes replaced the nuclear device and his hands replaced the electronic control to the variable speed gear drive.

As we have "progressed" we have all but lost the ability to bypass technology. Eyes and hands no longer replace the technology. There are few escape mechanisms for failed hardware or software. In some instances the technology is so extensive it is impossible to create hard bypasses as when the technological advancement exceeds manual capability (e.g. computers can perform mathematical calculations almost instantaneously that could not be solved manually in a lifetime). Obviously, if that type of technology "goes down," the system shuts down.

What is greatly troubling, however, is when the technology has simply replaced a normal manual operation like selecting a seat on an airplane. When the technology goes down, we have so "dumbed down" the operators that they can do nothing more than sit and stare at a blank screen. I don't know how many times I have called for some item or part only to hear a voice on the other end say, "I don't see one here on the screen."

"Well how about seeing if you can *see one on a shelf?*" I reply. "You know it is possible the screen may not have been updated from a new shipment etc." To many counter people this is incomprehensible.

Another favorite of mine is the telephone answering system. If you start out with voice mail and can in fact finally get to a real person on the other end you are still unlikely to get any satisfaction. The real voice invariably has no idea of the whereabouts of the target party, is incapable of taking a message, would not think of going to the target party's desk and putting a note in front of him or her, and seems stuck on repeating the message, "Would you like to have his/her voice mail?" I know that we used to play a lot of phone tag, but we also used to talk to each other rather than machines.

These areas are one of the places where small companies potentially have huge advantages over the big corporations. Big corporations invariably have access to far more sophisticated technologies than do the small mom and pop operations. As a result, mom and pop must continue to be responsive in a personal way. They cannot afford to be "dumbed down" to the level of the first line operatives of the big guys. They need to stay sharp because their first line of defense is their own knowledge rather than a "smart machine" of some kind. Even where mom and pop have access to the technology, they tend to retain their own intelligence as a *second line of defense* in case the first line goes down.

Larry Olson's Structural Engineering P.C. firm is one of those organizations. As a structural engineering organization, Larry has had to keep up with the technology that makes their jobs easier and even makes certain engineering operations possible. Yet, Larry continues to keep the feet of all of the people in his organization firmly planted on the ground. He and his people still have the ability and willingness to use old "rules of thumb" to get quick analyses in the field. Contrast this to many engineering organizations who can only take the data in the field and retreat to the office to plug it into the computer and "get back to you later!"

Of much greater importance, with solid backgrounds in why things happen in actual practice, Larry and his people have a huge leg up in trouble shooting problems that computers can't even see. In virtually all of our construction contractor coordination meetings, questions came up that got solved on the blackboard in one of our plant conference rooms. Imagine that, solving an engineering problem in long hand on a blackboard! You can bet the solutions were not only sound from an engineering analysis, they also met and surpassed the tests for common sense and logic. It was a rare case when implementation of one of those solutions did not result in superior performance.

In the early 80s, we had all of our maintenance managers attend a seminar on effective maintenance methods. As I recall, there was a wealth of information presented at this seminar. Most of this information dealt with the amounts of time that were squandered during the maintenance day and what they were squandered on. Ostensibly, this information was gathered from other top organizations around the country.

One of the key points made was that approximately two thirds of the maintenance time was spent on non-productive activity. A number of new technologies and information processors were available to change that. Principal among these were good definition two-way radios and data gathering programs to detail and track failures etc. A final point was we needed to do a better job of planning and scheduling the work.

Following this seminar we set out to make changes and move ourselves into the world-class category. We purchased radios and put them on key people. Throughout the years we eventually put them on all maintenance persons and all managers. We gathered data and we worked at the other issues. Certainly many other organizations in the world did the same. And we certainly did make some progress or so we thought. What we failed at were the people issues, planning & scheduling along with root cause elimination.

In 1998, I attended another very similar training session. By that time, there were virtually all new faces in the group. Only a couple of other people and me were common to both sessions. Interestingly, the meeting started off with the fact in most industry in 1998, about two thirds of the maintenance time was spent in non-productive activity. What had gone wrong that almost two decades had passed with little apparent progress? However, not to fear, help was available! New technologies were available to rescue us. Vibration analyses machines, lubrication oil analyses procedures, infra-red scanners, complex inventory and maintenance management software, ultrasonic devices, and a host of other technologies were just waiting to be our saviors.

Interestingly, we immediately moved to "acquire" these tools (often in sets of two). I will allow that my boss at the time, Matt Meyer, provided the platform that gave the best opportunity to change history with his championing of the cause. In addition to making use of technology, I do believe Matt will effect some significant progress in the planning and scheduling area, which he realizes is still more people than technology. I will not be around in Cargill for the next follow-up meeting in another 16 or 17 years, but it would be interesting to see whether two-thirds of maintenance time is still spent in non-productive activity in the year 2015.

Even with efforts like Matt's, however, my fear is non-productive time will still be at unsatisfactory levels. That is, unless we begin to focus less on the miracle cures, which interestingly all have to do with repair or detection of the problem, and focus more on how to prevent the problems from occurring in the first place. Maintenance efforts generally only fix problems that are broken in production. When will we learn to focus on eliminating the cause of the problem and putting the onus for that performance where it belongs? Not, I fear, as long as business leaders think we can secure enough technology to make the problems go away.

In the 90s one of Cargill's top managers reported to all employees that as a company, *Cargill had to move from an asset intensive commodities company to a knowledge based, solutions oriented organization.* There was no argument that historically Cargill had been asset intensive and also largely an organization that dealt in commodities. However, Cargill could not have survived and thrived for a century and a quarter without having knowledge and working hard to effect more positive solutions to problems than did our competitors.

So to what was reference being made in being knowledge based and solutions oriented? Certainly solutions oriented deals with meeting customer needs and solving their problems. I think many organizations today are focusing on providing solutions rather than simply providing products, and that is good. However, I do worry the advent of information technology has created a new product, namely information. By popular expression we have become an information based society. We tend to see information and intellectual property as the end product.

Certainly many highly valued companies peddle some type of intellectual property or information gathering, processing, managing, and/or disseminating apparatus or system. Many of these organizations have become very profitable by manipulating and massaging information.

There is something missing in this picture, however. Information cannot feed or clothe us; it cannot get us from here to there. It cannot house us. It cannot heal or even medicate us, and it cannot educate us. People and products do that. It is still goods and services that are the products that add value and make our lives better. Information is a useful tool and a very helpful means to the end, but selling information still only has value if the buyer can use it to create a good or service that directly touches the consumer. Absent those goods and services, all the information in the world is essentially worthless.

Moreover, we are at great risk when we equate information to knowledge. Information is one of the tools to acquire knowledge, but it is not knowledge in and of itself. The old slide-rules we discussed at the opening of this chapter were fascinating works of technology for the time and had 23 scales worth of information. However, that could only be turned to value by having the intelligence and ability to manage that hardware (slide rule) and software (problem solving expertise) to generate knowledge and create solutions.

Not much has changed other than the hardware and software are infinitely more powerful today. Nonetheless, human intelligence, ability, and movement to action continue to be the elements that turn information to knowledge and knowledge to solutions. *I only need one computer, but if I have one person who can do half of my work for me, then I will gladly take a second person of equal ability.*

# CHAPTER 12
# The Perfect "10"

For years, the number 10 has been used as a rating device. How often have you heard someone say, "on a scale of 10, I would call this a 7," or whatever the number. Gymnastics have long utilized the 1 to 10 scale to evaluate individual performance. Seldom were 10s given out as that was considered perfection, and we all assumed no one was ever perfect. In addition, if a 10 were given and a later performance proved superior, what would be left to rate the higher achievement?

That seemed to change in the late 70s. The movie "10," where Bo Derek was The Perfect "10" in beauty and critical female physical attributes, gave new meaning to the term "10." In effect it gave people license to declare perfection. This is as good as it gets! Advertisements boldly stated, "It doesn't get any better than this." People were no longer hesitant to assume someone or something had reached perfection. We all became much bolder in asserting that perfection had in effect been achieved and there was no other place to go but down.

While my conservative nature still makes me somewhat more hesitant to declare perfection in real time, I am less reluctant to evaluate people and events over a period of time and declare certain of them to have achieved that high level of perfection. In my career, I have encountered two persons who demonstrated such superior performance and characteristics; they have not been duplicated in my 35+ year career or 55+ year life. Further, while I cannot predict the future, I do not believe they will be surpassed. I confidently rate them "10."

At the top of that list is Joe Culbreath. Joe happens to be one of the first people with whom I had the pleasure of working in the industrial environment. As noted in an earlier chapter, my first plant assignment with Cargill was at the soybean processing facility in Memphis, Tennessee. After some initial plant site training and a short dual learning experience on the lecithin drumming operation, I was assigned to a shift supervisor position.

The shift supervisor position essentially involved just what the name suggests. Supervise the operation for an 8-hour shift. We weren't expected to do any strategic planning or worry about any long-term plans. We were tacticians. Our job was to administer the daily plan as laid out by the various department superintendents as well as Fred Brosius, the plant superintendent.

The shift supervisor's position was and still is one of the greatest learning positions in the world. This is especially true on third shift when one must weigh the cost of waking up a department manager versus potentially making an incorrect decision. A shift supervisor has the opportunity to work very closely with a small group of people, manage all technical components of the operation, administer the logistics of finished products and raw materials, and keep the mechanical components of the operation going. It is in this position that I established relationships with the likes of Tommy, Marcel I, Marcel II, and Vaughnsy, all of whom you have met in earlier chapters.

Joe Culbreath was a maintenance man with whom I normally would only have passing contact. In the position of shift supervisor, the only real contact I had with Joe was in the event of a mechanical failure on second or third shift when I would need to call in a maintenance man. Feminists, pardon the expression, but in the late 60s there were no maintenance women in our organization.

On Thanksgiving Day in 1969, I volunteered to handle the day shift operation since I had no family ties in the Memphis area. As luck would have it, I did encounter some mechanical problems early in the afternoon and started down the list to call in a maintenance man. I was turned down several times since most guys did not wish to come back in on a holiday, even for the premium pay. Eventually I came to Joe, and when I called him, he immediately agreed to come in and help me. Joe's loyalty was so great he would never decline to help out no matter what his personal preference may have been. Not once did Joe ever decline to come in and help, as you will soon see.

In a short time after I called Joe that Thanksgiving afternoon, he arrived at the plant. However, instead of Joe contacting me and then expecting me to go along and help him as I virtually always did with any employee, Joe found me and presented me with a home cooked thanksgiving dinner complete with all of the fixings. He then instructed me to eat it while he went out to correct the problem. I was dumbfounded and I did as he requested. The meal was delicious.

When Joe had completed the repair project, he returned and explained his actions. When I had called him, he was just getting up from their Thanksgiving dinner. Joe told me after he hung up the phone, he looked at his wife Betty, who is one of this world's classical beautiful women both externally and internally, and told her, "That young man is away from his family on this day and working all day at the plant. He will not have any Thanksgiving dinner or any other celebration. Would you please fix a plate of food for him, so I can take it with me?" Betty obliged (I'm sure happily) and I was the recipient of a great Thanksgiving dinner.

This was before the days of a microwave oven in every home kitchen and company lunchroom. It was no simple matter to collect a plateful of residual Thanksgiving dinner dishes, reheat them, and then get that delivered "hot" to a recipient 20 miles away. Betty had taken great pains to reheat and pack the dinner to keep it hot and tasty when it arrived. Joe had insisted I sit down immediately and eat it and not worry about helping him. I felt very honored to have received that kind of treatment. For Joe and Betty, I am sure it was not that Jim Roth was especially deserving, but rather any person in that position would have been deserving. Joe and Betty always considered the interests of others in equal proportion to those of their own.

Within a few months, I was promoted to the position of construction ramrod for a second plant, which we were preparing to move to the Memphis location from a closed plant location in Redfield, Iowa. In this position, one of my responsibilities was inventorying all of the equipment and materials that had been moved from Redfield. It was also my responsibility to get work scheduled on any transferred items needing mechanical integrity work. I scheduled this with Harold Cook, the maintenance superintendent, who would assign maintenance men to me to accomplish the work. I soon learned that Joe Culbreath and his normal partner Bill Cook, brother of Harold, were the superior maintenance persons. While a couple of the other maintenance men had a broader knowledge, no others combined the knowledge and the work ethic of Joe and Bill.

By early in the summer of 1970, we had completed the reconstruction and startup of the former "Redfield" plant. With two plants at one location, Memphis was now far and away the largest soybean operation in Cargill. With our expanded capacity, Harold Cook was promoted to the new position of general operations superintendent, and I was given Harold's old job as the maintenance superintendent. This was a key job in the operation and moreover, put me in position to work with Joe Culbreath on an everyday basis.

Among other things, one of my duties as maintenance superintendent was administering the day-to-day work assignments. On the basis of my past experience with Joe and Bill, I knew I could always count on them for the tough jobs. Certainly, Joe and Bill got more than their share of the tough, dirty, or nasty jobs simply because of their unselfishness and willingness to do more than their share.

We had installed a rotary kiln unit that caused us a great deal of grief with the trunnion rolls. It was a very greasy job as the main kiln tire was grease laden. When working on these trunnion rolls, it was virtually impossible not to get at least the upper part of your body in contact with this tire. I had a special hard hat that was covered with grease that I used for this particular job. Joe always joked (what a sense of humor) when he saw me walking across the yard to the shop in the morning with "that" hard hat on, he knew what he would be working on that day.

That Joe and I had become very good friends certainly worked to Joe's disadvantage in terms of getting those nasty work assignments. I knew Joe would not complain and he often "inherited" nasty jobs by that default condition. I do not think Joe ever considered he was at a disadvantage, and he accepted those challenges with enthusiasm. That I also virtually always went to the nasty jobs to assist after I had finished my administrative duties cemented the relationship between Joe and me. As I mentioned in Chapter 3, one of the key things my dad gave me was the sense of accomplishment in doing a tough job well. I don't know who instilled that spirit in Joe, but I know for a fact someone did. Enthusiasm and a sense of accomplishment were as natural to Joe as breathing.

While continuing to work closely with Joe as well as continuing to develop our friendship, I observed a whole other class of attributes necessary to elevate someone to the status of perfect. These included honesty, integrity, truthfulness, compassion, friendliness, fairness, and all those related characteristics. I found Joe to be both a devoted Christian and a devoted family man. Joe and Betty also have two daughters who they love dearly. Joe and Betty were (and are) every bit a salt-of-the-earth people.

As though one holiday experience was not sufficient to test a real friend, on Christmas Eve of 1970 I was forced into another. We were operating one shift supervisor short due to the resignation of one of our supervisors for whom the soybean operation was not a good fit. I had discussed the issue with Harold Cook and we decided that he could handle both the production and maintenance function for a few weeks. That would free me to pick up the extra shift supervision position until we could get a new person hired and properly trained. With that all in place, I was working the 4:00 P.M. to midnight shift on Christmas Eve of that year.

Between 7:00 and 8:00 P.M. we had a major breakdown on the "Interstate 40" belt feeding the new plant. This was so named because it was about a 500 foot long belt that was installed on concrete double tees and set on support bents about 90 feet in the air. From a distance it looked like an interstate highway bridge. One of the main head bearings on this belt had failed that night. I went down the list of eligible maintenance men without any takers until I got to Joe. When I called, one of Joe's young daughters answered the phone. Recognizing my voice, her response to my question as to whether I could speak to her daddy was a hugely disappointed, "I guess so," that was spoken with a sigh that said it all.

I apologized to Joe for calling him on Christmas Eve and explained my problem. He said he would come in, which he did. I am confident before Joe left home, he took great pain to apologize to his girls and wife for their temporarily spoiled plans. I am just as sure Joe also assured them that they remained special to him and they would pick up their celebration in the morning. Joe had the kind of home relationships that allowed him to alter plans without creating the feeling he was cheating his family. They knew he would make it up to them. I do not believe an employee can be an exceptional employee at work unless that person can create and maintain exceptional relationships in his or her personal life. Work cannot be a respite from personal problems or disappointments, nor can work compete with family life. Work and family must co-exist, and for Joe they always did and have.

For the next several hours in bitter cold, at least by Memphis standards, Joe and I hung out in mid air, 90 feet above ground level, removing the old bearing and replacing it with the new bearing on the I-40 belt. It was one of the most grueling tasks performed in some of the most difficult conditions I have encountered in my entire career. To this day, not a Christmas Eve goes by that I do not think back to how I "celebrated" it in 1970. More importantly, not a Christmas Eve goes by that I do not recall how special Joe was on that cold night in 1970.

I left the Memphis soybean operation in the summer of 1971, but I returned to Memphis in 1979 as the general superintendent of the new corn milling and refining operation there. I was again fortunate to have the opportunity to work with Joe. He had transferred from the soybean operation to the corn operation for the new challenge. During my short two-year stint in this position, I had the pleasure of hosting the 20 years of service anniversary party for Joe. It was a great opportunity for all of us to tell and show Joe and Betty how special they had been to all of us during those years.

I have been blessed to have had many other good employees and associates to work with in my industrial career. Many of these people did exceptional and exemplary things. You have read about and will continue to read about many of these people in the other chapters and what they taught me and how they impacted my life and/or career. However, none of these people have risen above the standard set and maintained by Joe Culbreath. Joe taught me a lot about plant maintenance. More importantly, Joe taught me that being an employee and associate, whether as subordinate, peer, or superior, can be raised to its highest level if the element of friendship is included in the mix.

The only other person to rate perfection in my experience is Eldred Swoboda. Eldred achieves this distinction in the category of union steward. Over the years, I have worked with a number of different unions and a variety of union stewards. In many respects, union stewards are a breed of their own. I've known many people (at one time including me) who would claim to be able to spot one of that breed from a block away. Eldred is one of the reasons I now make that statement in the past tense.

Growing up in rural Iowa, I had not had much contact with unions or unionized operations. We did regularly blame them for high prices of cars, farm implements and virtually all durable goods. Most of my perspective on unions was that they were power grabbers and the members were mostly out to get all they could. Certainly that perspective has changed. Even though it continues to fit some unions and members, it also fits at least some people and groups in just about all governmental and economic organizations as well.

When I became involved in the industrial work force, I discovered union members are ordinary people just like the rest of us. Certainly there are bad apples in the mix, but there are also normal apples and a lot of very good apples in that mix. It is also interesting to note and one can never forget why unions came into being in the first place. Failure of business owners to realize their most valuable resource was the people working for them and treat them accordingly was the soil on which unions could be planted and take root. I continue to find it amazing that even to this day, many business owners and managers do not believe in the Golden Rule of "Do unto others as you would have them do unto you." Somehow they think the "other guy" is very different from them.

At any rate, I did come to realize that unions do play a vital part in the economic process. Do they exist in places where they are needed? Indeed they do. Do they exist in places where they are not needed? Same answer! Bottom line is unions are a part of the industrial climate. Where union representation exists, plant level stewards must exist to provide the first line of representation. I do not think they have an easy position, and I do not envy any union steward. I would not want their position.

Too many union stewards believe their function is to get whatever the union workers want. Too few realize the real job of the union steward is to work to secure what is in the best total interest of all of the union workers. What any given person *wants* at any given moment and what is in the *best interest* of the group in total can be and very often are two very distinct and different things. A good union steward recognizes that difference and acts to effect the best interest of the group. A very good union steward recognizes sometime the direction needed may involve unpopular decisions, but makes them anyway. Accordingly, most politicians could not make the grade as very good union stewards. There are too few people in the world willing to do the "heavy lifting."

Eldred Swoboda was the quintessential union steward. Eldred

recognized his function was to protect both the stability of his constituent's jobs as well as the prosperity of those jobs. Of equal importance, he fully understood the implementation of that function involved both hard work and at times unpopular decisions. Like Doug Brooks, Eldred had the ability to "walk in my shoes" as well as the ability to "put me in his or his constituent's shoes." Finally, what should not be overlooked in this experience is all of us, Eldred and the plant workers as well as me and the management group, had a great deal of respect, admiration, and affection for each other. We all recognized each of our successes depended on all of the others.

Eldred's "modus operandi" was simple. First, was the issue an absolute? Was it a point of law in the labor agreement? If so, the answer was a simple yes or no! Second, was the issue a quasi absolute? Was there past practice on the issue? If so, the answer to this particular issue was again a simple yes or no, but if there were reasons why a change should be made, then a discussion and agreement should be reached now for future occurrences. Finally, were we plowing new ground with this issue? If so, if it was in the best long-term interest of both owners and workers, then the answer was yes. If it was not in the best long-term interest of both owners and workers, then the answer was no. Only if there were a real conflict in best interests between the owners and the workers did the opportunity or need for "negotiation" come up.

While that mode of operation seems incredibly simple, most stewards (and I should add most owners or managers) fail to see how mutually dependent each party is on the other. Higher wages or tighter work restrictions are not in the best interest of the worker if they render the business non-competitive. Similarly, low wages that are not sufficient to keep or more importantly to reward workers for their efforts are not in the best interest of the owners if workers continually turn over or are not motivated to achieve their maximum potential. Eldred fully understood this (as did I) and it made our relationship mutually beneficial. Win-Win is not a new concept!!

Under Eldred's leadership, most issues were handled between Eldred and the worker. Eldred was like Lyle Bowers in that he was firm in his convictions, but used logic, education and persuasion rather than an iron fist to move people to the proper way of thinking and action. When there was new ground to plow, Eldred would schedule time to meet with me and we would attempt to evaluate all of the pros and cons of the issue and then arrive at a decision. Often, we were able to come up with Win-Win scenarios, even when not apparent on the surface. That not being possible, we worked very hard to come up with a little less win and a little less lose so neither party got hammered. It was a very rare occurrence when higher levels of the union or of management had to be brought in to resolve labor/operating issues at Cedar Rapids East in those years.

Eldred's leadership can be contrasted with the leadership in another plant where I would find myself later. The absolute epitome of "non-logic" occurred one evening when we had called Bernie, the boiler expert whose seniority resided in the maintenance department, in to resolve a failure of the boiler. The following day the union steward was parked in my office complaining we had not called in Harry who was not a boiler expert, but a more senior maintenance man. He insisted we pay Harry for the time lost.

I simply said, "Look, let's assume the same thing happens tonight and we call Harry in and he is in fact able to solve the problem. Would you expect Bernie to file a grievance?"

"Sure," was the reply.

"And would you support that grievance and insist we pay Bernie for the lost time?" I queried.

"Of course!" was the steward's reply without hesitation.

Unable to control my anger at such ludicrousness, I looked at him and said, "Get your rear end out of my office and come back when you have decided which side of the fence you want to stand on. If you're having trouble deciding, I would suggest you error on the side of expertise rather than seniority, but at least pick one or the other!!" That ended that particular battle, but the war raged on.

Fortunately, most of the other union stewards I have dealt with were not of the caliber just described. Unfortunately, none of the others were of the caliber of Eldred Swoboda either. Eldred stands alone in my opinion in the performance of his duties as a union steward. He embodied high intelligence, an ability to cut to the chase and understand the issue, a hard work ethic, an even disposition, a skill at educating and persuading, and a burning desire to find or establish Win-Win solutions. I don't know if Eldred ever completed a "Management Grid" workshop to determine his dominant style. I can tell him he doesn't need to. He is a 9,9 ("Grid" rating demonstrating the rare combination of the highest rating for both a production driven orientation and a people centered approach to management)!! And all of that makes him a Perfect "10" in my book!

Like Joe Culbreath, Eldred Swoboda and I became very good friends. I have always valued Joe and Eldred for their friendship as much as I have the performance of their jobs. However, I do not for one minute believe our friendships and their superior performance were mere coincidences. I believe that friendships are critical to relationships, and relationships are critical to superior performance.

Joe and Eldred stand at the top. They will never have to look up to determine the standard!

# CHAPTER 13:
# Alpha & Omega–The Beginning and the End

In Revelations 22:14 Jesus said, "I am the Alpha and the Omega, the First and the Last, the Beginning and the End." Bible scholars can, and I'm sure do, debate what Jesus met by this proclamation. Certainly, one can make a literal translation in relation to His life on earth beginning with His virgin birth as the Alpha and His death on the cross and subsequent resurrection and ascension as the Omega.

One can also make the case Jesus' life was a continuum of beginnings and ends that often occupied the same space and time. Certainly His death and resurrection marked both the end in the traditional sense and the beginning in the sense Jesus was now the Intercessor for us in the presence of God. His ascension marked the end of His earthly ministry, but the beginning of the extension of the Christian faith throughout the world.

Jesus likely was also referring to what He could do for us. Alpha and Omega represented the outer boundaries of what Jesus was about. Accordingly, the Beginning and the End also included everything in the Middle as well. With Jesus as our Savior and Guide, we do not need anything or anyone else. We need only trust Him to direct our path. In fact the writer of Revelations seems to allude to this interpretation in subsequent verses. This makes Jesus the very Essence of life. His Way is the fundamental nature of how to get the most out of our life here on earth.

Jesus' Way was and is the Way of agape love. Agape means unconditional. Jesus loved without regard for whether He was loved in return. Jesus taught agape love as the beginning, end, and everything in the middle. It is how He lived His life and how we are to live ours.

Without trying to put us mere mortals on a par with Christ, I do believe in the work environment there is a similar alpha and omega.

There is one fundamental component in the work environment that is the initial focus of all successful activity and remains the central focus throughout the completion of all activity. This component is above all others and transcends all the others. The alpha and omega of the work environment is very simply *taking care of people.*

Shortly after we entered the pork business, Bill Leischner, who you will meet more intimately later, attended an Excel sponsored seminar for new supervisory personnel. During one of the social interaction periods during this seminar, Bill happened to enter into a conversation with Bill Fielding, then president of Excel. Fielding inquired as to Mr. Leischner's work. After some discussion, Mr. Fielding ended the conversation with this admonition, "If you want to be successful, go back to the plant and take care of your people!"

A number of years later, one of the Excel processing facilities brought in a high- powered consultant to identify what was needed to improve the operation. His recommendations were recorded and put on a plaque that hung in the office of the general manager of this facility. Each time I visited that office, I was struck by the message. The primary line of the plaque said, "Always take care of the product (meat)!" It then detailed several steps in how to do just that.

I could not view this plaque without thinking this consultant had it a bit out of phase. I thought back to Bill Fielding's admonition. More properly, the primary line should have said, "Always take care of the people!" That should then have been followed with the key steps to do that. I would expect to see steps like challenge, train, empower, support, recognize, and even express compassion. When people are taken care of, they will see to it that the product is taken care of.

In the mid 80s Excel began to look for a point of entry into the pork business. We had visited a number of single plant facilities as well as a couple of complete business entities. None of these seemed to be proper fits and we continued looking.

Rath Pāck, an Iowa based company with a primary facility in Waterloo, Iowa was an old line packing company that had been in business for decades. The Waterloo facility was the flagship plant and was a multistory unit with over 2 million total square feet of space. It was one of those old time fortresses where one can swing a headache ball into the wall to destroy it, and only one brick falls out. Over the course of time, the company had fallen on hard times and by January of 1985 was in bankruptcy proceedings.

In early February of that year the officials who were left at Rath contacted Excel searching for a white knight. The inquiry we received was presented to me one afternoon with instructions to follow up out of courtesy. I immediately placed a call and spoke to one of the officials who was extremely cordial. I asked for some basic accounting, marketing, and engineering data so we could do a very quick evaluation to determine if we had further interest. I was assured they could handle that request and would get it out to me.

The next morning when I arrived at my office at 7:30, I was greeted by a large package (box) from Rath with all the information I asked for and much more. To this day I have not figured out how anyone could have gotten that package 600 miles from Waterloo, Iowa to Wichita, Kansas in less than 16 hours by any normal courier method. Maybe someone drove it down!

At any rate, the information in the box was of sufficient interest to cause us to initiate some due diligence information gathering work. Over the next several weeks, Charlie Schieber and I worked closely with a small group of remaining Rath officials.

There were a number of things that made Rath look like a good port of entry including the best hog procurement area in the USA, some successful processed meats formulations and expertise, and the Blackhawk brand that still had very good brand name recognition and market acceptance. Beyond that, I thought the core group of gentlemen remaining in the company were experienced and of high quality and would give us an extremely valuable "been there and done that" business recognition. In spite of my recommendations we ultimately chose to pass on Rath. To this day, I think we made a big mistake. However, neither the fact of Cargill passing on the opportunity nor my opinion this was a mistake are particularly germane to this story.

As our work unfolded, I became friends with several of the gentlemen who remained. As we worked through issue after issue in an attempt to bring us (Charlie and me and ultimately Cargill) to a comfort level with our ability to be a *successful* white knight, I became increasingly aware of the critical nature people had played in the success and failure of the Rath organization.

My interaction with the Rath people during this due diligence work would often involve retracing steps through the gargantuan facility as we evaluated process equipment, old work flows, how fundamental improvements could be made in the operation, and future potential. As we would move through the multi story facility, I would often be privileged to hear stories from out of the past. The Rath guys were good storytellers and I never tired of the "history" lessons they taught me. I'm sure the stories were often told as reflection for the Rath folks and entertainment, or even amusement, for me. Even so, I soon learned they were also educational and there were valuable lessons to be learned in each of the stories about the *soul* of Rath Pack.

One day we studied an old workflow that had involved movement of product down through a number of stories (floors). As we rode one of a series of elevators between the floors, I could not help but raise the question. "I suppose in the old glory days the union demanded that each elevator had an individual operator!" I queried as a question, but more in statement form.

Sensing some of my old rural Iowa background and years in management were probably causing me to move to the point of view that the union had been the millstone around the neck of Rath, my Rath "guide" responded to my query. "Yes, that was the case," he said. Then setting me up for the kill, he continued. "Have you noticed at the opening of each elevator on each floor there is a door?"

"Sure," I replied. "Those are needed for safety purposes and have been a required fixture for years."

"Well, we had to have a person stationed at each door to each elevator on each floor. That person's sole job was to open and close the door whenever an elevator arrived," I was told.

I instantly did the math in my head and noted that while the person was operating the door at least two more people were present watching, the elevator operator and the person who had transported whatever product was being moved onto the elevator. I also did the multiplication math on the number of total doors with so many floors and elevators. I sighed in a way I'm sure signaled a union bias. My expression surely gave away my thoughts that no business could survive with such ludicrous labor inefficiencies and no union deserved the maintenance of jobs when they made such demands.

Smiling as he obviously read my mind he then continued, "Before you get too caught up in the inefficiency of that and any condemnation of the union workers, Jim, you should recognize the whole labor-management process at Rath cut both ways. I remember seeing a man collapse at his workstation on one occasion. The supervisor rushed to the point in the line where the man had collapsed and screamed, 'Someone get over here and drag this carcass out of the way so I can get another body in the line.'"

I stood dumbfounded by the inhumanity of that experience. I don't remember if I was told whether the collapsed man eventually died or not. More importantly, at the time of the incident, the supervisor did not know if the man had died or was dying, and yet his concern was obviously not for this man, but rather only to keep the line going and not lose any production.

I don't think the story was recounted to me to suggest all management personnel in the "old line" Rath management group were so cold hearted and certainly, I do not believe they were. Nevertheless, as I noted earlier, this story in concert with many others I had been told gave me some important insight into the soul of the old company.

There are people and human needs on both sides of all labor management issues. I hope I have been able to see these needs throughout my career. That labor and management ever see themselves in adversarial roles with each other is sad. By definition, the composition of both labor and management is people. People make the other tools and resources go so that goods and services can be provided. If the needs of any group of people are not being met or at least addressed, the activities in which those people are involved will most certainly suffer. I do not think any of the other resources of production (bricks & mortar, machines, procedures, materials, etc) can lay claim to such an overwhelming influence over all the rest.

Apparently over the years, people in the Rath organization, both labor and management, had become sufficiently desensitized to the needs of others that the degree of selfish activity rose to a level that destroyed the overall competitive effectiveness of the organization. Even a mixing of the two "warring" parties could not overcome the damage inflicted in earlier conflicts.

To be sure, the Rath organization did not go down because of one insensitive supervisor and a group of people doing nothing but opening elevator doors. Perhaps, however, the demise of the Rath organization was at least partly a result of the inadequate addressing of human needs and the inability or unwillingness to take care of people on all sides. I think a strong case can be made for that. I am not a Rath historian and without question my total exposure to this company that had existed for decades was no more than a few months. Nevertheless, I believe the evidence that remained in the wake of failure pointed somewhat conspicuously to a number of people related issues. Issues that seemed to be a result of an atmosphere where the needs of people at all levels were subordinated to other interests.

As you will see in Chapter 15: "The Family," the exceptional performance of the entire team at the Cedar Rapids East Soybean operation was made possible by the atmosphere of compassion and fairness. There are likely no other characteristics of human behavior that are more conducive to a feeling you are someone of worth than when you are dealt with in a spirit of compassion and fairness.

I once saw an interview with a leading Fortune 500 CEO. Following his predictions of how his company would do over the next several years, he was asked what he personally did to insure the progress of the company and how he saw his job responsibilities as CEO. The CEO responded he had several functions. However, the one that caught my attention was that he felt it was his responsibility to be the kind of boss the very best managers in the world wanted to work for.

I believe this man has it exactly right. And he can only be the kind of boss the best managers in the world want to work for if he recognizes them as people and recognizes their needs. These needs are not necessarily all personal needs. The need for challenge, stretch, and performance satisfaction go right along with support, encouragement, empowerment, recognition and reward. And I cannot imagine a person not wishing his or her boss to at least understand they are also an individual person with some individual and unique characteristics and challenges.

To be sure, the atmosphere created by the above noted philosophy and that which seemed to govern at least a part of Rath's history contrast sharply. One of the difficult questions is how do we establish concern for people and meet their needs without running the risk of having them trample us in the process. Interestingly, looking at the experience at Cedar Rapids East, it is easy to see people want to perform rather than trample. Most of them will perform and make us proud and successful, rather than sorry and a failure.

All of that notwithstanding, however, perhaps we should take another look at Jesus' example of unconditional love. Jesus' teaching and life example were to establish a concern for others and meet their needs *without regard* for whether they trampled Him in the process. Is that too much for us to risk?

In the early 70s, I had the good fortune to work closely with Leroy Venne. At the time, Leroy worked for Crown Iron and we had purchased an extraction unit from them for the CRE facility earlier noted. Leroy was the primary contact for the installation and was the on-site resource person for start up and wring out. Leroy and I became both working associates and friends. I was always struck by Leroy's good nature and his willingness to assist in any way. Leroy always gave me the appearance of doing whatever it took to make our job easier whether we afforded Leroy any reward for that effort or not. Many would say that was customer service and simply the Sam Walton way, and maybe that is correct.

A few years after the installation, Leroy came to work for Cargill. Unfortunately, by that time, I had left the part of the business that Leroy joined. As a result, over those many years, I did not have the opportunity to work with him in any significant way. In the late 90s, our son, Derek, went to work for Cargill in the same division as Leroy.

Derek recounts many times when Leroy has come to his assistance, shown great concern for him, and worked to help meet Derek's needs. In fact, Derek tells me when he has to call someone in the Minneapolis Operations office for advice or a permit approval, he always prefers to speak to Leroy. It is not that others do not have the skill or ability. Rather it is when Derek is speaking with Leroy, he (Derek) is the most important person in Leroy's sphere of activity.

Twenty-five years had not changed Leroy. He had and continued to have the ability to raise whoever he was interacting with to the level of the most important person in his world at that particular instant in time. Maybe Leroy was just a slick actor and it's all perception. I think not. I think Leroy understood the process of success *begins* with people and *ends* with people. Further, I think he understood success is also pretty much at the mercy of people in the *middle of the process* as well.

# CHAPTER 14
# Friends

In his book, *How to Sell Anything to Anybody,* Joe Girard talked about "Girard's Rule of 250." Mr. Girard explained that over the course of time as he attended funerals, he asked the funeral directors how they knew how many people to expect. Generally, that number totaled about 250. After a similar discussion with a wedding caterer who explained he expected about 250 from the bride's side and another 250 from the grooms side; Mr. Girard drew the conclusion 250 people are about the number of friends we are able to accumulate (and retain).

While I'm sure arguments can be made for numbers greater than 250, as well as less than 250, the key point is that we all have a circle of friends that has certain limits. It is my experience that friends fall into three major classes. First, are those people who we meet and with whom we deal in our everyday business life who rise above the simple level of business associate, customer, or supplier to friend. You have read (and will continue to read) about many of these friends of mine in these writings.

Working together is one of the best ways to cultivate friendships. Co-workers, like Eldred Swoboda and a host of others are classic examples. Like-minded suppliers and associated support operations are always a rich source from which to develop good friendships.

Forced togetherness is also a great way to develop friendships. Eric Skov Hansen worked for a Danish engineering firm with whom we contracted when building one of our processing facilities. I spent many days traveling in Denmark with Eric and other Danes observing the Danish swine industry, visiting equipment manufacturers, and becoming educated on swine genetics, breeding systems, and pork production in that country. Unless you have irreconcilable differences, which I think I have with very few people, traveling in a car, airplane, train, or ferry with another person for hours or days at a time creates an atmosphere from which friendship is almost sure to evolve. It did with Erik and the other Danes.

Lots of people are good hosts, but none top the Danes. My travels with Erik landed me in an old Danish castle, that had been turned into a hotel, for a one night stay while we were traveling in central Denmark. Hundreds of years ago the Lady of the castle supposedly murdered her husband in one of the castle bedrooms. My memory is fuzzy on the details of the story, but as best I recall, bloodstains on the floor in that room were her undoing. Legend has it that this Lady's ghost comes back to this room each night at midnight and works to remove the bloodstain from the floor. This was the room I was given for the night and although I remained awake until after midnight to make the "Lady's" acquaintance, if she was there she was too quiet and transparent for me to see.

The second friendship group is made up of those people with whom we maintain a personal friendship and with whom we share common bonds. I have often found that friends in the first group (business originated) frequently move into the second group of personal bonding.

When I first arrived in Memphis (Chapter 7: "Can You Speak the Language"), Bert Solden was one of the shift supervisors. Bert was thirty-two, but looked twenty-seven (his wife Mary never seemed to look much older than twenty-seven). I was twenty-two, but looked twenty-seven. We were similar in so many ways that a friendship just seemed to happen. Bert took me under his wing in the plant operations and helped me in more ways than I can name.

Beyond the work environment, Bert and Mary essentially made me a part of their home. Their young children, Scott, 11 and Terri, 8 at the time, became almost like a little brother and little sister to me. God often seems to put the right people in place to fill a need at given times in our lives and Bert and his family certainly filled a need for me.

Joe Culbreath also rose to this level of friendship as was discussed in Chapter 12: "The Perfect "10"". There are literally dozens of other people I could name who fall in this second class (perhaps most of my 250 limit). Some of them you have met in past chapters or will meet in future chapters. Mike Dallan is one person who you will meet in more detail in later chapters and who has steadily moved up through the friendship channels. Quite likely, Mike does not fall into the very elite final class only because he and I have never resided in the same geographic area.

There is then that last group of friends that is a very limited inner circle; persons with whom you develop almost family-like kinships. Many people refer to these people as "best" friends, while I prefer to think of them as "close" friends. These are people who you would die for. Happy is the person whose immediate family members fall into this inner circle. Unfortunately, many couples and families do not share this intimate friendship. Mine certainly do, but I do not choose to talk about them here as they have been discussed in much more detail in Chapters 3 and 6. I would, however, like to discuss some of my "non-blood" close friends.

My wife often says I have never really had many close friends in my life and I suppose that is partly a result of my more introverted nature. I also believe it is a function of my natural independence and high self-esteem and my lack of need to have constant reinforcement of my worth. Obviously, this can also result in arrogance and condescendence although I hope that has not been the case in my life. Chapter 32: "The Face in the Mirror" deals with this in more detail.

When I was growing up, my cousin Wes Boshart was my first close friend. We lived close together, attended the same one room country school, played together whenever we could arrange it, and were regularly together at family get-togethers. Wes remains a very good friend of mine today, but the miles separate us, and we are lucky to see each other once a year. Nevertheless, we always still have great times when we have the chance to get together.

My friendship with Wes was supplemented in junior high school and high school by Jim Henss. Jim lived right across the street from my Grandma, who I regularly visited for her wonderful grand mothering and cooking. Jim and I went to school together, played ball together, and chummed around together for 6 years as we went from boys to men. I can't say we studied together, as we neither spent a great deal of time with homework. Even beyond school and sports, Jim and I socialized together and often double-dated. We continued to be friends beyond high school, but again, with distance the close relationship eventually dissipated. Today I am lucky to see Jim every 10 years or so.

My college years at Iowa State University brought me to my next close friend, Ron Seipp (pronounced Sipe with a long i). Ron and I were both engineers and lived in the same dorm house, as well as being in a number of classes together. Ours began as somewhat of a more unusual bond since other than college, curriculum, and housing; we didn't appear to have a lot in common. We came from substantially different backgrounds. Ron's was more metropolitan and, although an Iowa resident for part of his early life, at the time of our meeting his parents resided in New Jersey, which was a world away from rural Wayland, Iowa.

I was a regular church attendee and Ron was not (at least at that time). I often joked I was always more comfortable around Ron because of Jesus' teaching of His Second Coming as detailed in Matthew 24 verses 40 and 41. Jesus commented that when He returned, "two women would be working together and one would be taken and the other left, two men would be in the field working and one would be taken and the other left." I always reasoned if one were taken and one left and if Ron was the other person, I stood a much better chance of being the one taken.

Ron and I spent a lot of time together throughout our college years and even shared a mobile home together our senior year. Although we didn't do a lot of house cleaning, we did do most of our own cooking. We would even have started the kitchen on fire one evening had it not been for Ron's alertness and fast action. Ron often came home to the farm with me. He loved my mom's cooking. We learned to cope with life's challenges living away from home and moving from dependents to independents.

What Ron and I did have in common was a real love for life and laughing. We often irritated both of our future wives with our casual and fun-loving attitudes. Neither wife was particularly enthralled with our decision to go pigeon hunting in my Uncle Elon's barn one New Year's eve. However, Uncle Elon, who was 63 years old at the time, did get a huge kick out of going up in his barn hay-mow with us. I'm sure it was one of the most active New Year's eves he had spent in years and I know he carried that memory to his grave.

Positive friendships, like marriages or business relationships, should result in each friend bringing out the best in the other. Although our wives would sometimes disagree, I do think Ron and I did that. Again, we were really kind of what each other needed at that time in our lives. After college, distance and time began to work towards a waning in our close relationship. To be sure, today we are still friends, but beyond the Christmas card/letter exchange we seldom communicate.

After Ron Seipp, no one stepped forward to fill the non-blood close friend role. Other than my wife who was (and is) my closest friend, my children who share a bond on a different level, and my father who until his death had always been a very close friend, there was no other close "friendship" bond. Although I continue to believe I got along just fine for the next couple of decades, I'm sure there was some missing part in my life. I think it maybe even bothered my wife some that I had no one other than her in whom to turn.

Then in 1987 when we moved to Beardstown, Illinois all of that changed. Within a few months, I had developed friendships with many new people and more importantly "close" friendships with two very special people. To this day, those two people remain my closest "nonblood" friends. The first of those two people is Dick Robinson who you have already met in Chapter 8: "Why Stationed by the Plow."

As I mentioned in that chapter, Dick and Dan Schnitker are the two hardest working guys I have ever met. Dick is fiercely loyal to his friends and his causes. Nothing is too tough for Dick and he can do just about anything. I think all of those things drew him to me. I hope some of those same things drew me to Dick.

Like Ron Seipp, Dick and I share a real love for life. My wife, who is a fairly casual person herself, was always mortified when I would come in about 8:00 or 8:30 at night and call Dick, "Hey, I'm going to the Dairy Queen to pick up some soft serve ice cream and a can of hot fudge. We'll be at your place in 15 or 20 minutes to eat."

"You can't just call up and invite us to someone's house," she would protest.

"I'm not inviting us to *someone's* house," I would reply. "I'm inviting us to *Dick's* house!!" And off we would go and always have a great time talking, laughing and eating hot fudge sundaes with Dick and his family.

The second person was Bill Leischner. Bill was a farmer in the Beardstown area and his wife Donna was the charge nurse at the Oscar Mayer plant we had just purchased. I had made Donna's acquaintance on one of the first days that I had been at the plant. I soon made Bill's acquaintance in a more accidental fashion.

We were reasonably sure our Beardstown assignment was going to be temporary so we did not sell our house in Kansas. Accordingly, we did not look to buy a house in Beardstown. What we were really wanting in Beardstown was to rent a small farm. My wife and daughter had scoured the area and we had the unbelievable good fortune to have found a 120-acre timbered farm with a large and grand old house that had a lot of character. The house had been built in 1915 by Archie Dunn's mother. The house was built after his father had died during an operation on the kitchen table of the old house that later was turned into a barn. The barn was still in service and we continued to use it for that purpose during our tenure. The "new house" had been inhabited only by Archie and his mother and later by Archie and his family until his death in 1986. Although Archie's two sons, George and Carl (who we found to be delightful people) had long since moved away from the Beardstown area, they could not bring themselves to sell the old home place.

We formed an immediate bond with George and his wife, Francis, and they agreed to rent us the farmstead and the 120 acres of timber. We became only the second family to live in the 70-year-old house. Even before our family made the move to Beardstown, I would stay in the house during the week. One of the first evenings I was there I went exploring in the timber.

Mostly, I was walking the fence line to see what kind of repair work I would have to do to put some stock cows in the timber. This was a dream that didn't ever become a reality, mostly because the fence line needed more work than I could give it. After nearly giving myself a heart attack by stumbling across an old cemetery, which later gave some interesting history lessons as there were stones dating back to births in the 1700s, I proceeded to find the east fence line. I followed it back north to what I thought would get me back to near the farmstead. As I emerged into a clearing area I could see the highway and also the neighboring house.

Upon walking a few more steps, I was startled as I came almost face to face with my new neighbor. He introduced himself as Bill Leischner. I asked if he happened to be related to Donna, as that was only the second time I had ever heard the name Leischner. He smiled and informed me that she was his wife. Bill and Donna had two sons, who were about the age of our daughter, Renee. It did not take long for Bill and me to become friends that evening, but I had no idea the impact he would have and how strong that friendship would grow.

Interestingly, Bill had farmed Archie's place for years until Archie's death. In addition to the 120 acres of timber on the bluff side, there were 240 acres of prime flat farm ground across the road. Through living on the place and listening to Bill's stories about Archie, we came to the point where we felt like we really knew the old guy even though we had never met him and he had died long before we knew he even existed. To this day, we have an International 806 and a Farmall M (both tractors) that belonged to Archie. We purchased these from George when we moved to the place and later hauled them back to Kansas with us. I cannot think of any circumstance that would cause me to ever sell those machines.

The 80s had not been a good time for many farmers and Bill, like many others, had suffered from drought and low prices. When we began reconstruction of the plant that we bought, Bill came to work on the construction crew and later the maintenance crew. He soon became a supervisor and worked his way to the position of environmental manager in the early 90s. In this position, he and I had the opportunity to continue to work together on an almost constant basis as we worked to move Beardstown from somewhat of an environmental problem child to environmental poster child in the eyes of the Illinois EPA.

Although Bill and I worked together at the plant, it was through Bill's totally unselfish acts as a neighbor that brought us to such a deep friendship. Bill helped us get our small farming operation established and stopped by virtually every day to see what kind of help we needed. On those instances when I had to be out of town, there was *no virtual* about it, he stopped every day to make sure Chris and the kids were OK.

Soon after we arrived, I wanted to clean up some old piles of wood in the pasture, so Bill brought his caterpillar dozer over for me to use. I later used it to clear a spot for a basketball court. I had a great time playing with the dozer; then one day it was gone. With his farming operations limited, Bill had no further use for the dozer, which was a maintenance hog in its own right. He had a chance to sell it so he did. I was heartbroken! Even today I often joke about what kind of neighbor would sell a caterpillar dozer right out from under my nose after he had gotten me hooked on using it to have so much fun.

Even with all the help Bill gave us while we lived on the old farm, the most giving acts came as we left and returned to Kansas. We had moved all of our "farm stuff" to Beardstown in a 16-foot livestock trailer that we had bought just prior to the move. When we left Beardstown, it took 6 loads with the livestock trailer, 10 loads on a 32-foot flatbed trailer that we purchased, two loads on our little Toyota pickup and 2 loads on a 16-foot flatbed trailer. For three months, we worked at loading throughout the week, leaving on Friday night for Kansas, unloading on Saturday, and returning on Sunday afternoon.

Bill not only stopped frequently in the evenings to help with the loads, he and Donna spent two of their weekends helping us drive loads and vehicles out to Kansas. Bill is always an upbeat-smiling type of person who you seldom see angry. The second trip Bill and Donna helped us make was the day that Bill stopped smoking. He had been told the best time to stop was on a day when you would be doing something totally out of the ordinary. Well, pulling a livestock trailer full of farm supplies and equipment 500 miles was certainly not Bill's ordinary day.

On that particular day, I had left a little earlier pulling the 32-foot flatbed, since I traveled slower. A couple of hours later, Bill and Donna left pulling the livestock trailer and Chris left with one of the cars. We had two-way radios in everything, but Bill hardly spoke to Chris. He seemed like an unhappy, angry man and for most of the trip Chris was sure we had pushed our friendship one step too far in accepting Bill and Donna's latest offer of help. It was not until they were almost to Kansas that she realized Bill's demeanor was based on nicotine withdrawal and not on anger at "having to help those dumb neighbors again!"

A couple of weeks later, as I was preparing to leave the old farm for the last time, Bill saw my car in the driveway and stopped in. We stood in a kitchen barren of things and yet overflowing with memories. We each choked out a few words; then we just hugged each other. Bill left and I spent my last few moments in the old house quietly crying. More than a decade and a half has passed since Bill and I were neighbors in Beardstown and yet our close friendship remains and continues to grow stronger.

My family does a very good job of keeping me grounded and keeping life in perspective. Yet, I do think it is important to have "near family" close friends like Bill and Dick to supplement that effort. There are certain times in life when non-blood relationships are necessary. When those times come in my life, it is reassuring to know Bill and Dick are there, no matter how many miles may separate us.

For me there can be no consideration of friends and keeping life in perspective without eventually coming around to Joe Kauffman. Joe "Goodpliers" as he was known to all of his acquaintances was an enigma to me for the first several years I knew *of* him. When we moved to Hesston, Kansas in 1980, Joe had a small and somewhat unkempt repair shop in Zimmerdale, a wide spot in the road about 3 miles south of town. We would pass his shop frequently and we would occasionally run into this big man with large hands and semi-clean overalls barbecuing chickens for fund raising events. Beyond that we generally kept our distance.

In 1991, we purchased a farm with 160 acres and a farmstead located about a mile from Zimmerdale. We became a neighbor to Joe by default. Joe was not a man of many means and certainly on some days he was not a man of *any* worldly means. Yet, when Howard and Anna Ruth Beck, the couple from whom we had bought the farm, had their farm equipment sale, Joe gave them a supreme gift. He chartered a small plane and flew over the sale area and farm and took a number of rolls of pictures. No one knew what the overhead plane was doing. Several days later, Howard and Anna Ruth showed us an album Joe had just given them that was arranged neatly with a series of memorable pictures. It represented the culmination of seven decades of farming and over a century of relatives living and farming that particular ground.

That evening, Chris and I commented about what an incredibly thoughtful and selfless gift that had been from a man of so little worldly means. We decided this man may be something far more special than we had thought him to be. We determined we should at least give him "a try" as a repairman when things broke in our new farming operation. What started out as "a try" turned into "life-blood." I traveled quite a lot in my work and whenever I would be gone and anything would break down, Joe became not just the mechanic, but the ultimate backstop. He would drop anything he was doing to help Chris.

Joe's life was about helping, and Joe would help anyone, especially his friends. One evening during a severe thunderstorm he drove over to the farm where only our daughter was living at the time, and simply stayed in his car in the driveway through the storm to make sure that if Renee needed any help, he would be there. What I find so amazing about his life (Joe died in January of 1999) was that due to the fact that he was not your average person, most people did not avail themselves of his friendship. Unfortunately, that group included us for several years. I could tell you stories on end about Joe, but I simply refer you to the "More Stories" section for *"Goodpliers" Remembered,* a copy of the tribute to Joe that I wrote for the local paper after his death.

Joe inspired me and taught me a lot about life and friends. For those of us fortunate enough to listen to him and learn, Joe taught us all what friendship is really about.

*When we fail to be friends, we fail to carry Christ's message of love. When we fail to open ourselves to the friendship of others, we fail to give others the opportunity to share that message with us. Ultimately, we fail to receive the blessings of life that Christ intended for us to have.*

# Chapter 15
# The "Family"

In the early summer of 1971, after I had spent the first two years of my Cargill career at the Memphis soybean complex, I was given the opportunity to transfer to another operation for further development. I was given the choice of either going to Gainesville, Georgia or to Cedar Rapids, Iowa. The Gainesville plant was a relatively new facility and was located in majestic topography just outside of Atlanta, Georgia. The Cedar Rapids facility (known as CRE) was an old plant with some of the oldest technology in the industry. It was located in the center of that east-central Iowa town.

Given those circumstances plus the fact we had really come to enjoy the warmer climate of the South, choosing Gainesville would have been only natural. There was, however, one more item in the mix. Our first child, Renee, had been born on Good Friday (April 9) of that same year. Choosing between being about 100 miles from each set of grandparents and being 1200 miles from them weighed much heavier in the decision mix than climate and topography, so we picked Cedar Rapids. Both sets of grandparents were thrilled with that choice.

While I was confident at the time this was the right decision, it would be 26 years later before I would realize just how critical that decision had been for them. I discovered one of the ultimate joys in life for myself in November of 1996 when Renee and her husband, Jon, presented us with our first blood grandchild, Titus. Titus lives in the same town as we do and we thoroughly enjoy him. Jon and Renee's second child (Kayla born in 2000), as well as two additional grandsons (Benjamin born in 2001 and Lucas born in 2003), children of our son Derek and his wife Kris, reconfirmed this ultimate joy of grand parenting. Whoever said grandparents and grandchildren are natural allies certainly knew what he or she was talking about.

When I arrived in Cedar Rapids, however, I did have serious second thoughts about our choice. The plant was a vintage 1940s plant with old equipment and an equally old work force. Most of the workers were in their forties or fifties and had been at the plant for years. The management team at the plant consisted of the plant superintendent, the maintenance supervisor, and me. As time progressed, I would come to a full realization of just how such a limited management team could be highly beneficial to an operation, but murder on individual managers. Jeff Stanley would soon join the group as a construction assistant when we began an expansion project.

The plant processed 25,000 to 30,000 bushels of soybeans per day. While that may seem like a lot of grain to go through a process in one day, it was relatively small even in the early 70s. Plans for expansion had already been made and capital money approved when I arrived in the early summer. For all its old equipment and systems, this was an incredibly efficient facility. Of most importance, however, it possessed one of the greatest collections of workers God ever assembled in any one industrial environment. It was of no wonder to any of us who ever worked at this plant why the CRE plant was continually at or near the top in performance efficiencies.

Soon after I arrived in Cedar Rapids, the plant superintendent left Cargill and was replaced by Uli Sander. You have already met Uli and his wife, Marianna, briefly in Chapter 7. Uli was one of the most unique people I have ever met. Uli had experienced life as most of us can only read about. He was born and raised in Germany. His mother died when he was only 6 and he was reared by his mother's sister and her husband who were very well to do. Uli was in his teens at the time of World War II and that is where life began to get very difficult. Uli was arrested by the Russians as they pushed into Germany. The Russians treated Uli very well, but upon his release by the Russians, Uli was immediately arrested by the Poles who put him in a concentration camp where he was treated very harshly.

Uli was hesitant to talk about his past as I'm sure most of the memories were anything but pleasant. Yet on several occasions he did talk to us in some detail. I'm sure a part of this was to let us know "where his shoes had walked" so we would understand him better. One day as we were leaving for lunch, one of us commented, "Let's go to Bishops (a popular cafeteria in Cedar Rapids)."

"You guys go ahead, but I prefer not to go along. I refuse to stand in line for food again," was Uli's reply. He later informed us why he refused to stand in any line for food again. He then told us of his experience of being sent to the concentration camp earlier noted. People incarcerated there were treated quite harshly and with no regard for human sanctity. Uli continued to tell us the amazing story of how he eventually found freedom and maneuvered his way back to normal life. What most of us take for granted, Uli had to fight an incredible battle to achieve.

Uli eventually wound up in San Francisco. Uli's father was half Jewish and had to flee Germany at the time of the war and landed in Manila. After the war he immigrated to the United States where he was later able to pull the necessary strings to get Uli into the United States. Uli eventually found his way to the Cargill copra (coconut meats) processing plant and refinery in San Francisco. At that facility, he worked his way up through the ranks, got an engineering degree during the nights and ultimately became the plant superintendent there. He also met and married Marianna in San Francisco.

There is likely no woman in my past with whom I have had anything less in common and yet enjoyed being around so much as Marianna. Perhaps it was just my sport of trying to turn her into a pragmatic conservative as she was trying to make me into a romantic liberal. We neither one succeeded, but we gave Uli and others (my wife, Chris, included), many hours of laughter and enjoyment watching us spare. In addition, I forced a lot of steak down her mouth whenever they were at our house and enjoyed every minute of that. In return, she forced whatever concoction she called food down me when we were at Uli's and took great delight in that.

Marianna taught me you can have irreconcilable differences with another person and yet enjoy their company. You can take whatever differences you wish with their positions without compromising the relationship you have with their character or the joy provided by their presence.

In addition to being a person for whom you held in highest regard for his survival and determination if nothing else, Uli was also the right guy at the right time for both the plant and for me. I had quickly won my position with the people in the plant. They recognized my strong intellect and understanding of the soybean processing operation and they were comfortable with my approach to people.

The downside was that with the expansion process and start-up of a new operation came a lot of mechanical and system problems. With no management people at the plant from about 6:00 P.M. when we left until about 7:00 A.M. when we returned as well as most of the weekend time, I was in a vulnerable position. Any problems that were encountered during those times were usually referred to me via telephone calls. The telephone calls were bad enough, but often the problem required me to return to the plant in the middle of the night. As time passed, I was becoming worn down and frustrated. Uli was instrumental in keeping me focused and seeing the light at the end of the tunnel.

Uli's management style was very much like mine. I would also suggest Uli's style reinforced mine at a time when I was probably still somewhat impressionable. Uli believed you expected certain behavior and results from people, you gave them the tools and training to achieve that, and then you stepped out of their way and let them do their job. This worked perfectly at the Cedar Rapids East plant, first for Uli, and a year later for me when Uli left and I was promoted to plant superintendent.

Interestingly, one of the reasons it worked so well was the result of one of our predecessors. One of the prior plant superintendents had been an autocrat and for years the crew had worked under absolute totalitarian rule. No one turned a valve without his approval. He was feared, but highly respected, revered for his knowledge, but hated for his methods. One of the guys at the plant once told me, "I went to his funeral just so I could walk on his grave!" I never met the man, but I think he was highly responsible for my success at Cedar Rapids East. The crew there had without question learned from his excellent process knowledge. The shackles he had put on their independent thinking created an unbelievable opportunity for each of the superintendents who followed him, including Uli and later me, to unleash their high powered and creative juices simply by turning them loose.

When I first arrived, the CRE crew was made up of a group of solid performing operators, maintenance personnel, and support workers. Over 30 years later, I can still name them all by name and position, which I really think bespeaks their individual and collective *impact* on me.

They had this kind of impact and they made this kind of impression for two key reasons. First, they were all important persons to the operation at Cedar Rapids East. Second they were a part of the family at Cedar Rapids East. Not everyone was equal in his ability or contribution, but everyone was a part of the family. That family also included the management group; Uli until he left, Jeff Stanley, Virgil Tharp when he arrived, Bob Foote during his stay, John Kinney when he arrived, Ron Dirks, and me. It was almost an aura. While you were a part of the Cedar Rapids East plant you just felt like a part of the family of the people I named.

I do not use the term family loosely, nor do I use it in the sense of blood relatives. I use it to describe a condition in which everyone was bound to a common objective and dedicated to helping each other achieve our goals. This group was no more tolerant of each other than my kids are or were at home (the bigger always prey on the smaller). But like my kids, where no one outside the home is a greater supporter or more quickly rallies to their defense, the people at CRE looked out for each other's good and the good of the group in total in the general business and industrial environment with a bloodlike bond.

The practical results of that family were twofold. First of all the plant operated very well. Of the thirteen domestic oilseeds operations of Cargill at that time, CRE was virtually always first or second. When we expanded the plant, the rated capacity was 55,000 bushels per day with expectations we could peak at 60,000. In 1973 when margins were very good, we were able to run upwards of 75,000 bushels per day through the plant. Everything had to click just right, but with the caliber of people we had and the manner of working together that existed, clicking just happened!

The second major benefit was that work was fun. Even when I was worn down and frustrated, it was still fun to work in the group. Moreover, rather than just allowing fun to happen at work, we all helped create it. We had dinners and parties for all of the guys including their wives on several occasions. We did little things at the plant for each other. We rallied around each other in times of trial. Most importantly, we all enjoyed the sense of accomplishment and the joy of group success. We all shared in the individual successes of the other's, and we genuinely rooted for each other to succeed.

One night while I was at home, I received a call from the extraction operator. The extraction operator was the charge person at night when there was no management person there. He informed me one of the workers had not shown up for work. As with all of the people in the CRE crew, this particular man was a good worker. The guys at the plant obviously wanted him at the plant for his own good as well as theirs. They volunteered why he wasn't at work and told me exactly which bar I could find him in.

Now being in a bar when you are supposed to be at work would be grounds for dismissal. No one at the plant would put a fellow employee in the position of getting fired, nor would anyone at the plant put me in the position of having to fire someone *if* they felt that were the only choice I could or would make. However, the guys in the plant were confident that first, I would treat him as family, or at least as a friend, and second, being confronted in the bar by me would likely help him stay on track in the future. I have never seen that kind of trust displayed in the industrial sector anywhere else.

Yes, I did go to the bar and yes, I did in fact find our absent worker. His first reaction was one of horror followed by one of resignation and then almost one of relief. I still remember his words to me when I walked up to him. "Would you like a drink?"

I smiled and indicated I was not there as a social visit. I did not have a drink, but I did sit down on a bar stool next to him and conversed with him for the better part of 30 minutes. I did explain that his actions were not acceptable and we would have to fashion some form of discipline to fit the circumstance. I did reassure him his job was safe from this episode, but obviously he had to refrain from similar activity in the future. We then talked about a number of non-work related issues. Although I cannot remember what the other specifics of our discussion were, I do remember his words as I got up to leave, "Thanks for coming, Jim."

Perhaps that was said sarcastically. Perhaps it was said matter-of-factly as the way anyone is spoken to similarly when leaving. I think, however, it was spoken with at least some degree of genuineness. What I know is I didn't ever have to go looking again for him (or any other employee for that matter) when he was supposed to be at work.

For most of us, the CRE family was our second family after our blood family. For some, however, it provided the primary family. Many of the guys would come in early for their shift and sit down in the lunch-room to converse with each other prior to the start of the shift. One of the elevator operators was one of the guys who regularly did this. One day, we were summoned to the lunchroom where he had collapsed in his chair.

We immediately called for an ambulance. Some of the other guys in the lunchroom attempted to resuscitate him before the ambulance arrived and transported him to the hospital that was only a few blocks away. A short time after the ambulance left, we called the hospital to check on his condition. We were told that he had been dead on arrival at the hospital. They did ask us for next of kin so they could call them to the hospital. We could not find any in his files. The people at CRE had provided more family to him than even we realized.

I have often tried to identify the specific things that created and sustained the CRE family. As the plant grew and new people came in, a certain amount of the family bond began to fragment, but even then there was still a distinct atmosphere that to this day has not been matched at any other facility I have been a part of. I have tried to cre-ate that same atmosphere and have on occasion come close with sub-groups, but I have never once even began to see the same results on a total plant basis.

Perhaps it was not so much what we did as what we did not do. Subsequent chapters will deal with many of the burdens we put on our-selves and our workers today in the name of some other effort or on some other front to satisfy some other management discipline. Many of these efforts have the exact opposite result at the operating level of the company.

In fairness, one of the things that made it possible at CRE was the relatively small number of people in the crew (less than 30 initially including the production management group). It was possible to really get to know each person and more importantly for each person to know you really knew him and personally cared about each of them.

I do believe a key element was 10 years before empowerment became one of the management buzzwords, we did that with the CRE crew. It wasn't the result of some seminar and new "program" that we embarked upon; it was our way of life, our means of existence. We didn't just talk about empowering employees; we did it in no uncertain terms and without reservation. When a plant operates two-thirds of the time with no management personnel on site, that is empowering the workers! No one wondered if they had been empowered and no one questioned that empowerment. Further, no one second-guessed decisions made as a part of that empowerment. That is not to say we didn't learn from mistakes; we did, collectively.

Beyond that, we encouraged the ideas that everyone had. No one knows better what is needed in a given area than the person who works 8 plus hours a day in that area. Recognizing that axiom, we acted on those ideas when they were forwarded. Nothing makes a person feel more valuable and worthwhile than when their intelligence is honored. We made each person a part of the solutions to our problems. When we struggled with our safety performance, among other things, we laid out our total budget for safety related activities. We then enlisted the help of the entire crew to identify where it could best be spent to improve the work place from their perspective. What we had left unspent, we distributed to them. Our safety performance improved.

Each person on the crew had many years of experience. The fact that most of the crew had come from farming backgrounds and had high work ethics and that most of them had worked for years under an autocratic system—that tended to deny the ability and worth of the person's intellect—were important elements in molding the family ties at the CRE operation. That Eldred Swoboda was the union steward who so effectively led by both example and by helping craft win-win solutions to labor issues can also not be overlooked or under-estimated.

Yet for all those indigenous things to CRE that have not been replicated, I continue to believe the single most important element to the success of that operation was the spirit of compassion and fairness. Everyone treated everyone else as they wished to be treated. There was an open, honest, and transparent exchange of information brought about by trust. It was not part of a program or a process, *it was just the way we were and the way we operated.*

Whether it remains possible in today's environment to create that same kind of spirit is debatable. In any event, I count as one of the significant blessings in my life the chance I had to be a part of the *Cedar Rapids East family.*

# Chapter 16
# Team

In athletic events, as players break a huddle at the start of a game, at halftime, or after a timeout, there is often a clasping of hands and one common word shouted. The word often chosen is "Team." This is ostensibly a reminder that each person is but one part of a larger group, and only with the combined effort of the larger group can the objective of winning be met. Interestingly, many times immediately after that, players go out and perform without any regard for the workings of a team. Teams don't just happen, nor do they come into being as a result of a singular or group proclamation. Teams must be built and just as in any building, a foundation must be laid first.

A number of people would challenge my use of family in Chapter 15 and suggest what I experienced at the Cedar Rapids East facility was simply the workings of a well-tuned team. Perhaps! Certainly, I do not dispute that there were several team functions at CRE. The key distinction between team and family is one of implication, function, and intent. Team implies the bringing together of a number of people (or even animals like a team of horses) generally for a specific purpose. Further, the value of a team is in synergy, the sum of the group being greater than the sum of the individual parts. As long as that happens, the team is of value. However, at such time when the value of the team as a whole is less than the value of the sum of the individual parts, performance is no longer served by the team. Family, on the other hand, is a binding together of a group on a more fundamental basis. There is at least some degree of permanency beyond merely optimizing a certain performance. Families are bonded together by something more than simple synergy.

Athletic teams as earlier noted are generally pulled together for a single objective, which is usually winning a contest. These specific purpose teams are normally put together to accomplish that more singular objective. In the business community, there is often the overriding concept that entire operations, even entire divisions, are really teams. In many respects this is true. However, even here, managers often believe that simply proclaiming a business unit a team in this global sense will in fact result in superior performance. Yet in actual performance, the results accomplished are generally less than the potential. Why?

Those things that are critical to success on specific purpose teams are also critical to these more global teams. A close study of what drives success or failure in specific purpose teams can be very instructive in why "global" teams succeed or fail.

The simplest team I have been a part of was when I first arrived at the soybean plant in Memphis in 1969. Soon after I arrived, Fred, the lecithin operator, left the company. Fred had been one of the original employees when the plant began operations in the mid 50s. For years, Fred had operated the lecithin system. This included operating the pre-coat leaf filter, filling 55-gallon drums with finished lecithin, and loading the drums two-high in boxcars. When Fred left, Jimmie Williams, who was also one of the original plant employees, bid for and was awarded this job.

This particular job was one of the plums in the plant. It wasn't easy, but it was interesting. It was a day shift, Monday through Friday position, and it was largely self-directed. Jimmie was a good worker and a great guy. Everyone in the plant was happy he had "won" this position. However, Jimmie was not particularly mechanically oriented and he had not been previously exposed to a process type operation. Jimmie struggled through the training period with Fred prior to Fred's departure. He continued struggling on his own after Fred left. It was becoming increasingly apparent Jimmie and the position were not going to come together. No one wanted to remove Jimmie from the job, but both Jimmie and the job were suffering.

I had been at the plant only a few weeks and did not have a specific assignment other than to learn the overall plant operation. I had spent no more than a part of a day in the lecithin operation so I was far from an expert there. Nevertheless, I approached Fred Brosius, the plant superintendent as you may recall from meeting him earlier, and offered to work directly with Jimmie for a few weeks. I thought perhaps together we could get the operation under control and Jimmie comfortable with running it. Support functioning was a way of life for Fred and he quickly agreed. Jimmie and I became a team.

Jimmie and I both came into the team with something to gain and something to offer. Jimmie was desperately trying to succeed at a new job and retain his position. I wanted to help him do those as well as get some early supervisory experience. Further, Jimmie knew what was supposed to happen in lecithin production, and I understood how to make equipment and processes work. The marriage of those two capabilities allowed us to run the lecithin operation successfully even though I did run the leaf filter off the track the first day, much to the amusement of the maintenance people who were dispatched to help us get it back into position. Actually that helped cement our relationship as working together in adversity often helps create a bond that is useful in team performance.

Within a few weeks the lecithin system was running smoothly and I had transferred enough of my equipment and process knowledge skills to Jimmie that he had become comfortable in the total operation. There was no longer a question as to whether Jimmie could handle the job. I had received some very valuable lessons in the supervision and management of people and processes on a small, but very intense basis. In addition, with Jimmie's success at stake, something of real importance was riding on my involvement. We had achieved synergy and had both benefited personally from it. Without question, the foundations necessary for a successful team had been laid.

I was later a part of a much more diverse team that was assembled in the early 90s to develop the pork operation plan and facility for Cartai, our sister company in Taiwan. The Cartai people had been very successful in the feed business for 20 years in Taiwan. However, this group had no experience and only limited knowledge of pork processing. On the other hand, those of us from Cargill USA had years of collective experience in meat processing, but none of us had set foot on Taiwan soil prior to this project.

Further compounding the process was the fact that the principal geographic market for our product was Japan. Neither the Cartai people nor we understood the Japanese market and yet we both thought perhaps the other brought some knowledge of this to the table. Although we invited representation from Cargill's sales group in Japan to join our team, they functioned more as an advisor than as an integral team member. Finally, recognizing that Danish pork was favored in the Japanese market as well as the fact the Danes were ahead of us in certain meat technologies, we added a design and construction group from Denmark to our team.

This team spanned three continents, crossed two major oceans, and involved four different languages. Fortunately English was at least to some degree the common language. It made a real impression on me how demanding we are of the rest of the world in international communications. Basically if they want to work with us in any way, they better speak our language because we are not going to speak theirs. I muse at the thought of how much our balance of trade might shift if we learned to speak a few other languages.

More than the language or distance barrier, however, was the cultural barrier. Trying to learn what several thousand years of culture had ingrained in a people was beyond even the Doug Brooks' method of Chapter 2. We did our best to "walk in their shoes" and "put them in ours," but there were still a number of sticking points we encountered as we progressed.

Even with the challenges we faced, the results of the efforts of the team were exemplary. We managed a project with limited money relative to the needs and desires. We put together a world class operating facility that was the envy of the rest of the Taiwan and Far East pork industry. Additionally our joint training efforts helped smooth out many of the rough edges that are inevitably present at commissioning.

That we were able to do this with the diversity of the team is a tribute to the tenacious spirit and effort displayed by all team players. Moreover, I think it speaks volumes about the need for friendship, respect, and a spirit of comradery in building foundations for a team. We quickly established a mutual respect and friendship with the Danish Intercool people. More importantly, Fue Ju Wu (Wu), who was the principal player for the Taiwan nationals, and I had a great appreciation for each other's abilities from the get go. Wu and I developed a deep friendship at the very beginning of the project. When Joe Nalley joined the team later, he also became good friends with Wu. Joe, Wu, and I remain good friends today.

During the project, we were all able to take opposite positions with each other to the point of violent disagreement and yet never lose site of our goal. Once settled, the argument was behind and forgotten, but the goal remained in full view ahead. More importantly, everyone's character remained unscathed. The Taiwan project reinforced another critical element of a successful team and that is confidence in each other. Certainly, that allowed us to disagree and yet continue to move forward.

As earlier noted, observation of successes in specific purpose teams can often be a key to what makes global teams work. In addition, it is also possible to find global teams that work well and learn from direct observation of them.

When I originally arrived at the Memphis soybean plant in 1969, there was a real team spirit at the plant. People tended to move toward team action. This was somewhat ironic in many respects as the plant work force was about half black and half white and desegregation was still in its relatively early stages. However, you have already met the man who was the top operational manager at this facility, Fred Brosius. Fred was the consummate leader of the day. He would ask no one to do what he himself was not willing to do. He communicated effectively and he supported everyone in his or her individual and group effort. Fred gave each of us responsibility, coached us constantly, and was quick to thank and compliment us for both effort and performance. He led the cheers at work and also at play. In short, Fred created the atmosphere for team activity to flourish. He laid the foundation.

Like Fred, there must always be an effective leader who can lay the foundation and clearly understand and define the roles each member of the team is expected to play. The leader must also be able to get each member to understand and accept his or her role. An atmosphere must be created for synergism to take place. The value of the whole will never be greater than the sum of the individual parts if there is not an atmosphere of cooperation and a willingness to give *and* get assistance.

One of the early failures of the "Taiwan" team previously noted was that we did not have adequate knowledge of the Japanese market. The more critical failure was that *we didn't know what we didn't know.* The Taiwanese contingent counted on us filling that role as a result of our understanding meat sales to Japan on the basis of our USA experience. Unfortunately at the time, our USA sales were primarily frozen versus mostly fresh sales for products of Pacific Rim origin like our

Taiwan operation. Fresh and frozen products were two very different product lines!

Conversely, we counted on Taiwanese and Japanese cultures and meat consumption habits being somewhat common and, more importantly, being fully understood by our Taiwanese team members. They weren't and they didn't! Finally, knowing the Japanese had a preference for pork products from Danish processing facilities, we all thought the Japanese liked the Danish process methods and the Intercool people brought that expertise. What we ultimately found was the Japanese didn't care much at all about the Danish processes; they just liked the Danish PIGS!!

We had not laid the required knowledge foundation and secured the necessary talent in that area. We can assemble a team of great athletes, but if the sport is football and we've assembled a group of world class tennis players, the team will most likely still not achieve the desired result.

In the last half of the 90s, Cargill contracted with a consulting group to hold "high performance team building" seminars for all of their management people. These seminars were intense 3-day sessions that were a combination of classroom study, interactive communications, and physical activity geared to push people to their limit individually and as a group. The goal of this exercise was commendable and should have been considering the hundreds of thousands of dollars that was invested in these seminars. The explicit take home message was that collectively in our business, much more could be accomplished as a team than as mere individuals.

We had spent three days in supposedly open and vulnerable communication interchange. One of the implicit messages sent in the team building exercise was our relationships were therefore now going to be fully transparent and we could have full confidence in each other. We could now all have the kind of intense disagreements Wu and I had without any character assassinations or fears of reprisal. Above all, we could know our input was desired, expected, considered, and really mattered.

The explicit message was that each business unit would function as a team. In fact, many of us in the corporate management group attended the team building session in the middle of our strategic planning initiative that culminated with the downplaying of the old VP positions and the emphasis on new team leader positions. Essentially, since we had now proclaimed we were to function as a team, and further, since we had been effectively trained by experts in how to do that, *it would in fact happen.* We had set the default condition to team action.

Unfortunately it didn't happen as predicted. Certainly there was evidence of team efforts after the session. Perhaps team effort was even somewhat greater than it had been before. But it did not become a way of life and most candid observers would have noticed little difference a few months following these sessions compared to pre-seminar conditions. Indeed, before long, as much reference was made to VP positions as to team leader positions. Even the professional organizers of the sessions lamented there was not nearly as much open exchange in the follow-up sessions as there had been in the primary sessions.

Why had the desired change not occurred? Briefly, change did not occur because the system *foundation* did not change. Proclamations and training sessions do not in and of themselves create and sustain anything. I am reminded of a key operating principle: *You act your way into a new way of thinking, you do not think your way into a new way of acting.*

Ultimately, functioning as teams must be a way of life. We need to do that even when we are not thinking about it. One of the mistakes made on so many issues is we continue to believe we can "put on and take off" modes of operation like a shirt. We can do the team thing when it works to our personal advantage and bypass it when it may not. It does not work that way! Foundations must be laid. We must have a natural bent for open and transparent communications as well as a supportive and empowering approach to human issues.

There are few organizational entities as effective as well assembled and directed teams. There are few as inconsequential as poorly assembled and misdirected teams. Like most things, effective team action comes about from intelligent direction and hard work. More critically, it also comes about from effective leadership and solid foundation support as is more fully detailed in Chapter 17: *Bedrock.*

Clasping hands and shouting "team" only assures that noise is made and sweat is transferred. It doesn't make teamwork happen.

# Chapter 17
# Bedrock

One of the most popular parables of Jesus is about the wise man and the foolish man and where they choose to build their houses. I am sure a great many of you know this parable well from the song you sang as children. As you recall, the wise man built his house on the rock and when the rains and the floods came, his house stood firm. On the other hand, the foolish man built this house on the sand and when the rains and floods came, his house collapsed with a mighty collapse. Obviously, the point of the parable is to build your *life* on a solid foundation. What a great lesson for life in everything we do.

Jesus doesn't speak to why the wise man chose to build on the rock, or more importantly, why the foolish man chose to build on the sand. Ostensibly, we could predict the wise man was aware of the effects of wind, rain, and floods and therefore knew that without a foundation on the rock, his house would not stand.

What about the foolish man, however? Even simple logic would suggest a rock foundation would be more substantial than one of sand. And certainly, his architect, his builder, or his insurance agent could have been expected to guide him differently. So what motivated the foolish man? I would suggest laziness or, giving him the benefit of the doubt, perhaps lack of financial resources. If you have ever tried to hew something out of stone, build with stone, or even just move stones around, you know you have engaged work. Sand on the other hand is fairly easy to move around and work with.

I am always struck by how effectively Jesus used earthly examples to convey a heavenly meaning; in this case build your *life* on Jesus as the Foundation. Yet, I am always amazed at how the earthly examples in these parables of Jesus so closely touch the real fabric of daily life.

One of the TV channels I like to watch is the Discovery Channel. Some of my favorite subjects they address are on the marvels of construction (bridges, dams, skyscrapers etc.). In all of these examples, the foundations must go to something that is absolutely solid - *bedrock*. Often it is not where they are going, but how they get there that is the real story. It is amazing how bridge piers get constructed by first pumping out water and mud down to bedrock at the bottom of the river through water tight sheet pilings. Once that is completed, there is a "building back up" with concrete, which is a substance with rock like characteristics. If the foolish man was lazy or had limited financial resources, he would have had no chance to succeed on any of these foundations for sure.

Even in our own construction projects we often used piling when we needed to have exceptional foundational support for high loadings. While this was occasionally pipe or pole pilings that rely principally on the friction of the ground against the sides of the pipe or pole, it was usually of the concrete caisson type. In this type of piling, a hole of up to 36 inches or bigger in diameter is drilled in the ground and cased. This hole goes down to some solid underlying rock formation (bedrock) where the bottom is cleaned, a column of reinforcing steel is inserted, and then the hole is filled with concrete as the casing is withdrawn. When all is done, there is a concrete column that extends from the surface down to bedrock. There is no better foundation than this. One can rest assured no matter what type of building or load is placed on this column, if designed and constructed correctly, it will not fail.

Just like the foundations previously described are necessary to keep a building standing and properly functioning, foundations are just as necessary to keep people and organizations standing and properly functioning. When I started work for Cargill, as noted in Chapter 1 as well as in other chapters of this book, one of the key foundations I found was the principle of integrity and fairness. I had also learned that lesson well from my parents.

Principles like integrity, honesty, fairness, and compassion are the key foundation components to any worthwhile operation. They are the bedrock-base. However, it is the people in the organization and the manner in which they live out the principles who are often the concrete pillars or caissons that connect the underlying solid rock to the "building" itself.

I had only been working at the Memphis plant for a few months in the fall of 1969 when we received approval to transfer the solvent extraction equipment from a closed plant in Redfield, Iowa to the Memphis location and reconstruct them. In Memphis they would become a second plant in tandem with the plant in existence at that time. This combination of two plants would make Memphis one of the largest soybean complexes in the world.

As a young engineer, I was very excited about being a part of this. What was even more exiting was I was assigned the job of construction ramrod. While this entailed a number of duties, one of the main ones was to get all of the Redfield equipment transferred, unloaded, stored, inventoried, scheduled for repair, and ultimately readied for reconstruction.

Harvey Marxhausen was one of the Cargill assistant general superintendents in the Minneapolis office at the time. Harvey was over a number of the plants including the Memphis plant. Harvey was also the executive supervisor of this construction project and spent a couple of days in Memphis almost every week.

I was unmarried at the time and at least one night of each week Harvey was in Memphis, he would invite me to have supper with him at the restaurant in the Quality Inn Motel just off of President's Island. This was always a great meal for a single guy and the hostess in this restaurant had jewelry in some interesting places (at least for that point in time). However, of even greater importance were the conversations Harvey and I would have. Harvey became my dad away from home and the friendship and camaraderie we developed in those evenings lasted until the time of Harvey's retirement in the early 80s. I should note I continue to hold Harvey as a dear friend. However, as with many business generated friendships and working relationships, when the business or geographic connection ends, the opportunities to be in each other's company become infrequent at best.

Much more than just the friendship and camaraderie at the time, however, Harvey laid a foundation for me in training, education, caring, support, empowerment, advocacy, and mentoring. These played a key role in my development in the organization. Harvey's work not only aided my development, it also showed me how to become a person like Harvey who could and would help others.

For all of the importance of these things, however, the real "bedrock" of Harvey's effort was it left no question in my mind but that I was important to Harvey and through him, I was important to Cargill. Other than my father, there has been no other person who has had as much influence on my work life as Harvey Marxhausen. Other than my father, there has been no other person in the world with whom I would rather work. Do you think a young (or even an old) Jim Roth would not put out 125 percent effort for Harvey Marxhausen and thus Cargill??

I am sure there are still people in the organization like Harvey Marxhausen, but I do think they have become harder to find. More importantly, I think the rewards for their efforts are much harder to codify.

After my first year of work in Memphis, my wife Chris and I were married. I worked a lot of hours and sometimes some rather strange hours. Chris became involved at the church, but other than that, her circle of friends was pretty much Cargill wives. The wives in Memphis were included in a great many activities and were made to feel as much a part of the operation and Cargill as possible. Little things like small gifts or dinners that just said, "Hey, we appreciate your husband's efforts and your willingness to share him" were frequent in nature. These built strong foundations with our wives, and they felt very much a part of the overall plant efforts. As the years went by and the company size and complexity increased, it seemed like these efforts were no longer recognized for any foundational value. In fact, at times it seemed like the entire concept of foundations based on personal touch was gone.

When we started the plant in Taiwan in the winter of 1993, I asked six other Excel USA operations persons to accompany me to Taiwan for the initial start-up (others would follow later). In order to get to Taiwan in time for the appointed start up time, we had to leave the USA on Sunday morning, February 14. I felt bad about taking these guys away from their wives, especially on a Sunday that happened to be Valentine's Day.

Prior to leaving and remembering my past history, I asked my secretary to have a flower arrangement sent to the homes of each of the seven wives, including mine, on Monday, February 15 as a combination thank-you/peace offering. Lisa thought that was a great idea but had her own twist, "Let's not do it on Monday. We may get some of the left over flowers that didn't get sold for Valentine's Day. Let's do it about Wednesday. That way we will be sure of getting fresh flowers, and also the wives will have had a couple of days to miss their husbands. Finally, let's send the flowers to where the wives work. That way we'll get some extra mileage from all the other people who work with them as they comment on how nice the flowers are and what a thoughtful company their husbands work for."

Lisa was so dead on target; it amazed me. Of course why not, she was a wife herself, so she was just putting herself in their place and analyzing what she would react to. I took off for Taiwan and left it up to Lisa to make the arrangements. She did and we batted seven for seven.

Every one of the wives thanked me personally either by card or call (except my wife who thanked me in other ways). I still have some of the cards. They all commented on how neat it was, what a great gesture it was, how it brightened their day, and how they were the envy of all of their co-workers. I felt like I had put in place one of the lessons I had learned years earlier from Harvey Marxhausen. Show people you care about them and appreciate their efforts and they will respond.

Several weeks went by and one day in mid May when I was in the office in Wichita, the pork division controller called across the wall for me to come over to his desk. When I got there, he tossed an invoice across his desk to me. "Do you know what this is?" he asked.

I looked at the invoice and it was for $230 for 7 arrangements of flowers delivered on February 17. "Sure," I replied as I laid it back on Bob's desk, "That is for the flowers I had Lisa send to the wives of the guys who went over to Taiwan with me for the start-up. Hasn't it been paid yet?"

"No, it hasn't been paid," commented Bob, "I thought that is what it was for so I sent it up to accounts payable that way and they returned it. They said we do not have any mechanisms set up to allow that kind of expenditure."

I absolutely blew up. In fact, my boss came running into Bob's office wondering what was going on. "I haven't ever heard Jim use *that* word before!" he mused.

"Look," I steamed, "We spent $35,000 getting these guys over there and back. Their time value was another $10,000 to $12,000 per week while there. And as an organization we have no mechanism to pay for the most valuable $230 we have spent in the whole process. Give me the invoice and I'll pay it out of my own pocket!!!" I stormed as I grabbed the invoice.

"No, no," Bob said as he quickly reached out and took the invoice back from me. "I'll figure out some way to get it through." Bob did find a way to get it paid, but that was not the issue. The issue was we no longer had the flexibility to do the kinds of little things that build foundations and pay back huge dividends in good will and a feeling of care and appreciation. I knew the value of those kinds of efforts, but even I became more reluctant to battle the system to use them. When I did, I just did as Bob and found some way to hide them in something else. However, I know most people simply fall in line. If the system doesn't allow one to do it, then don't do it, case closed. In the process, we allow at least some of our foundations to be built on sand.

In many circumstances, one can find examples of integrity failures, less than honest responses, non-compassion, political posturing and inflexibilities as noted above. Certainly these overt things weaken the foundations that have been built up by years of solid effort and solid citizens like Harvey Marxhausen. However, I am of the opinion that perhaps most damage is done incrementally by erosion that is often done without any apparent recognition of its occurrence.

In the early 80s, several of us who were long time Cargill employees were asked to transfer to Excel Corporation, then named MBPXL, shortly after the purchase of that company. At the time of purchase, Cargill retained the employee benefits package in force at Excel. No attempt was made at the time to convert it to the Cargill benefits package.

Since a number of Cargill benefits were notably better than those corresponding benefits at Excel and recognizing this was going to make it difficult to get some of the key people the Cargill leaders wanted to transfer to Excel, the leaders told us we would be retained on the Cargill benefits system. We would be employees of Excel to be certain. Excel would pay our salaries and incentives. However, we would be retained on the Cargill benefit system rolls even after our transfer. This would assure we did not lose what we had worked for, become accustomed to, and counted on.

For me this was a key component of the transfer package as three of the Cargill benefits were highly important to me. Among these were the Cargill pension plan and the survivor's benefit component of the life insurance plan that had become a part of my long-range financial plan.

Additionally, I had just come through two lower back surgeries and was fairly sure I would be facing more surgeries. The Cargill surgical and hospitalization plan seemed to be superior to that in effect within Excel. With the Cargill benefits package retention assurance I, along with others, accepted the transfers.

One day, several months after we had made the transfer, a Cargill manager came into my office and casually informed me all of us who had transferred to Excel were being converted to the Excel benefits package (Cargill would continue to backstop us on the pension plan, but everything else was converting to the Excel plan). I was both dumbfounded and furious, as were most of the others. I asked how Cargill could even consider such a move, as it was against the one very thing I thought we stood for, namely *our word was our bond.* Moreover, it made me feel as though I was not a very important spoke in the wheel if I could be cavalierly treated in this manner.

My comments were shrugged off and I was informed that some of the Excel managers were unhappy we were treated differently and ostensibly better than them. Cargill "leaders" (whomever they were in this case) apparently determined it was in the best interest of the company for all of us to be placed on common ground. Perhaps there was value to that, but unfortunately if it could only be accomplished by disregarding past promises and commitments one had to question where the value started and stopped.

"Fine," I replied, "Then convert all the Excel managers to the Cargill system and not only will we all be on the same ground, but we will also remain on common ground with you and all the other Cargill leaders and Cargill divisions. That is the way you handle this situation without destroying your integrity or reneging on your word and promise!"

I'm sure my words were heard, but it certainly seemed like they went right into outer space. The theme continued to be this was necessary to achieve intra-company harmony and therefore that made everything OK; sort of an *ends justify the means.* The leaders felt confident this was in the best overall interest of the Company. To this day, I wonder at what level in the organization this decision was made. It was so out of character with the fundamental principles (the bedrock) of the company. Then as well as now I think it must have been a more independent decision of persons (caissons).

As it turned out, we all accepted the decision, but none of us liked it. In the end, some of my words were heard as I was given assurance that if I did have another surgery (which I did), the Cargill plan would back up the Excel plan and I do give credit for that action. However, as earlier noted, foundations include both the bedrock *and the caissons,* and the unfortunate byproduct was that day turned me from an employee who put his full trust and confidence in the company he worked for to an employee who was forced to accept the fact any word or promise could be suspect. Accordingly, I have not been able to have an *unabridged trust* in Cargill to deal fairly and equitably with me, or others, since that time. That is not to say Cargill has not done that. What it is to say is I could no longer count on it unequivocally and without reservation?

The damage to Cargill was (and is) the foundation of integrity and honesty that so many people worked so diligently to build over the years and decades got eroded. These insidious situations are the most damaging since they are often unseen and unknown. Little by little the foundation underpinnings are worn away until small or large collapses occur and we wonder what caused the building to fall.

Fortunately there are people in Cargill, and I'm sure other organizations as well, who continue as foundation builders and repair persons. Just as it is possible to reinforce or rebuild damaged construction foundations before catastrophic collapse, so is it possible to repair damaged foundations in organizations.

Another boss of mine who continually worked to build foundations was Ray Larson. Ray was as different from Harvey as night from day in terms of education, talent, and general skill set. However, Ray was like Harvey in that he knew the value of inclusion, support, and devotion. Of all the managers with whom I have worked in Cargill, no one has been more fiercely loyal to his employees than Ray Larson.

I first worked with Ray in Cedar Rapids, Iowa in the mid 70s as peers. I was the head operations person and Ray was the head merchandising person. Then in 1978, I transferred to the Memphis Corn Plant as the operations manager where I reported to Ray who was the general manager. Ray and I both lived in the same suburb of Memphis, so we rode together to and from work most every day. This 30 to 45 minute commute both ways gave us great opportunities to discuss operational concerns uninterrupted. In addition we also often shared non-business concerns and both learned to appreciate the other as both manager and friend. We even discovered we shared the same birthday, although Ray's was five years prior to mine. We also both had a love of humor and fun.

It was through these discussions I came to recognize what a strong sense of ownership Ray had in each of his people. I do not mean owner- ship in the sense of slavery, but rather in the sense Ray was responsible to see that each person was treated with dignity, respect, and common courtesy as well as supported in their efforts to succeed in their particu- lar job. This trait in Ray was never so apparent as when a young very attractive female sales trainee was assigned to the Memphis operation. While we all found this young lady to be easy on the eye, none of us gave it much further thought.

This young lady was assigned to syrup sales. Accordingly, she was assigned to the sweetener sales manager who was a great guy, but one of those people for whom it was so easy to poke fun because of his predictable and often nervous nature and behavior. His wife, a delightful person herself, gave us the impression of being highly protective of her husband which we always found ironic as he did not seem to us to have the capacity to wander.

Nonetheless, he did take the new trainee "under his wing" with almost a reverence for her. I am sure to this day most of this was a result of his desire to help her succeed. Perhaps the fact she was very pretty made it easier, but I suspect he would have done much the same for any other trainee of lesser physical attraction. Nevertheless, it was apparent around the office that special attention was given to our newest manage- ment person.

A few short weeks after the arrival of this young lady, Kris Thompson, the merchandising manager and another comrade of mine in making work fun, strolled into my office and announced she had inter- esting news on our young lady friend. It seemed one of the young men with whom this young lady had come in contact on her training rounds in Minneapolis had since been continually haunted by where he had met her before. Finally, after weeks of brain recall activity, he recognized he had not met her in person, but rather on the pages of *Playboy* magazine. She had been one of the Big Ten conference playmates.

Kris told me this news was making the "lower level" rounds in Minneapolis and would likely soon be well known throughout the company. I told Kris the whole idea was preposterous and she was crazy. She told me to get a certain issue of *Playboy*. Since *Playboy* was not one of the periodicals I purchased each year on the senior class magazine drive, we had to do a little digging. However, upon successfully uncovering (no pun intended) the issue in question, it was fairly easy to see this was indeed either the same girl or a twin sister.

Kris and I then proceeded to explore all of the ways to exploit this bit of information to add some life to an otherwise somewhat dull piece of time. In this process we mused at how much fun it would be to be at the morning coffee in the Lake Office (Cargill top management headquarters) with all the senior officers when this information was made known to them. While they were a highly intelligent group, they also were a highly conservative and fairly stoic group who would most likely not knowingly or openly be thrilled about the employment of former playmates.

Kris and I decided while this may be lots of fun, it was out of our reach. What would be within our reach, however, would be to have a sort of Memphis manager's get together dinner and include the wives. During the course of the meal, Kris and I would casually remark about the new sales lady's progress and then slip with the remark about her past escapades. Since this would be news to all the others in the group, including the sales manager; they would be shell-shocked and speechless. The presence of the wives would make it even more fun. Kris and I, along with Ray, could get a giant laugh and ultimately the others would probably see the humor as well.

Kris and I then went in to see Ray; first of all to break the news his newest salesperson had an interesting former life and second to suggest our plan for having a little fun with the others. Ray was dumbfounded by the initial news and appalled by our suggestion. It was first of all obvious that to Ray, this former playmate and a person for whom he had not asked; had yet become one of his people and as such deserved not only his support, but also his compassion and devotion. Ray's concern was not so much for how the "coat & tie group" would respond when they found out about her past as it was for how any of those responses, plus those from lower levels, would impact her in the attempted performance of her job as well as leading her life in any form of normal fashion.

While Ray acknowledged our ingenuity in breaking the news to the others, he let us know in no uncertain terms there were far better ways to do that and none of those included doing it in front of any wives to see their reaction. The males in the group could each decide how he wished to break that news after he recovered from his own shock. Ray made it easy for Kris and I to see that he was correct and our "fun" could only have been accomplished at someone else's pain. After further discussion, Ray helped us decide we could best support all of the Memphis people by continuing to operate as though we knew nothing and supporting each other in that manner. We would just let the normal grapevine channels take their course if they were to do so.

Those channels certainly did take their course and the news was soon known throughout all of Cargill. Ray handled the issue in a most professional, supportive, and compassionate manner. Within a short time, our saleslady left the company and moved on, both geographically and with her life.

I sincerely hope she didn't leave because those of us at Memphis made her uncomfortable, and I hope today she is able to lead a normal and proper life. Certainly everything Ray Larson did in Memphis was geared toward helping that happen. I think we all learned from Ray the strength and endurance of foundations built on support and devotion.

I'm sure there are times when we all struggle with what we are going to use as our foundations. I think a lot of our decisions on these issues come from our backgrounds. Even so, people like Harvey Marxhausen and Ray Larson can show us ways to build new foundations, shore up our existing foundations, and/or put down a few more extra support columns or caissons. The foolish man in Jesus' example may have simply never had any good mentors to help him understand the difference between rock and sand!!

# CHAPTER 18
# Stained Glass Windows

During his high school days, our son, Ryan, went to church at the Eden Mennonite Church in rural Moundridge, Kansas. The quality of a church is unquestionably the result of the people in that church, and not a function of the building within which those people happen to worship. Nonetheless, the Eden "building" is a most attractive facility. Each time we visit there, I am struck by the beauty of the stained glass windows that flank the platform/pulpit area at the front of the sanctuary.

While the beauty of these windows strikes me, I am also fascinated by what stained glass windows do and do not do. Certainly they are things of beauty to behold. They allow a limited amount of light to enter and yet shut out the glare of bright sunlight. The arrangements of the various colors and shapes may create a specific image or tell a particular story. On the other hand, stained glass windows are opaque, they do not allow a person to view what is happening inside from out and vise versa. I think it is the combination of both the beautiful and opaque natures of stained glass that gives it much of its desirability and utility.

I'm certain the stained glass windows at the Eden Mennonite Church as well as those of thousands of other churches, synagogues, and cathedrals around the world are there for beauty, and not to hide actions on the inside from those who would view from the outside. On the other hand, in the business and industrial climate, I think a great many stained glass windows have been installed where transparent glass formerly existed. In these instances, the transparent characteristics of honesty and understanding have been replaced with perceptions of beauty or utopian conditions as viewed from the outside, but where very different conditions exist on the inside.

Transparency is the most important element in ascertaining honesty that exists. If we can truly achieve a totally open nature, we are likely to get to the truth. You may recall meeting Ron Dirks in Chapter 9: "What Makes the World Go Round." Ron was the guy who stumbled on to the right answer for us in the upside down condenser episode. Ron was also the absolute best employee candidate interviewer I have ever had the pleasure of working with. Ron achieved this through two characteristics: first, he was a bright guy, and second, he had a penchant for creating the atmosphere that left him on an absolute equal level with the interviewing candidate.

At the Cedar Rapids East plant in the early 70s we had a relatively small total crew with low turnover. Accordingly we did not have an HRD staff to handle employee relations including hiring and firing. That work fell to me as the production manager as did numerous other "staff" responsibilities. Generally, we did not have major hiring efforts with advertising, etc. We took walk-in applications from day to day and when an opening occurred, we drew from the pool we had accumulated.

Ron Dirks was the plant clerk. This was a relatively low paying thankless job that entailed doing all of the odd administrative jobs none of the rest of us on the management team wanted to do. Ron was an unmarried, hippie appearing, Vietnam veteran, who was leading a relatively loose life style at the time. [Note: That changed in 1975 when Ron got married and he ultimately became a truly solid person both personally and professionally]

When applicants would come into the office, Ron was the person they would encounter. Ron would give them an application form and then begin the conversation with him or her, although in those days it was mostly "hims," as they filled out the application form. While Ron's appearance and demeanor created an instant feeling of "brotherhood" with most of the applicants, he also cultivated an additional sense of ease between himself and the applicant. What the applicant put on the form was of only cursory value. What he or she told Ron was what keyed our decisions to hire or not to hire.

Ron would bring the application in to me, toss it on my desk and say either this person fits or this person does not fit. He virtually never missed. I got to the point where Ron had 95 percent of the vote in selecting new employees. What is interesting is many people will view this situation as an unfair and misleading procedure on our part. We were in effect "sneaking up" on people and *catching them in the act of being honest.* Certainly, most, if not all, of these candidates were unsuspecting of Ron's impact on the hiring decision. Had they been suspecting, would that have given them license to bend the truth?? No, it wouldn't, although that is precisely what likely would and often does happen. People tend to fear transparency. They wish to appear as something they are not.

By being able to get absolute honest responses, we were able to find the people who best fit our needs at the plant. However, what usually gets lost in this entire discussion is the fact that by achieving this absolute honesty, we did not hire people who would likely not have been as successful in our operation or perhaps successful at all. They went on down the street to the next opportunity that was likely a better fit for them. Did we do them a disservice? Again, on the contrary, their honesty helped us funnel them in directions of more likely success on their part.

I have spoken many times in this book about the need for transparency in establishing open and forthright relationships. It has been my experience and observation that transparency exits in the business world in an indigenous or native form under two specific conditions. First, where there is a genuine desire for a win-win atmosphere, where people generally recognize their success is directly related to the success of others, and where common knowledge and understanding are recognized as the prerequisites for mutual achievement. The second area is where size or skill makes it possible for business leaders to be able keep in touch with all or most phases of a business unit down to the lowest levels. While there is transparency in both of these conditions, the motivations for such are very different.

The earlier example of Ron Dirks may have also helped you recall Chapter 15: "The "Family"" and the discussion of how the entire Cedar Rapids East group stayed together in the sense of supporting and uplifting each other. This is a very good example of the first type of motivation where transparency is embraced because people recognize that it creates positive value. We all knew the more each of us knew about the other's job and how all the jobs were inter-related, the easier and better our own job would run. In like manner, the more we each knew about the personal needs of each other and the more each of the others could know about our own, the more we were able to support each other on the personal side as well. Chapter 31: "Three Million Dollar Handshake" cites numerous examples of relationships that thrived and continue to thrive because of this type of transparent interaction. Once exposed to transparent relationships, it is difficult to accept anything less.

For years, hog carcasses in most USA plants were graded manually by sight. As carcasses went by at speeds of 12 to 16 per minute, a person would observe each carcass and make a determination of the thickness of the fat layer on the outside of the carcass (from less than 1/2 inch to well over 2 inches) as well as the lean muscle structure of the carcass (in six different categories). At the speeds noted, even the best and most experienced operators could not begin to do this with any degree of accuracy. As I studied this in one particular facility, I noted over 80 percent of the time the operators simply noted a fat layer category of 3 and a muscle category of 3 as well.

It did not take any stroke of genius to note 80 percent of the hogs coming to us did not fall in the exact same class. In the 1980s, the Europeans had begun to use electronic measurements for the fat and muscle structure on carcasses. Although not perfect, this removed a lot of the subjectivity and made measurement at the high chain speeds more of a match to the actual carcass merit.

In the early part of 1990, a few of us in the Excel Pork Division succeeded in convincing the rest of the management group to install one of these electronic devices (called a fat-o-meater or FOM). We viewed it as a very transparent device. It would grade a supplier's hog carcasses objectively based on electronic measurement with little opportunity for packer subjectivity. Producers have always tended to view packers with a huge dose of suspicion and distrust!!

We hoped the FOM would give the producer greater confidence in our grading of his animals. Nonetheless, we knew we would have to do a great deal of training of hog buyers, producers, dealers, and virtually everyone else in the production chain to achieve this confidence. We conducted side by side tests with the old methods, held producer and buyer meetings in the field to explain the system in detail, included descriptive material with producer's checks, and jumped through about any hoops the producers held up to educate them on the new system.

Sure enough, following months of education and the opportunity to see the merits of the system, producers not only accepted the FOM measurements, they preferred them and in many instances demanded them. We had succeeded in creating a transparent relationship between the buyers and the sellers at least on the measurement issue.

Interestingly in the late 90s, under a different management group, a decision was made that the FOM system could be made better and even more accurate by changing certain elements of the formula used in conjunction with the measurements. Quite possibly, accuracy could have been improved with this change. However, this time it was done and implemented without any fanfare, and more importantly, with no attempt to inform anyone other than a few key people involved in the change.

While the objective was to attempt to create a more representative grade, one of the effects of this change was to reduce the value of some of the top-end animals that graded better with the original FOM formula. Perhaps the question should have been raised as to why producers, who had been conditioned to improve the quality of their animals in a given direction, would suddenly be okay with a change that took money out of their pocket for apparently doing just that?

I was not involved in the last change, so I cannot pass judgment why this change was made with no fanfare. Perhaps there was simply no recognition of the need and desire to know on the part of producers. In any event, when it eventually became known, Excel became the subject of a Packers and Stockyards (one of the regulatory arms of the United States Department of Agriculture) investigation that ultimately resulted in the USDA filing a complaint against Excel for significantly underpaying producers as a result of the formula change. Without transparency and education, there was no chance to even get to the argument as to whether this revised formula was *actually* a better reflection of the true value of the animal or not.

Interestingly, one of the things the P&S people spent a good deal of time reviewing was how thoroughly we had documented, communicated, and educated our producers with the first switch to the FOM with the original formula in the early 90s. Attempts to bridge the gap in time to allow them to both understand and begin to change the characteristics of their herd won acceptance of the new technology. The regulators obviously viewed this favorably. I'm sure they had trouble understanding why this same course had not been followed again.

The company's failure to follow that same path also had costs in producer loyalty and confidence. Producers worry that if you were not open and transparent with me yesterday, why should I expect you will be open with me tomorrow. Further, if you are hiding something from me, then it must be to my disadvantage and to your advantage. Human nature is not that hard to figure out!! Moreover, if we can't see clearly, we will usually expect the worst. This is especially true if we think someone has helped make the viewing fuzzy.

One of my most unique experiences of transparency occurred in the mid 80s while I was heading up the analysis of the leather business. I was fortunate enough to get to spend the better part of a week traveling the eastern quarter of the country from Maine down through the Appalachians to the deep Southeast. My traveling companion, or more properly my guide, was a principal at one of the companies with whom we did a lot of business. During these travels, we visited leather tanneries of all shapes and sizes. Bob was a most gracious and informative host, who made this experience fully educational and fun for me. To this day I am not sure I ever properly thanked him for his effort.

One of his personal friends was a gentleman who was the principal of one of the best leather tanneries in the New England area. Knowing the reputation of this man's operation, I asked about the possibility of visiting there. Bob made the call and got the ok for us to visit. As we walked up to the entrance, Bob looked at me and said, "I don't know how Jack will react to this visit. He may give you a tour and he may throw you out!" Words like that are a little scary when you're on foreign turf.

Nevertheless, we went in and were promptly ushered into Jack's office where he was seated behind his desk. Jack complimented me on the leather coat I was wearing (a gift from my parents 10 years earlier). He and Bob exchanged a couple of pleasantries and then Jack explained he had a severe cold and the only reason he had come to work that day was to meet us. I fidgeted just a bit.

Jack then looked at me and addressed me with a couple of pointed and probing questions relating to why we were chroming our hides in the manner that we were. I answered his questions as directly and in as straightforward a manner as I could. Jack went on to explain why the process we were using was not a particularly good one and why many good tanners would not buy from us for that reason. We proceeded to discuss that issue in depth, with me very much the listener as I was most interested in learning from this man.

Suddenly, he stopped and said, "So what can I do for you, young man? What is it you would like to know about the tanning business?" I was a little shocked at his directness, but I responded with some form of general question about the key operational parameters of the business. I assumed this kind of question would give him the opportunity to give either a direct answer or, if he thought I was being too forward, he could generalize some type of noncommittal answer. Or, I guess he could throw me out of the office!!

To my pleasant surprise, he responded in the most direct and forthright manner. He went to the point of giving me information beyond my request. His answer prompted a question about operating costs for which I had hoped to get at least a generic answer. Jack listened to the question then called to his secretary to bring him in the past month's P&L and operating statements. He proceeded to invite me to come over behind his desk where I could see his books, and he then turned page after page showing me his exact costs and results.

After some period of time poring over these statements, Jack picked up the telephone and called one of his top operational assistants. He introduced us and then said, "Here, give these guys a tour. Answer any questions they have and show them anything they want to see. I'm still not feeling well and I'm going back home." With that we shook hands, and I thanked him for all of his help and invited him to visit any of our operations anytime he wished, and he left. His assistant gave us a thorough tour of the operation. It was the most enlightening visit and experience I had on the trip.

Later, as we walked back down the sidewalk toward Bob's car and actually in about the same place where Bob gave me the "ingoing" warning, Bob looked at me and said, "I have never seen Jack act that way to any stranger before. He certainly took a liking to you. I'm sure very few 'outsiders' have ever seen Jack's books the way you did."

I don't know to this day what caused Jack to be so transparent with me. I suppose there was something about me he liked. Moreover, I'm sure he had an air of confidence (not arrogance) that his was an operation that set the standard. If we wanted in the business, then we should at least know what standard to shoot for. Mostly, however, I think Jack was the kind of guy who preferred transparency. It was his first choice as a *modus operandi.* If Jack did not always follow that first choice, it was probably more testimony to the nature of the people with whom he was often interacting rather than his own indigenous preference.

He also impressed me as an intelligent man who knew just about everything there was to know about his own operation. Given this knowledge, I would very much expect all of Jack's subordinates would be very transparent in their dealings with him. I suspect Jack had transparency for both reasons noted earlier. First, he recognized the win-win nature of directness and honesty. Second, he was so well versed in his operation that no subordinate would be stupid enough to try to pull the wool over his eyes. Transparency existed because it was desired and also because it was imperative.

When I joined Cargill in the late 60s, it was small enough that the top officers in the company were able to maintain a grasp on both the overriding company strategies as well as most of the general plant level operational happenings. This "vertically integrated" knowledge on the part of the leaders created an atmosphere of honesty and transparency out of necessity and fear if not desire.

As the company grew ever larger, however, it became impossible for the key corporate leaders and policy makers to be sure all their desires and policies were adhered to at lower levels. As more and more levels get added between the top and the work, more and more stained glass gets layered in from level to level, both consciously and unconsciously. Managers are often able to tell their superiors what the superiors want to hear (the beauty of stained glass) with little fear that superiors will ever gain knowledge of the real conditions (the opaque quality of stained glass). In addition, when superiors must view through several layers, the simple process of layering creates opaque conditions even without intent. When enough stained glass gets layered in, it becomes difficult to track real performance and company politics often become the principal management effort. I do not wish to get in a discussion of company politics here as that is handled in detail in Chapter 20: "We Have Met the Enemy."

For all of the problems with lack of transparency already noted in this chapter, I believe perhaps the most pervasive and of the most ultimate damage to a company is the "dummy down effect." As upper and mid level leaders become more distant from the day to day operations, there is a natural tendency to rely much more on set task and operating procedures and rules than on the ability of subordinates to manage and make the right things happen based on simple business principles, goals, and objectives.

Leaders often gravitate to creating a series of "audit procedures" to track adherence to their rules and procedures. As this process continues, the perceived need is to establish procedures and rules the most incompetent subordinate in the organization can apply. This in effect "dummies down" the entire lower management structure to the level of the least competent underling, or worse yet, the one perceived to be the least competent.

A classic example of this is in project management. For decades, those of us in project management were given wide latitude in doing just that—managing the project. We understood company principles, as well as business objectives, and we were held accountable for the project budget, scope, and schedule, and we were expected to get those accomplished in a safe manner and with quality that met requirements. We were charged with doing the right thing. When we did that, we were rewarded, personally with career enhancement and divisionally by being awarded more capital funds to do more projects.

One of the tools available to limit risk in construction contracts is performance bonding. For a cost of about 1 percent of the contract, the owner can in effect get an "insurance policy" that helps reduce the pain of a contractor defaulting. It needs to be noted that bonds do not have anything to do with default, just a reduction in pain if that happens. For years, we were trained to make proper evaluation of a contractor's ability to perform and thus the need (or lack of need) for performance bonding. We evaluated the contractor and project to determine:

Did the contractor have a solid credit rating?

Did Cargill have past experience with the contractor or did we have contacts in the industry that did?

Was the size of the job well within the contractor's financial capability?

Would all or most of the work precede the payment schedule?

Was the work of a non-highly specialized nature?

If a contractor and the work fell through all of these funnels, then bonding would most likely be spending 1 percent or more to insure security we had already "insured" by proper analysis. We saved the cost of the bond and proceeded to manage the work and the contractor. Over the years, I had been involved in some quarter billion dollars worth of construction. I bonded only a couple of jobs that were of a highly specialized nature. Because we managed the risk, we did not ever have a contractor default on any of these jobs. Through proper front-end analysis efforts, Cargill saved something in excess of 2 million dollars in bonding costs on these projects.

In the late 90s, performance bonding became a virtual mandate. Project managers had essentially no authority to waive bonds no matter what the risks were or were not. Only vice presidents could waive bonds and they were reluctant to do so as the audit trail would pick that up. It looked better on the audit to have the bonding box checked.

On one small bond of roughly $1000 (about $100,000 worth of extra work on an existing contract), we failed to increase the amount of the original bond to handle the extra work with this particular contractor (who happened to have a long term spotless record with Cargill). When the work was audited, the auditor criticized us for not securing the bond. I quizzed her as to whether she ever evaluated the bonding issue from the point of real risk management. In other words, did we secure a bond when good risk management would have said, "Save our money."

"No," she replied, "that is not our charge. We are to insure the procedure of bonding is followed and if not, that is a *markdown* on the audit." Unfortunately it is really a "*dummy down*" to the level of the project manager who is incompetent to evaluate the risk factors noted earlier and be counted on to do the right thing.

It is indeed sad as these insulating layers get added in an organization, the organization loses some of its ability to be proactive as well as its ability to be consistent in character from top to bottom. Moreover, when procedures become more important than principle, integrity suffers. Even when it is not the intent to subordinate principle to procedure, that is the natural evolution when the audit trail tracks procedure and not performance.

Where policy at the top and performance below do not coincide, one must conclude that business leaders *are surrounded by stained glass and apparently satisfied with the view from the outside.*

# CHAPTER 19
# Putting Up the Numbers

As you may recall from reading Chapter 1, I have always been a football fan. One of the great football dynasties was the Pittsburgh Steelers of the mid to late 1970s. While I was not a Steelers fan, anyone who claimed to be a football fan had to marvel at the machine-like effectiveness of this team. The thing that most impressed me was how this team of superstars was melded into a homogeneous group with a singular purpose of destroying the competition. Performance was the order of the day each and every Sunday when this group took the field.

Each person on this team had a task to do on each play to make the entire team successful and they each did it. The result was victory after victory and championship after championship. And yet, no one person had to make the big play time after time. Accordingly, when Lynn Swan, a premier wide receiver on that team along with John Stallworth, was first eligible for entry into The Pro Football Hall of Fame, he was denied.

Ostensibly Swan was not a solid candidate because he had not "put up the numbers" during his career. In other words, he didn't have enough pass catches, yards gained, or touchdown passes to warrant entry. All he had were a number of years in the league where he was one of the big play makers and a whole handful of Super Bowl rings to prove he could get results. The fact that he alone didn't have the big "statistics" was due to the fact every player on the team was an equal contributor. Further, with the dominant defense of the Steelers, the offense was often working with a short field. Short fields are great for putting points on the board, but not for racking up offensive statistics. Fortunately for football fans, Lynn Swan finally made it into the Hall of Fame on a subsequent vote. That he did not make it on the first ballot is testament to the fact that our society focuses on statistics and not on performance that yields results.

Some time back, my youngest son, Brandon, told me about an

article in one of his sports magazines. In this particular issue, all the NFL quarterbacks had been rated for the previous year. Brandon read me the formula. Simple passing statistics made up 45 of the total of 100 possible points. Leading the team back from a fourth quarter deficit to victory was worth ½ of a point. If a quarterback would have led his team back to victory from fourth quarter deficits in each of the 16 games of the regular season, he could only have amassed a total of 8 of the possible 100 points, less than 20% of what he could get by just playing the statistic's game between the 20 yard lines and "putting up the numbers." If I am looking for a guy to quarterback my team, I want the guy who can *lead* the team back from fourth quarter deficits to victory. I'm going to give the most points to the guy who can lead.

The business and industrial arena is very much like that just described. Too many times, rewards are based on putting up the numbers with only passing regard for whether there is or has been performance that gets real results. To some degree, I think this is the result of the metrics craze (not meters instead of feet and inches, but measurement in general). We have become highly focused on measuring above the bottom line.

Understandably, this is to be able to gauge performance, make course adjustments, and thus impact the bottom line positively. I certainly support this theory. The theory breaks down in practice; however, because is it is much easier to manipulate the numbers above the bottom line than it is to manipulate the bottom line number. Just as in the quarterback case above, leadership is the key. It takes effective leadership to establish the metrics so performance, and not manipulation, is driven. It also takes leadership to drive performance so manipulation is not needed.

Above the line measurements are especially critical where it is difficult to quantitatively gauge the impact of a given performance by reference to the bottom line. Of course it is also much easier to manipulate the numbers in these cases as well. Safety performance has always been one of these areas. We all know poor safety performance results in poorer bottom line performance because of compensation costs and more importantly, lost productivity. Compensation costs are quantifiable (although often not easily), but lost productivity costs are impossible to quantify. Accordingly, safety performance has historically been evaluated with above the line measurements like number of accidents, number of lost time accidents, number of days lost and even dismemberments or deaths.

One can read books like *The Jungle*, written by Upton Sinclair in the early 1900s, and gather that safety in the workplace is at best a mid 20$^{th}$ century phenomenon. This can probably be tracked directly to what was just noted. Without recognition of lost productivity and with little or no compensation costs, why worry about safety? The answer to that is simple; *concern for our fellow workers.* However, even that phenomenon did not seem to take root until the mid part of the 20$^{th}$ century.

When I joined Cargill in 1969, there was no OSHA and only a limited number of federal workplace safety regulations. Cargill had suffered a couple of disastrous accidents in the previous decades that resulted in the loss of several lives and critical injuries to others. Feeling the pain of losing comrades, Cargill took several aggressive safety measures and made employee safety a critical operating parameter. I was, and remain today, proud of Cargill's early approach to safety. Even with the emphasis placed on safety at the time, there still existed some of the macho intellect that continued to make safety management difficult. We did measure our safety performance by many of the metrics noted in a previous paragraph. Although I was not at a high level in the organization, it did appear to me the numbers were reported and processed in a transparent fashion.

Then in the 70s, the government stepped in to "help" other companies, who had not been as proactive as Cargill, manage their safety efforts. In typical governmental fashion, they attempted to do this by passing reams of regulations. These regulations sometimes helped improve safety performance and sometimes hindered safety performance. Of course, companies such as Cargill were sucked into the regulations by default. If you were a part of the industrial community, the regulations were for you!

As is noted in detail in Chapter 23: "Do You Solemnly Swear" the safety and environmental laws of the 70s changed forever the approach of business to these issues. What had been "at best" a humanistic concern for people and the environment and "at worst" an economic consideration, now became a consideration of fear driven by the regulations. Leaders were more worried about fines, government intervention, and the whole realm of legalities. With fear a more powerful driver than either human or economic considerations, safety performance became a more critical parameter.

At this point leadership often faltered and failed. With government regulators looking at the measurements, it became critically important to "put up the numbers". Certainly leaders also wanted to "put up the performance," but the numbers drove the system. Leaders at the top pressed for good numbers and leaders at the performance level began to manage the numbers as much as the performance.

Make no mistake, as just noted, performance was also desired and certainly as the years have passed, significant progress has been made in improving employee safety. I am thankful for that and proud to have been a part of it. However, as the years have passed we have also become proficient at "putting up the numbers" in spite of the performance.

One example of numbers management comes from light duty programs. Many organizations have installed these light duty programs to provide work for employees as they recover from injuries. I think this is commendable and serves the needs of both employee and company. However, this does provide a platform for number manipulation and unfortunately sometimes even further risk.

As I have traversed the American workplace, I have been in plants where employees still under medication and medical attention have been returned to work almost immediately after an accident to prevent them from becoming a lost time number and/or rack up lost days. I have seen an employee with a digital amputation be returned to the plant and shuffled from department to department to just sit while still under sedation. I have noted other similar examples as well. Perhaps there is limited danger to these persons since they have not been put back in their normal work situation. Nonetheless, "safety" numbers are being created that are not really reflective of actual safety performance.

Who is hurt by this numbers game? Some would suggest it is all internal and no harm is done. Others would suggest the government is being cheated in the numbers reporting. Still others may suggest the ones being cheated are those in an organization who are really working to drive performance and not simply the numbers. Perhaps all of the above are partly true. Irrespective of who one may think is most hurt, the real problem is that we have the false sense of security provided by good numbers when perhaps all of the processes are not in place to provide good performance. Accordingly, we all remain at greater risk than we think. Historically, the slower decline in work related deaths, for which there are no manipulation opportunities, as opposed to the improvements in the other safety "performance" measurements may be testament to this fact.

Safety is not the only area where numbers get massaged. In the mid 70s MBPXL, the predecessor company to Excel, began chrome tanning hides. This process continued after Cargill purchased the MBPLX operations. The plants in Friona, Texas and Dodge City, Kansas chrome tanned part of the hides they processed, but the facilities in Plainview, Texas and Rockport, Missouri did not.

Day after day, month after month, and year after year, the hide merchants would run through the formula pricing numbers showing the gross margin on chrome hides was just under $7 per hide greater than for brine curing, which was the default condition. With the standard costs of chroming being in the $2.50 range versus something in the $1.50 range for brine curing, we were apparently taking $6.00 to the bank on each hide we chrome tanned.

However, month after month, the blue book (the P&L statements for each area of the operation) showed we had a greater net profit in the Hide Operations at the Plainview plant that did not chrome than at the Friona plant which did. Both plants were in Texas and both processed similar cattle with similar labor conditions. Certainly, the blue book numbers did not square with the "above the bottom line" metrics perpetuated by the merchants.

Following the collapse of our effort to get into the full leather making business (Chapter 24: "Used Cars"), Bill Fielding approached me with an assignment. Bill, then President of Excel Beef, told me he wanted me to resolve why the blue book on hides did not square with the measurements above the bottom line. "Look," Bill told me, "No one in the company knows more about hides and leather than you do right now. I want you to go to Texas and find out what is happening between Friona and Plainview on the hide operations. I don't care how long it takes or what resources you need! Go, get it done!" To this day, I credit Bill with one of the prime examples of leadership where a manager actually recognized and challenged contradictory numbers above and at the bottom line.

I went to Friona with a certain amount of trepidation about how I would be received by the local group. Vaughn Blum, the plant general manager, jumped up from behind his desk when I told him of my assignment. He marched around his desk to where I was sitting and stretched out his hand to shake mine. "Finally," he said, "I get so frustrated every month getting beat by Plainview when everyone is telling me what a great deal chroming hides is. You'll get our absolute support here in Friona!" With that he called in a couple of his department heads, and instructed them to assist me in any way I requested. Bill was the hide department manager who quickly became and remains a friend of mine. Diane was the plant controller. Bill and Diane made my job fun.

The rest of the story is one of detail after detail as we sorted through several years of documents. Ultimately what we found was we were normally not selling the chrome hides against the generally acknowledged formula. In order to sell short-cycle, Challenge mixer processed hides that were perceived to be of poorer quality than long-cycle drum processed hides, we often discounted to a flat price instead of pricing with the formula. In addition, yield weights between chrome and brine hides did not favor the chrome hides as we were led to believe. Finally, actual processing costs for chrome processing were substantially above the "standard" cost customarily accepted.

With Bill and Diane's assistance, as well as their crews and support people, we were able to reconstruct actual numbers that squared almost to the penny with the blue book. For all the fanfare, we were loosing our fanny in the chroming process. The challenge was given to the hide merchants to solve these problems or we would exit the chrome business. When we could not resolve these "real" economic problems and in the face of growing environmental concerns, we exited the chroming business.

In the first couple of years we were in the pork business, we struggled with profitability and, in fact, bled a lot of red ink. I have alluded to this in other chapters. Obviously this caught the attention of managers all the way up the line to the top of Cargill. Leaders wanted to know what it took to turn this business around. Certain people in the organization felt increasing the production rate was the key component to improving our profitability and the division took steps to effect that rate increase.

Following the increases in the production rate, I sat in on certain meetings where performance was being reviewed with Cargill higher managers. The division personnel had set up a series of above the bottom line measurements to "track" how much we were improving versus the prior year. These above the line numbers showed operating improvements in the millions of dollars. And yet, the division P&L (the blue book) for this year continually showed higher losses than the previous year. As I listened to the discussions of this great improvement, I was shocked as I saw it apparently being swallowed hook, line, and sinker by intelligent managers who certainly should have known better. Unfortunately, we sometimes are so desirous for good news that we will accept at face value news that is *too good* to be true.

What I found to be the most amazing in this process, however, was the fact that at no time did I see any of the higher ranking officials challenge what were apparent contradictions between the measures above the bottom line and the bottom line itself. Some of these were as easy to observe as simply comparing two numbers as Bill Fielding had done earlier on the chrome hides. If it's too good to be true, it probably isn't, and in this case it certainly *wasn't!!*

Sometimes, the system itself invites distortion. When I was managing the soybean operation in Cedar Rapids, one of the measurements we were evaluated against was the daily production rate. Our objective was to process 65,000 bushels of soybeans per day. This number was calculated at the end of the month by taking the total number of bushels we had processed, dividing that by the number of hours of scheduled running time and then multiplying by 24. While that seems simple, straightforward and essentially tamperproof, it still contained a very significant wiggle point. How one defined scheduled running time had a dramatic effect on the average daily rate.

At one particular point in time when rail transportation was particularly difficult to secure, we were forced to reduce the production rates by some 50 percent for several days because we had inadequate transportation equipment to move the finished product. At the end of the month, we calculated the amount of lost bushels due to transportation failures and backed into a number for the scheduled operating time. It was easy for those of us in production management to justify as we had little or no control over the transportation function. The result was we were still able to "make" our average production objective of 65,000 bushels per day. As an overall business, we did not process as many bushels as the numbers would seem to indicate on the surface. Also, we did not put money in the bank and therefore impact the business positively, but we were able to "put up the numbers."

When I moved across town to manage the operation of the corn processing facility, we had some different metrics. Instead of calculating the average daily production rate at the end of the month, we calculated it at the beginning of the month. We determined what we should run each day. We then agreed on how much scheduled downtime we needed for maintenance etc. From that we calculated the total number of available production hours and from that the total number of bushels of corn we should be able to process for the entire month. That then became the total monthly production objective.

Manipulating this fixed number was essentially impossible. This made everyone focus attention on achieving the number rather than manipulating it. If the transportation function was having difficulty, we all rallied to their support, whether we felt we had any control or not. Amazingly, the combined efforts of all the different disciplines often resulted in problem solutions. In order to put up the numbers, we had to "put up the performance."

Metrics in a perfect world would do just that, they would insure that only by performance could we count on the measuring device rewarding us. However, even in that perfect world we may encounter less than perfect people. In the soybean operations, in spite of the flawed daily production rate metric earlier noted, we did have a number of other production measurements that in fact demanded performance. One of these was white flake fat. This measured the amount of oil left in the soybean flake after the extraction process. The extraction process was geared to removing the oil from the soybean. The most critical measure of how well that had been accomplished was to measure the amount of fat (oil) left in the white flakes (soybean) after the process.

The Cedar Rapids East (CRE) facility had a huge advantage compared to all the other facilities. We operated two shallow bed extractors as opposed to the deep bed extractors in all the other plants. This allowed us to "squeeze" the beans into very thin flakes to deliver to the extractor. Thin flakes exposed more cells and allowed more oil to be extracted. However, the thinner the flake, the more fragile it was. In deep bed extractors, the very thin flakes would tend to break up and cause poor solvent drainage and thus impede removal of the oil.

While we would run flake thickness as low as 6 thousandths of an inch at CRE, all the other plants would have to run flakes at 10 to 12 thousandths or more. The result was we would absolutely kick all the other plant's butts in white flake fat—all the other plants except for one. One of the other Midwestern plants would always seem to be right down there in the 0.8 to 0.9 percent residual fat range with us. The only difference was they ran the thickest flakes in the company, at times approaching 20 thousands of an inch.

In addition to measuring how one has performed, metrics are also wonderful learning tools to utilize to improve performance. All the other plants looked to CRE as the standard bearer for residual white flake fats. The CRE experience suggested both good drainage and thin flakes were the keys. But wait, the experience at the other facility suggested flake thickness had no bearing. With the very thick flakes they ran, one could conclude drainage and therefore solvent flow was the key.

Certainly CRE had good drainage because of the shallow bed extractors and the other guys had it because of the thick flakes. Those of us at CRE remained dumbfounded with the results, however, as we knew each time we allowed flake thickness to increase, residual fats went up in almost direct correlation. Other plants were confused, and as a division, we were unable to define a standard method for optimum performance.

This went on for an extended period of time until one week when both the production manager and the lab manager at this other facility 'went on vacation the same week. The lab manager from another location was sent to fill in for the week. Amazingly, the residual white flake fats at the "fat flake plant" that week were not 0.8 to 0.9, but rather pushing 2.0. The lid was soon blown off of what turned out to be a huge misrepresentation scam. This facility put up the numbers, not by performing and not even by manipulating the numbers. They did it by changing the numbers to what they wanted them to say.

Pressure to "put up the numbers" and the associated rewards

for so doing create temptations too great for many to resist. While it is usually weak persons (or sometime persons simply caught in weak moments) who succumb to this temptation, it has been my experience the sword cuts both ways. Companies often do a poor and inadequate job of matching above the bottom line measurements with bottom line impact. This is an example of the leadership I spoke of earlier.

A very close associate of mine once suffered through a year at the processing plant where he worked with a rather dismal plant performance as measured by the numbers. Yet it was a year with good margins and his plant had been able to push through production when it counted to the bottom line. Of particular interest was that it had been a year with very poor raw material quality. Other plants in the geography refused to accept and run certain grades of this low quality raw material. With the low quality, however, came an even lower purchase price that resulted in very large processing margins.

His plant accepted the material, and although difficult to run, they continued to push it through the system. This resulted in two things. First, it resulted in good profits being generated for the company. Second, it resulted in the plant having to struggle more to make the measurement objectives since the poor quality material made efficient performance difficult, if not impossible. Inability to get the above the line measurements changed to match the bottom line performance resulted in overall sub-standard ratings for the crew. Exemplary bottom line performance could not overcome the inability to "put up the numbers" and was subsequently not met with appropriate reward!

I recently saw a marquee sign that read "An ounce of image is worth more than a pound of performance." Lynn Swan was a performer who apparently lacked the "necessary" image! So have been a number of other persons in many different walks of life. Perhaps finding better ways to match "above the line" measurements with the actual "bottom line" results could help create marquee messages that would read, "An ounce of performance is worth more than a pound of image!" That would be leadership progress!

# CHAPTER 20
# We Have Met the Enemy

There used to be a cartoon called Pogo in which one of the main characters, I believe Pogo himself, was frequently noted saying, "*We have met the enemy and he is Us!*" Obviously, we are not our own enemy all the time, but there is a large dose of truth in Pogo's proclamation.

Throughout my entire career, I have found numerous examples where the enemy was in fact us. This book is full of examples where we brought adverse conditions on ourselves because of ourselves. The upside down condenser installation of Chapter 9 is one shining example. Other good examples abound. Many of these individual episodes of "fighting" against ourselves are just that. They are individual episodes borne of ignorance, lack of focus, mental blindness and so forth. There is no pervasive underlying element to all of them that creates the "condition of adversary".

That is not the case, however, for the greatest internal enemy of them all, *Politics.* Politics in the business environment is the one thing that can turn person against person within a company, making absolutely true the statement "the enemy is us." More importantly, however, *politics create the effort of proper positioning in the space formerly occupied by exceptional performance.*

Even in the absence of enemies in the sense of person against person, the results of political positioning usually cause us to perform in a way that is not in the best overall interest of the organization. It may be due to personal agendas and personal gain or it may be through simple inaction because there does not seem to be enough wind to point the political weather vane in a specific direction. Finally, it may be due to fear; fear of not succeeding, fear of not complying, or simply fear of holding the high ground when the support troops do not seem to be arriving for backup.

Certainly some of the elements of politics are apparent, but not necessarily pervasive. In the mid 70s, all of the business and operations managers of the Cargill Processing Division were "invited" to Minneapolis for training in EEO, equal employment opportunity, issues. This was at the time the equal employment laws and associated quota systems and prima fascia discrimination suits were at the fore of American business concerns. I did not ever share the fear many top executives did of governmental intervention, but then I had only my operation to worry about. I knew while it may not have met the strict quotas, it was not because of a failure on our part to be supportive of any of the protected classes. Top officials on the other hand had to be worried about all of the Cargill operations and as I later learned, not all managers shared my philosophy.

At any rate, we were summoned to Minneapolis to be part of a seminar put on by a firm that had set itself up as an authority on teaching managers how not to discriminate. I always marvel at how many of these "upstart" consultants have been made highly successful or at least highly wealthy as organizations rush to be sure their people have been "trained" by experts. That notwithstanding, I must admit some parts of this training, like the "random" poker chip draw, were genuinely of value to some of us.

As the seminar proceeded, one of the issues the consultants raised related to dress codes. They noted many companies had strict dress codes that would not allow an Indian or Muslim or similar ethnic employee to wear a decorative costume of their native land or culture. Of course they expected unusual or flamboyant dress would also not be openly welcomed in the Cargill operations of that day. They proceeded to lull us into a sense of superiority and maybe even a little condescendence.

As we sat around a large open circle, the consultant continued, stating that while it may be understandable to look unfavorably on native costumes because of their disruptive effect, it was nice to be working with an organization that was not so trivial as to insist on any other types of dress codes." He ended his comments with a statement/question; "Cargill certainly does not have any written or unwritten dress codes for people like you attending meetings like this, do they!?"

As we all nodded in agreement, the consultant exploded, "Like H___ you don't! Look around this room at everybody's feet." It was an all male audience. "How many pairs of boots do you see?? I only see two!!" Only one other manager, a kind of a cowboy in his own right, and I had on boots. Everyone else had on wingtips or loafer dress shoes of some type.

"Now look around the room at everyone's neck and see how many people you see without a neck tie on!" he continued. "I only count one!!" This time I was the only one as I had on a turtle neck sweater as opposed to everyone else's dress shirt and tie. "Now don't tell me this is all coincidence. You guys are all marching in step with an absolute expectation on the part of the hierarchy as to how you will be dressed when you come to these meetings. I don't know how to explain the guy without either dress shoes or a tie!" Interestingly, for over 30 years, few other people in the organization were able to explain me either.

As noted at the onset of this story, there is nothing necessarily pervasive about it. I tell it for it's value in understanding the long standing expectations of robotic like behavior on many issues of a rather trivial nature. Certainly dress codes have been relaxed through the years and, contrary to being the most causally dressed person, today I am probably one of the more "traditional" dressers. I dress with what I am comfortable in and I know I can properly perform my duties in. Whether I look like everyone else is not of my concern. In fact, I will only look like everyone else if everyone else happens to look like me, as it will seldom be the other way around.

Unfortunately, while things like sameness in dressing are fairly innocuous, they are "attitude multipliers" and tend to set the stage for a perception of sameness and follow-the-leader mentality for things much more critical in nature. Things that need independent action based on the facts and what is in the best real interest of the organization and not on some politically correct position.

During the recovery from the Ottumwa fire noted in Chapter 31: "Three Million Dollar Handshake," one of the "non-engineering supervisors" commissioned the repair of one of the production rooms damaged by fire. This supervisor called the local lumberyard and had extruded polystyrene and FRP (fiberglass reinforced plastic) board delivered and used to rebuild the wall coverings in the room. In the general construction of the 80s, we had been using expanded polystyrene (the foam coffee cup type material) with a FRP cover as the internal wall covering on these walls.

As time progressed, it was discovered that the expanded polystyrene had some poor moisture saturation and fire retarding characteristics. We stopped using the expanded polystyrene and began using extruded polystyrene. This is frequently referred to as Dow board, although several other companies make similar products. This was the standard through much of the organization and the work authorized by this supervisor was not inconsistent with general company design criteria.

In the pork operations, as well as some other operations, however, we had actually been going one-step further and using extruded polystyrene "sandwich panels." These panels utilized metal covers in place of the FRP board. This had even better fire retarding capabilities. Although these metal clad sandwich panels had been recommended by our insurance department, they had not been mandated by the corporate safety people. Had one of us with an engineering background made the call on the room in question, we would have specified the sandwich panel with the metal cover and been on the way. Nevertheless, the call made was not improper with general company construction standards at the time and the room was repaired.

As the room was essentially completed, but not trimmed out, one of the Cargill safety inspectors made a plant visit. He noted the extruded polystyrene that had been installed was not the blue Dow board, but rather a green material made by a competitor. He instantly demanded we remove all of the green board and replace it with blue board. When we offered resistance, he passed the information on to our business unit leaders who, assuming the safety guy had a legitimate consideration, told us to comply with the safety inspector. We told them we needed to do further investigation, as we did not think this change would result in any safety improvement. Further, we did not think it was inconsistent with generally accepted company construction practices and standards.

When we checked specifications, we found blue and green and yellow and pink to all be of the same quality. We also found other Cargill installations had used, and were continuing to use; whatever color the particular supplier would send out for a given installation. When confronted with this, the safety guy told us the blue board from Dow had a UL (Underwriters Laboratory) inspection listing, which meant it had passed UL safety testing for the application in question and was therefore the superior choice.

When we followed up with the UL people we were told the UL listing on Dow board was for a different application and no UL testing had been done on the specific wall application for which we were using it. He informed us UL could not consider Dow to be any different than any of the others. He could offer no safety advantage using the blue Dow board over any of the others. However, even when confronted with these facts, the Cargill safety guy refused to change his opinion or position.

With the safety guy unwilling to bend, the business unit leaders reaffirmed their position that we needed to comply. We again told them that to change as the safety guy directed would do absolutely nothing of value for Cargill in reducing risk. It would only result in the spending of another $20,000. If they did not wish to continue to challenge the safety guy, and further, if they really wanted to *improve* the safety condition, we encouraged them to authorize an additional $10,000 above the $20,000 needed to simply comply with the safety guy's desires. For $30,000 we could replace the green board and FRP with sandwich panels with metal covering which would in fact make a *real* safety difference.

To our chagrin, the business unit leaders told us to just replace the green with the blue. It was politically correct to be a "team player" and do just as the safety guy requested whether he was right or wrong and whether that did anything of real value for the company or not. While an upgrade to the sandwich panel would result in better fire protection capability, there was apparently nothing to gain politically from this move. As a result, we chose to throw away $20,000 for political purposes, but chose not to add another $10,000 to get real benefits. Unfortunately, once expectations of "falling in line" are in place, it becomes politically difficult to march outside of formation.

Fortunately, there are times when we see the damage the enemy (ourselves) is about to inflict and are able to thwart the attack before the hill is lost. Such was the case in the early part of 2000 with one of our water treatment suppliers, Walling. You will meet salesman Paul Reinartz and the Walling Company in more detail in Chapter 24: "Used Cars." For several years, Paul Reinartz and the Walling Company had done exemplary work in servicing our plant in Beardstown, Illinois.

The Walling Company was a relatively small company from South Dakota that had a rather limited base of customers and geographic reach. They had used this to their advantage in giving very personal service and meeting customer needs in the most proactive way. Over the course of the years they had not only made dramatic improvements in the Beardstown water quality, they had branched out to some of the other Cargill facilities and had done exceptional work there as well.

In the late 90s, the Cargill corporate central purchasing group had determined the company had too many suppliers in all aspects of the business and the organization would be better served to limit the total number. The company would select some preferred suppliers who could serve Cargill worldwide or at least country wide and with whom substantial overall discounts could be negotiated. The concept of this was sound, but the application left something to be desired. Ostensibly, this would cut out people like Walling who had the ability to serve limited parts of Cargill very well, but had neither the resources nor the desire to serve Cargill worldwide.

As the new policy unfolded and as selected suppliers became "knighted" as preferred suppliers, it did appear there was room for the existing small and relationship based suppliers like Walling and we continued to use them. Then, one of the major water treatment companies that had been given preferred supplier status mounted an unsuccessful campaign to replace Walling in Beardstown. The preferred supplier could match neither the pricing nor the service capabilities of Walling.

Unable to win on the battlefield, the preferred supplier took his battle to the political arena. He complained to the Cargill central purchasing hierarchy that he was the preferred supplier and therefore he should in essence be handed the Beardstown account on a silver platter. The hierarchy apparently agreed and instructions were sent to the people in Beardstown to switch.

Most of us were appalled we could even consider doing that to a customer service representative like Paul Reinartz and a company like Walling, who had so totally committed themselves to our service for years. That they continued to have the best pricing and service made this all the more unconscionable. The operating people put up all the resistance they could, arguing from positions of integrity, but they were continually rebuffed from positions born of political correctness. Again the concept of "we must be perceived as team players and that means not challenging the hierarchy be they right or wrong" became the recurring theme.

Don Nagle, one of the Excel corporate engineers with whom I worked at the time, refused to accept this nonsensical approach and would argue the point with anyone who would listen and even to those who would not. The "noise" Don made eventually fell on the ear of Matt Meyer, our boss, whose engineering mind was able to quickly see past the political finagling and to the disaster that was about to occur.

With Matt's action as well as other support that continued to surface for Walling's past efforts and proactive plans for the future, the mandate to remove Walling was rescinded. It was a refreshing victory for pragmatism and performance over politics. Victories such as this are critical in the life of a company as they give renewed hope to those who continue to work toward a performance based atmosphere rather than a politically based one.

As long as the spirit can be held high among the guerrilla warriors (as we sometimes have to be), the battle can continue to be fought. What is interesting is that as long as politics compete with performance, it is in the Company's best interest for this guerrilla warfare to continue and be successful. As Pogo would likely say, *"We have met the enemy and he is Us. We have defeated Us and thus claimed a victory for Ourselves!"*

# CHAPTER 21
# The Scissors

One of the people with whom I crossed paths on both a macro and a micro scale in my career at Cargill was Ernie Micek. Ernie was my first supervisor at Cargill and I find it hard to refer to him as Mr. Micek as my relationship with him has always been on the basis of Ernie. Ernie was the top officer within Cargill for most of the mid and late 90s. More than just having held the top positions late in his career, I believe credit for Cargill's dramatic growth through the decades of the 80s and 90s can largely be laid right at the doorstep of Ernie Micek. Ernie made a career of making the right decisions for Cargill's benefit without regard for how that may affect him personally.

Ernie was able throughout his career to break a number of barriers. He is a man of only modest height. Regardless of any "nondiscriminatory" claims people make, taller men and attractive women are always at an advantage in both the business and social world (indeed, studies have proven the same). Ernie was a graduate of Wisconsin University in chemical engineering. Although engineers are often the very best managers because of their problem solving ability, there is often a stigma attached to them that says they are high IQs with low human feel. As a result, they often find it difficult to break out of the technical positions and into the top management positions. Ernie had to overcome a number of obstacles to ascend to the top position in Cargill.

My first encounter with Ernie was on my recruiting visit to Cedar Rapids, Iowa before I had accepted Cargill's job offer. Ernie had just returned from Tarragona, Spain where he had been the plant superintendent at the soybean processing complex there. He had accepted a position in the processing group corporate operations office. I had only modest interaction with Ernie on this trip, but did find him to be a rather dynamic guy.

I suppose by virtue of being the youngest and newest member in corporate operations, Ernie inherited all of the new engineering trainees in the spring of 1969. I was the first of five to start that spring and, like the others, was under Ernie's wing for my five weeks training period in Minneapolis. Apparently, I impressed Ernie enough during that time that six years later I was invited to transfer to the Corn Processing Group that Ernie then headed.

It did not take long to understand what Ernie was all about. I was right in my first meeting in finding him to be dynamic. He also fully understood knowledge at the local level virtually always exceeded that of mid and upper levels when it came to the tactical components of an operation. Who else knows more about the operations, customers, and suppliers than the people who are in the middle of the action every hour of every day! Another of Ernie's operating theses was "he who hesitates is lost." Opportunities come and go and you better be ready, willing, and able to grasp them quickly when they come or you will watch them as they go.

Ernie's philosophy, whether stated or unstated, was to be successful and impact the business positively, you better have people of superior intelligence at the local level who understand the business, can operate it more efficiently than the competition, can recognize opportunity, can expeditiously formulate action to seize the opportunity, and then do whatever it takes to move on that action.

I would submit many business leaders and scholars, at that time and today, would suggest Ernie was not then nor would now be alone in espousing that philosophy. However, I would also submit if one looks closely at many large company actions, you will find that they fail on two of the critical components. [NOTE: In order to fully understand what someone truly believes or where someone is actually coming from you must carefully *listen to what they **DO***] The first component of that failure is people of superior intelligence are often not *"wasted in local positions,"* and if they do get assigned there, no mechanism rewards them for staying there. They are subsequently moved out to mid or high level corporate staff positions. Second, companies are often willing to "do what it takes to move to action" to seize an opportunity *only* after it has passed all of the upper level political scrutiny and pin-pricking and meets the pet interests of the group at the top.

So, how was Ernie able to turn his philosophies into concrete achievements and move Cargill forward? First, Ernie worked hard to get some of the best talent within Cargill into the corn business. He then kept them at the plant levels and empowered them. Even after we had grown dramatically and had a number of plants, the corporate staff consisted principally of one person, ERNIE. Where other "corporate" positions existed, the people filling them still headquartered in one of the plants so they could never get very far away from the real operations. Money was made in turning corn into starches, sweeteners, germ, and feed by-products. While a number of other disciplines and functions supported that, take away the process of converting corn to those products and all of those support functions would dry up and blow away.

Ernie also knew the value of inclusion and making people feel a part of both the process and the team. Ernie understood the need for foundations (Chapter 17) and worked to build them. Dinners, parties, and even weekend getaways with our spouses were frequent and extended the inclusion message to our families as well. Maybe Ernie just wanted to show off his wife Sally, who is a most gracious and delightful person herself. My wife was always happy to see Sally at any get-together as she (Sally) had the gift of making everyone feel comfortable and important. We often joked (behind Ernie's back of course) that Ernie had "married up."

Perhaps the most defining part of Ernie's make-up was his passion for moving to action. As I recall, Tom Peters, in one of his presentations in the mid 80s regarding the "search for excellence," noted that in many instances where managers are able to cut quickly to the chase and make good things happen they do it by "cheating!" Not cheating in the sense of doing something that is illegal or immoral or against society norms, but rather "cheating" in the sense they know how to get around the system by creating ways to circumvent the red tape and political processes that pervade the higher management levels of an organization. Ernie had a sharp scissors and was a master at using it on the "red tape" processes. In addition, if there were no known ways to cut through the red tape and if creativity also failed, then before losing an opportunity, Ernie used a third element. *Ignore the red tape and the political process altogether and move forward as though they didn't exist!!!*

Not long after I had transferred to the corn processing business in the mid 70s as general superintendent of the Cedar Rapids, Iowa Corn Plant, Ernie became determined to get in on the ground floor of ethanol production for fuel use. An old processing plant in the St. Louis area had closed down and a number of vessels and pieces of processing equipment indigenous to the corn processing industry were for sale at bargain prices. Ernie determined we could purchase most of this equipment at 5 or 10 cents on the dollar and use much of it to create a small pilot ethanol plant at our Cedar Rapids facility. We could get our feet wet in the process with very little cost and risk and then be able to move to full scale easily.

Ernie quickly went through all of the proper corporate procedures, explaining to the upper management people what was planned. The result was they rejected the idea. Undaunted, Ernie tried again and failed. By now Ernie was running out of time on the purchase of the equipment so he proceeded to make the purchase without corporate blessing, approval, and probably knowledge. At that time he asked me with tongue in cheek, "How much room do you have in your backyard. If I can't get the corporate guys to approve this, you and I may need to store this stuff in our backyards!"

Ernie tried a couple of more times to gain approval for this project and continued to be turned back. On the surface it appeared Ernie and I would have tens of thousands of dollars worth of used equipment and vessels resting in our backyards, Cargill would have forked out good money without their approval (and perhaps knowledge), and the whole thing would have exploded in Ernie's face.

Well, the surface would be partially right! I doubt if many of the top guys who said NO to the project even today realize their money got spent anyway. We stuffed the purchase costs into other work we were doing. Ernie and I did not store the equipment and vessels in our backyards, but we did store them in the boneyard at the Cedar Rapids plant. And the original plans for use of the equipment and vessels did not materialize.

So the final result of this was failure? Not so fast! There is a saying "Good things come to those who wait if they work like the dickens while they wait." There is also a saying "the harder you work, the luckier you get." The point being, the key to luck is patience and work. You have to make your own luck and create your own positive results.

A short time later the price of sugar, the world's benchmark sweetener, rose. Inasmuch as the principal end product of corn processing is sweetener, the profits in the corn processing industry became very good. Production capacity was at a premium and everything that could be done to squeeze an extra bushel of corn through the process was done. We looked for any action, process, or system that could get us a few extra bushels quick.

Recognizing our refinery capacity was limited not by the amount of dry starch solids in the slurry feed stream, but by the amount of total liquid, we as a group had been tweaking the milling process to get as high a starch concentration as possible in the slurry feed to the refinery. In one of those efforts, one of our department superintendents remembered the "apparently" useless St. Louis equipment in the boneyard.

Recalling a string filter in this equipment, Loren determined that if we took a side stream from the finished slurry from the mill, filtered that through the string filter and then added the "dry" solids from this filter back to the principal slurry stream, we could increase the solids content in the finished slurry stream by 7 to 10 percent. The net effect of this would be to increase the capacity through the refinery by 7 to 10 percent at virtually no new cost other than some relatively minor installation and piping costs. We proceeded to install this system and pumped literally hundreds of thousands of additional dollars into the Cargill coffers over the next few years as a result of it. All made possible by Ernie "ignoring" the red tape and proceeding to seize an opportunity, even though the final opportunity was not what was originally planned.

Over the years we made use of other parts of the St. Louis inventory, but the string filter alone paid for the entire purchase many times over. I can recall numerous other instances where the red tape lay in ribbons after the passage of Ernie. Probably the most far-reaching was when he moved quickly with Coca-Cola to seize the opportunity to cash in on their movement from sugar to HFCS (high fructose corn syrup) in their flagship brand - Coke. Without Ernie's actions, Cargill quite likely would have been left in the dust in this chase as the ante was very high in terms of capital dollars. While I was not as close to this (and don't think my backyard was ever at risk for a storage location on this venture), it is my understanding corporate approvals again lagged Ernie's own commitments as he raced to secure a spot for Cargill in serving Coca-Cola's burgeoning needs.

For most of the 70s, 80s, and early 90s, the corn processing businesses of Cargill were principal contributors to Cargill's net earnings on an annual basis. The foundations of these businesses were laid by Ernie. The profits from the corn businesses fueled the dramatic growth of several industries within Cargill as well as a number of acquisitions. Without the corn business, Cargill would be a fraction of the organization it is today.

To gain a full understanding of Ernie's impact, one need only look at the growth of the corn business within Cargill. Cargill entered the business in 1967 with the purchase of the plant in Cedar Rapids that had a capacity of 20,000 bushels per day. In 1970, when Ernie became responsible for the corn operations, daily capacity was a little over 30,000 bushels per day. By the early 2000s, daily capacity was measured in seven figures with multiple plants in the USA, Brazil, England and the European mainland. In addition, the simple operations of making starches and syrups had been expanded to include a myriad of complex Cargill operations, making all sorts of products out of the corn constituent parts and additional ventures where corn derived side streams were provided to joint or independent ventures as the raw materials for the making of even more complex products. And Oh yes, ethanol operations too!

Do I have only good things to say about Ernie? Certainly not. I often took issue with Ernie on specific components although I always supported his master plan. I sometimes prevailed in the issues of conflict, I sometimes succumbed, and I sometimes wondered why I put up with working for him. Yet throughout all of that I recognized the genius of him. Without question, Ernie had a significant impact on me as I watched him move in the best interest of the company—and at times at significant risk to himself—whether others recognized the move as that or not. That was and remains my first criterion in any decision I make, "Is it in the best interest of the organization regardless of what others think or want?" In addition, Ernie and I could take issue with each other and not let that affect personal feelings, relationships, or how we dealt with each other in the aftermath.

As earlier noted, eventually, Ernie ascended to the top position in Cargill. I believe he did a lot of good things there. However, in my humble opinion, one of Ernie's failures as the top man in the Company was his inability to create or maybe re-create an organization that fostered many of the very things that resulted in his success. Certainly none of Ernie's predecessors in the top positions had effected much change in that "re-creation" process either so he was in good company. Tom Peter's discussion on fast movers and cut to the chase people did not stop with his pointing out they do it by circumventing the corporate systems that stifle everyone else. He continued to point out that as these people ascend to the top positions, which they frequently do because of their ability to make things happen, they remember all the tricks they used to outmaneuver the system on their way to the top. Unfortunately, they often then move immediately to create new checkpoints and road-blocks to prevent the rest of us from using those same avenues.

I do not know if Ernie fell victim to that phenomenon or not, and I have never quite figured out why executives do it if in fact they do. I do not know if it is arrogance and they believe no one else is as smart and savvy as they are or were. Perhaps they fear allowing independent action will get the organization into trouble. It could be simply a function of organization size and CEOs can do little to stop the locomotive motion. Maybe it is as simple as the demands of time. I suppose it is possible CEOs don't even know or realize the phenomenon is happening. Nevertheless, it is a shame that it is not possible for a CEO to look at what he/she did "on the way up" and then say, "Wow, if I was able to do that when the system resisted me, how much more we could do if we created a system that would support the kind of efforts and actions I took."

For sure, I for one thought Ernie would be able to create that more "move to rapid action" friendly organization. Certainly, if that system could be created, scissors wielding men and women would be able to refocus their efforts from cutting red tape to cutting the competition to ribbons!

# CHAPTER 22
# Uncle Sam & Friends

Many of our citizens look *to* the government for help and assistance. Many others look *at* the government as the single greatest hindrance to progress and forward movement. Regardless of whether you are one who looks *to* the government or *at* the government, one fact is undeniable; Uncle Sam is going to be a part of our corporate and private lives whether he is an invited or an uninvited guest.

We are all sure there is no way the founding fathers expected the voluminous amount of legal code our government has and continues to put out. Government was put in place to manage those functions that could not be effectively managed in the private sector. In Utopia those things would generally be limited to law and order systems, domestic and international. We do not live in Utopia, however, so we need to include a few other things like education systems and transportation systems. Then, because we are a people descended from persons of charity and compassion, we wish to add a few more things like social and economic welfare.

Even the above list would be manageable if it stopped there, but it does not; the government has legislated or adjudicated laws and regulations that cover everything from a to z and then some. From where does the government draw such a right? Unfortunately, we in the private sector have invited, if not solicited, virtually every regulation we have. Even in the incredibly out-of-control position government is in today, Uncle Sam still largely gives us in the private sector the first opportunity to regulate ourselves. That failing, he will gladly step in and do it for us.

The problem lies not in the fact that Uncle Sam must step in and do the regulating, but more in the sad fact that *we* are in possession of the best information on how to most effectively regulate ourselves. The government must regulate from a position of moderate or total ignorance. We then wind up with regulations that often serve no one except perhaps the lawmakers.

Once regulations are written and put in force, many private sector entities tend to take the position of minimum compliance. Minimum compliance means one simply follows the requirements of the letter of the law. As you will read again in Chapter 23: "Do You Solemnly Swear" I have long been a believer in compliance with the spirit of the law and not simply the letter.

The spirit of the law is what good people acting in good conscience adopted to right a wrong or protect a value. The letter of the law is quite often how lawyers and politicians, often more lawyers, penned the letters and words to serve their own needs or those of favored classes. I have often held out that if we all work to comply with the spirit of the law, the letter of the law will take care of itself. While this is generally true, it is not always safe.

In his ignorance, Uncle Sam often writes in letters that have nothing to do with the spirit. These "extraneous components" are there either from ignorance or political expedition. Failure to recognize them and therefore comply, may land the unsuspecting in harms way when Uncle Sam comes "a calling." While focus needs to be on the spirit, I must yield at least a bit to those who want assurance all the letters have been accounted for.

The other interesting thing that happens when the letter of the law gets out of control is even the governmental entities find themselves shackled in their ability to make the *right* thing happen. Over the past several decades, the most frustrating thing for me when working with government agencies is that the avalanche of articles, paragraphs, subparagraphs, sentences, and words in the regulations have caused even the government workers to loose site of what a law or regulation is trying to accomplish for the public good. These government "overseers" become no more than regulators against a set of words demanding actions that may or may not be in the public good. The *right* thing to do gets subordinated to the *regulated* requirement.

The first car I purchased new, and in fact the only car I ever purchased new, was a 1965 Chevy Impala Sport Coupe. This car carried me through college and through the eventual courtship with my wife. It also carried me on earlier dates with other girls, so it is fortunate it cannot talk or I may have had to shoot it long ago. It took me to my first full time job and brought our first child home from the hospital. Even when relegated to second fiddle in the mid 70s, it was still somewhat a work of art. It was known affectionately in my workplace as "the Roth-mobile." In 1977 I discontinued driving the Roth-mobile, stopped licensing it, and placed it in protective custody in the old turkey pole barn (Chapter 3) on the farm. I did start it every year for a few years and drove it around the farm to maintain its mechanical integrity, but that ended in the early 80s.

In 1994 when I sold the farm in Iowa, I loaded the old Chevy up on the flatbed trailer and moved it to Kansas. I pulled it over to Joe Goodplier's shop (Chapter 14) and had Joe get it back in running order for me. Joe worked over the radiator, gas tank and brake lines, tuned it up, gave it a little Joe TLC and drove it over to the farm for me. There was no big push to use it and I knew we might have to do some regulatory hoop jumping to get it re-licensed in Kansas, so it just sat for a few more years.

In 1999, when our middle son Ryan got his drivers license, he thought it would be neat to drive the old 65. Again, noting cars cannot talk, I thought this would be a good time and circumstance to put the old Roth-mobile back on the street and contributing to society. I instructed my wife to begin the process of getting it licensed in Kansas. I had my wife do this because she is around home much more than I am and more importantly because she is both much better looking and much more persuasive than am I. I'm sure she only accepted the assignment because she did not know what she was getting into.

Making connection with the appointed representative of the governing body for car registration was the first challenge. When that challenge was finally met, Chris was confronted with the main problem. The main issue of registration was to insure the car had not been stolen. Only if the VIN (vehicle identification number) on the tag by the door and the VIN on the engine block matched the VIN on the title could we prove it had been mine and was now still mine. Since this guy could not find the VIN on the engine block he could not register it. All the discussion of how long it had been in my possession and its history meant nothing. Chris was instructed she had to take it to the next city, Wichita, for a more advanced inspector.

At the encounter with the Wichita inspector, a new problem surfaced. The rivets holding the VIN tag at the door were not of the same type. One had a round something and the other had a square something; a clear indication to the inspector the VIN tag had been tampered with. Our pleas that the car had been in my possession for 34 years and the tag had never been removed or tampered with fell on deaf ears. Never mind, how do we explain the rivets?

After several weeks of exasperation, Chris finally rounded up an old-timer at a GM place somewhere who indicated it was in the 65 model year the Chevrolet Division moved from the rivets with the round something to the rivets with the square something. He theorized that in the transition process the rivet bin probably had both types of rivets for a short period of time in moving from one to the other. My car happened to be one of the lucky ones to receive one of each.

Chris continued to jump through hoop after hoop and only achieved success through a combination of wearing down the bureaucrats and by finally producing a maintenance logbook GM provided to new purchasers. Incredibly, this was still buried in the glove compartment. This book had the signature of Dick Johnson, the owner of Johnson Chevrolet in Winfield, Iowa, from whom I had bought the car. It was assigned to Jim Roth! Even though the inspector assured Chris this was only anecdotal evidence the car was not stolen, he would allow her to register it as our possession.

I recognize regulations exist and procedures are developed to help provide assurance the public good is protected. It is hard for me to believe there could not have been far easier ways to insure I was indeed the owner of the Roth-mobile. Even that fact and the process of ascertaining that fact got lost in the battle over rivets. I would venture most every reader of this book could recount similar stories.

The Roth-mobile pales in comparison to some of the amazing regulatory battles I have been a part of in the industrial setting. Probably the "mother-of-them-all" was our attempt to remedy the wrongs unintentionally imposed on the environment around our Beardstown facility. The wastewater treatment system at the Beardstown facility had been designed for a one-shift operation. We had determined we could extend it to a two-shift operation of about 12,500 animals per day without adverse consequences.

However, those production rates were exceeded beginning in 1989. The higher rates continued for a series of years. These actions resulted in overloading of the waste treatment system. The overloaded waste treatment system pushed out excessive hydraulic and organic loadings and resulted in overloading the agricultural land base with water and nutrients. This in turn raised the nitrates in the ground water above the Illinois Environmental Protection Agency (IEPA) Class 1 standard of 10. We were out of compliance with the letter of the law.

Although the spirit of the law may have been trampled early on in this process, once there was evidence of elevated levels of nitrates in the groundwater, the effort was initiated to take remedial steps by up-grading the waste treatment system. Unfortunately, due to internal company politics and other difficulties, this did not get beyond the talking and investigatory stage.

In 1994 I had just finished working on the Taiwan project and was assigned to clean up this mess in Beardstown. Mike Richtig, one of the most valuable right-hand persons anyone could ever ask for, and I began aggressive work to identify the best system to upgrade the wastewater treatment operation. We were met with an unbelievable barrage of negativity from the IEPA with almost every effort. The first system proposed was rejected by the IEPA almost without discussion. After going back to the drawing board and spending several months and thousands of dollars in investigation and design development, we proposed a second system, manufactured by Biolac.

This was the same system we had put in effect successfully in Taiwan and was operating in meat plants throughout the world. The Biolac system was similarly rejected outright by the IEPA. We asked for and were granted a meeting to try to understand why. Only low-level bureaucrats showed up for the meeting. The best they could do to explain why they would not accept our design was the clarifier was not round and there were no other similar systems in operation in Illinois they could reference or look at.

No one could answer our question on why only round clarifiers worked in Illinois! To the invitation to go visit a similar system in another state, the bureaucratic position was they could not go out of state for such a visit. One can barely fathom the ludicrousness of such a position: "We will not approve anything we cannot see and we will not go out of state to see anything." I am very thankful Illinois was able to build roads, bridges, railroads, and airports before these bureaucrats arrived on the scene or I am afraid Illinois would be a little backward and likely not enjoying much prosperity today.

We refused to accept this position and proceeded to challenge the IEPA. We did win the challenge and in February of 1995, the IEPA did approve the design of the Biolac system we had proposed. What we did not realize was the battle had not even yet begun. In April of that year, the IEPA refused to renew our operating permit, charged Excel with non-compliance with permit requirements, and informed us of potential legal action. Our legal people scrambled to enter into an interim consent decree to allow us to continue operating while we proceeded with corrective action.

The hinge pin around which our corrective action swung was the Biolac system. With that in place, we would not be overloading the treatment system and that in turn would eliminate the overloading of the agricultural land with water and nutrients, which in turn would eliminate the opportunity for nitrates to migrate to the ground water. Accordingly, one of the keys to the consent decree was an aggressive timetable to install the Biolac system.

Designing the Biolac and the system around it was up to the Biolac engineers, our local engineers, and us. Purchasing the necessary equipment, materials and systems was up to us. Arranging for and contracting for the construction was up to our chosen contractors and us. Submitting applications for construction and NPDES, National Pollution Discharge Elimination System, permits was up to us. Reviewing and signing off on those permits was up to the IEPA.

By September, we had done all of those things noted above and were ready to begin construction in strict accordance with the consent decree as agreed upon with the IEPA. Amazingly, the IEPA was not able in that time frame to sign off on the two permits. Without the NPDES permit, the IEPA would not OK the construction permit, and without the construction permit they would not allow us to initiate construction. Without initiating construction in September, we would be in violation of our consent decree. Who ever said governmental action needed to make sense?

Many organizations may have chosen to sit back and say, "Hey, if you don't let us move, then lack of progress and compliance with the consent decree is not of our doing!" By now, the Beardstown situation had the attention of the very highest levels of Cargill and our marching orders were we would not be in violation of our consent decree. This was not inconsistent with the path Mike Richtig, Bill Leischner, and I would have chosen anyway so we moved ahead.

In discussion after discussion, the IEPA continually warned us not to start without the construction permit (which was in their hands). To each question of ours as to when they would sign the construction permit they responded, "Not until the NPDES permit is approved!" And they had told us they had no idea when that may be, but it was not on the immediate horizon.

I finally drafted a letter to the IEPA entreating them to approve our construction permit with Cargill accepting full responsibility for any problems created by our construction in the absence of the NPDES permit. Reluctantly, they agreed. We started construction in September of 1995, completed construction by March of 1996 and had the system on line by May of 1996.

Amazingly, the IEPA finally OK'd the NPDES permit in January of 1998, fully 30 months after the time necessary to comply with the consent decree. By the time the NPDES permit was granted, we had been operating the system for almost two years, we had substantially reduced the nitrate concentration in the groundwater and we were well on our way to achieving full compliance.

The IEPA regulators were so caught up in regulating they totally failed to acknowledge by their action that getting the nitrates reduced in the groundwater was what we were all working toward. We at Excel were working toward that and they, the regulators, were working toward regulating. They had totally missed their real charge! The sad thing is in the entire process we worked with some highly qualified and highly capable people in the IEPA. Unfortunately, they often simply seemed to be stuck in the mire of regulation rather than in the focus on protection. IEPA (Illinois Environmental *Protection* Agency) was more IERA (Illinois Environment *Regulation* Agency).

Following these actions on our part, we did become an organization that was respected by the IEPA personnel. They recognized as much or more than any other group with whom they worked, we did what we said we would do. As time went on, the Beardstown facility became an example to other organizations for the IEPA. I know I have been and remain very critical of how the IEPA and most other governmental agencies go about their work. I believe this is largely system driven rather than people driven. Many of the IEPA people, and government regulators throughout the land, are very fine people.

It is just difficult to move to correct action when Uncle Sam demands *regulation* and not *performance*.

# CHAPTER 23
# Do You Solemnly Swear

I think virtually all of us have some prejudices and stereotypes of certain professions or occupations. I am certainly no exception and must confess the legal profession is one of the groups that fall in that category for me. There is no question that I have told my fair share of "lawyer" jokes and laughed at countless others over the years. I must also confess a good number of those jokes certainly did not see the first light of day in a Sunday school classroom.

One of my favorite satirical remarks about the legal profession is that it is "unfortunately a profession where only 95 percent of all the lawyers give the other 5 percent a bad name!" I find this reversal of the normal number distribution in this bit of wit to be rather funny. I also believe that to be funny and effective, irony and satire must have some elements of truth to them. Perhaps the ratio is not 95 to 5, but I do believe the lawyers themselves have created the negative images that plague their numbers.

While I am not a big fan of lawyers, I have found some of that 5 percent or whatever percentage the good ones number. I will talk about them in some detail a little later. However, in much of my experience, I have found most lawyers to be irritating in several ways. First is their overwhelming desire to control and manipulate rather than an unbiased search for the truth. Second is a condescendence to anyone outside of the legal profession. Third is their absolute "letter of the law" perspective and their blatant willingness to dismiss the spirit of the law as irrelevant.

Unfortunately, in the line of duty, I have found my way into a number of depositions and hearings over the past few decades. Almost without exception in those circumstances, the opposition lawyers came right out of the box with an offensive push to try to thoroughly intimidate me, the witness. If in fact the objective of this exercise (be it a deposition, hearing, or trial) is to ascertain the real truth, why is it necessary to try to intimidate anyone? The answer to that question is that most of the time the end result does not seem to be to get to the real truth, but rather to "make the *truth* support a predetermined position or agenda." We need only look at some of the well-publicized trials in the general populace to see that lawyers are rated and rewarded, not for their ability to get to the truth, but rather for their ability to spin the information to their clients' advantage.

Christianity puts a high value on telling the truth. In Jesus' Sermon on the Mount in Matthew 5, 6, and 7, Jesus says, "Do not swear an oath, neither by Heaven for it is God's throne nor by earth for it is His footstool, but rather, let your yes be yes and your no be no." Mennonite theology is that Jesus was saying two things in this text. First, swearing an oath on some *thing* is meaningless as we are powerless to bring about any action as a result of that oath. Second, and more importantly, we should always tell the truth no matter what the condition or situation. We should not need an oath to force us to tell the truth.

As a result of these interpretations, Mennonite teaching is to not take an oath by swearing on a Bible. Rather, we make the simple statement that we affirm to tell the truth. The laws of the United States entitle us to this right. Interestingly, this is not well known to most people, and most lawyers seldom, if ever, encounter it. While I make my affirmation in the most serious consciousness, if it happens that the opposing attorney is administering the "oath," the results are usually most interesting and even humorous.

As I noted earlier, virtually all lawyers come out of the box on the offensive and the tones of their voices in the administration of the oath, "Do you solemnly swear to tell the truth, the whole truth, and nothing but the truth, so help you God?" are geared to frightening the devil right out of you.

I always sit very quietly and look the lawyer squarely in the eyes while he is reciting the oath. When he is finished, I very forcefully but politely say, "I affirm."

At that point the lawyer usually fumbles the ball in his own end zone, and I recover. He is immediately put on the defensive. The lawyer now has to go back through the entire recitation and say, "Do you affirm to tell the truth the whole truth and nothing but the truth?"

To this, I smile and say, "I do." Whammo! The damage is done, and the score is already 7- zip in my favor!

While this seems simple enough, it absolutely takes the wind from the sails of many of the lawyers doing the interrogating. Many people, who believe as I do and may prefer to affirm, do not know they have that right, and many more do not have the courage when put on the stand to take that position. Most lawyers know that and immediately begin to question, "What kind of guy am I about to interrogate? He could be or is going to be a problem." This internal questioning, coupled with their gut distaste for anything that upsets their interrogation plans, turns the tables on them. Their very acts of trying to intimidate and establish control from the beginning result in their losing control, at least initially.

From that point on, I do exactly as I have promised to do; I tell the truth. If it hurts my case, then it hurts my case. If it helps my case, then it helps my case. I do not try to level the playing field in the sense of truth. Truth is truth and should not be compromised. I do not hesitate, however, to level any playing field in the pursuit of getting to the real truth. I also firmly believe there is pragmatic value in telling the truth. As is frequently said, "If you tell the truth today, you do not have to try to remember tomorrow what you said yesterday."

I think the truth seldom hurts you if you live your life by a couple of simple rules. First, do unto others as you would have them do unto you. Second, understand and abide by the spirit of the law. The first of these is obviously both common sense action as well as the Golden Rule, which we have been taught since youth. The second is not so apparent. In most instances in life, we are taught to understand and follow the letter of the law. We are also often taught to use the letter of the law to find the loopholes and then operate inside of them. As I have noted before, the spirit of the law is what good people acting in good conscience adopted to right a wrong or protect a value. The letter of the law is quite often how lawyers and politicians (often more lawyers) penned the letters and words to serve the needs of themselves or the favored classes.

Beyond the often times failure of the letter of the law to abide within the spirit of the law, there is also the ponderous nature of excess legalese and the countless articles, paragraphs, sub-paragraphs, and more sub-paragraphs of supposedly defining terms. From a strictly pragmatic nature, this makes it virtually impossible for the average citizen to understand *the letter* of most laws and regulations.

From a business operations perspective, the regulations (laws) that have had real defining impact, starting in the 70s and continuing on to today, have been the environmental and safety laws. These, along with the equal opportunity laws of the 60s, constitute the bulk of the regulations that drive industrial operations management today. I do not have any idea how many thousands of pages of regulations have been recorded in the Federal Register relating to these three issues in the past 30 or so years. I do venture to suggest there are no normal or even abnormal mortals in existence who have read, much less understand, all of the *letters* of those laws.

The aforementioned paragraph notwithstanding, there are probably very few regulations recorded in history with much more simple and concise intents than those three regulatory areas named above. The intent of the environmental regulations is to leave the natural resources in equal or better condition than the way we found them. The intent of the safety regulations is to protect the worker and return him home at the end of the day in just as good of physical condition as when he started the day. The intent of the equal employment laws is that all persons should have equal access to any and all positions and pay, based on qualifications and nothing else. Of course, activist groups have taken great license with these laws and forwarded agendas that often have very little to do with the real spirit of these laws.

Accordingly and unfortunately, in the scramble to make sure every single particular situation and special interest is covered by the letter of the law, the spirit and intent often are trampled in the process. Throughout my career, I have tried to abide by the spirit of those laws. Interestingly, most of the seminars and educational materials with which I have been "coached" focus on the letter of the law. At the end of the day, the humanitarian in you will always feel better if you have spent the day living in the spirit of the law. My experience has been that *generally* you will also be better off *legally.* I have found it is very difficult for most judges, juries, hearing officers, regulatory enforcers, and even IRS examiners to hammer you on the letter when the overwhelming evidence shows you have unquestionably operated within the spirit and intent.

In the mid to late 90s, I had the opportunity to work very closely with LaRaye Osborne, one of the staff lawyers within the Cargill organization. A lot of LaRaye's work was in the environmental areas, and she assisted us with some groundwater compliance issues we had at our Beardstown, Illinois, facility. LaRaye is a unique lawyer who is able to stand in middle of the spirit of the law while being fully cloaked in the letter of the law. While she always kept us conscious of those necessary elements of the letter of the law in our discussions, deliberations, and corrective action plans, she also shared an equal concern with us that we ultimately did solve the problems. She was not simply content to achieve a legal victory of some type that made the compliance issue go away.

LaRaye is also interested in environmental activity. I said activity, not activism. I have long held the real environmentalists in the world are not the high profile activist organizations, but the real people whose lives, vocations, and even avocations put them in the middle of nature. Farmers, foresters, horticulturists, landscapers, outdoor sportspersons, even waste treatment system operators and environmental lawyers are among that group of people who drive *real* environmental progress. It is impossible to work closely with nature and not appreciate the incredible balance God created. We don't have any special interests or agendas; we just seek to do our best to protect that balance.

I fully believe LaRaye also understands the ultimate legal value in abiding by the spirit of the law. In several minor "flaps" with regulators and even citizens during our attempt to rectify the omissions and commissions of past generations, our position was always made stronger by the record we had begun to establish as working in the spirit and intent. Living in the spirit and intent made the legal arguments easier and more effective.

LaRaye Osborne notwithstanding, the corporate lawyer I had the most appreciation for was Greg Strobl. Greg was a good lawyer in the sense that he understood the law. However, Greg had one very important "non-lawyer" trait. He had an ability to define the applicable, potential legal consequences of an action and then jump out of his lawyer suit and into his client's work clothes. Most lawyers recite the absolute, most conservative legal position, doggedly insist it is the only acceptable course of action, and then wash their hands of any alternative.

Greg took just the opposite approach. He became one of us in every sense of the word in the business decision-making process. He helped us understand the legal ramifications and risks, but he also then expected us to educate him on the business ramifications and risks. We were always more than happy to do that. With the education all in place, we worked as a team to come up with the best overall posture for Cargill. None of us were worried about any personal rear end coverage. We were all in it together.

I remember one particular disagreement we had with a predecessor company over an issue following our purchase of a Midwestern processing plant. We met together with the former owners and both of our legal representatives to work out a solution. Although we had strong legal grounds for our position, there was some nebulosity, and there were some issues of spirit and intent as well. After hearing each other out, we retreated to private conferences where we all, Greg included, reluctantly agreed it was in the best interest of Cargill to meet about halfway. We proposed our solution and the other guys reluctantly accepted it.

Following the meeting, the other lawyer asked if he could ride to the airport with us to save someone else from having to drive him there. We were happy to do that. On the way, no one said very much of anything until Greg finally broke the ice. "Well" he commented, "everyone on both sides seemed to be equally *unhappy* so I guess we got an equitable solution!"

I found that comment to be very interesting, then and now. Then, because Greg was absolutely right. We were all equally dissatisfied, but still aware we had reached the best solution. Now, because I think it is the microcosm of most legal proceedings. Once it gets to the lawyers and even if you are fortunate enough to have a guy like Greg Strobl on your team, it will seldom be a win-win. It will only be some combination of pain sharing. See Chapter 31: "Three Million Dollar Handshake" for a classic example of a win-win by keeping the lawyers out.

Unlike Greg and LaRaye, many of the corporate lawyers with whom I have worked have not been willing to consider much of the spirit if it conflicts with their interpretations of the letter. This always caused me frustration in getting construction agreements in place. The documents we (Cargill) as the buyer used were written for the benefit of the buyer, and that is understandable. I did not have a problem with that until it infringed on the common sense rights of the seller or unless it demanded compliance with terms that we refused to accept when the roles were reversed and Cargill was the seller.

I simply waived the language that was unfair. The lawyers were always greatly incensed by this, especially when I was dealing with a small contractor who could not afford high-powered lawyers or who was very much at our mercy in needing work. I was regularly told that other divisions of Cargill would simply force this language down the contractor's throat, so why couldn't I? My point was not that I *couldn't*, it was that I *wouldn't*. You do not build relationships by taking advantage of someone because he or she may be weaker or may simply be in a weaker position at the time.

What has always amazed me is how other divisions would allow the lawyers to do this. It was absolutely not in the best interest of Cargill to insist on language that essentially made litigation against the contractor easier. Relationships aside, most of the small contractors we used were of high value to Cargill. They filled a key niche and were either able to get mobilized quickly, meet specific time demands, or work more efficiently and inexpensively. To be able to put one of these guys out of business, as was done on occasion, for a few tens of thousands of dollars, did nothing except perhaps add a notch to a lawyer's belt. Most critically, putting one of them out of business took a vital resource out of the arsenal of the company and likely cost us many more tens of thousands of dollars in lost performance.

Although we had a number of corporate lawyers, Cargill relied heavily on outside, local legal counsel on many matters. It was just one of these matters that brought me together with my favorite lawyer, Bill Zimmerman. Bill was a principal in a major legal firm in Kansas City who we retained to help us resolve an issue with one of the RECs (Rural Electric Coops) that served one of our facilities.

Bill is a jovial guy who failed to push himself away from the dinner table too many times. He has a great sense of humor, remains very much a kid at heart, and is a very good trial lawyer. In the REC case, we had shut our plant down permanently because of economic conditions. In our electric power agreement we had what is called a "ratcheted demand" clause. A ratcheted demand basically assures a power company that no matter what the power demand is in a given month, the user (Cargill in this case), will pay at least some percentage (often 75 percent) of the peak demand over a past time period, which is usually 12 months.

The spirit of this clause is that since the user still wants power reservation, the basis for the demand charge in the first place, he should be willing to pay at least a major portion of what he will continue to want. This clause is especially useful for power companies when dealing with businesses that are very seasonal in nature. The power company must reserve the capacity for all months even though the customer uses it for only a few. The spirit of the provision is not to hammer a business that has ceased operation with 12 more months of demand charges. That is, however, precisely how the REC interpreted the provision in this case.

We shut the plant down and the REC continued charging us 75 percent of our maximum monthly demand charge. After a few months of paying this, our accounting people said, "Hey, the plant is down. We can't be continuing to use tens of thousands of dollars worth of power every month!" and they stopped paying the invoices.

By the time I was called in from a technical perspective, battle lines had been firmly drawn. I researched a number of the other Cargill facilities that had ceased operations in the past years. None of the power companies in those instances continued to attempt to enforce the ratcheted demand charge. I called some of the power companies at plants where we were still in operation and asked them how they interpreted this provision in their agreements. They all indicated that in the case of permanent shutdown they would not continue to charge on the ratcheted demand provision.

Armed with this information, we held a series of discussions with the REC administrators and asked for some middle ground resolution. We were told no middle ground existed, and we should pay up. Otherwise, they would shut off what little power we had remaining, which was only some security lighting and fire protection pumps. We continued to seek some dialog, but we did not make any payments. True to their word, the REC abruptly cut off our power and sued us!

Enter Bill Zimmerman. "Z" as he was called and a couple of other lawyers from his firm were brought in to help us defend ourselves. I was assigned to work with them as Cargill's representative as well as to be the "technical expert." Bill and I quickly became good friends.

Although we were vastly different in our lifestyles, we were very much alike in our love for life and laughter. We were also both intelligent investigators.

We started building our case on the basis of the spirit of the contract provision and our understandings of how similar clauses had been handled in numerous other cases. The REC was absolute in their position that the letter of the provision said they could hammer us (my terminology), and they intended to do just that. Obviously, courts generally focus on dotted i(s) and crossed t(s) so we were more than a little concerned about our chances. Nevertheless, we did begin the discovery process. That was where the fun began.

We did not discover anything that changed the letter of the provision nor anything that showed there was a different intent on the part of the framers of the agreement. What we did discover was that over a period of many years the REC had done an incredibly poor job of contract administration, rate-change notification, meter management, and internal transparency.

Based on the *letters* in our agreements, we were able to identify several hundred thousand dollars of overcharges to us that had been made over several years. Now the key point was that none of us would have argued the rate charges were not justified nor would we have argued that, in the spirit of our relationship, they were not reasonable. However, we were being hammered on the letter and not the intent, so we hammered back on the letter and not the intent. While this may sound paradoxical for me, I was simply trying to get the REC to recognize that we should both focus on the spirit. The REC continued to turn a deaf ear so we pressed on.

Bill was a masterful interrogator. He was also very polite and accommodating in his deposition interrogations for those witnesses who were straightforward and simple. While he stayed polite and civil, he was absolutely ruthless on those witnesses who were arrogant, cavalier, and tried to maintain a debonair character. He would cut them to ribbons. I found this to be particularly entertaining as I consider myself very straightforward and simple, and I do disdain arrogance.

Ultimately we settled this case by paying the REC a small sum as a face-saver. We could have arrived at that point in our very first meeting, as this was still well to our side of "middle ground." Nevertheless, I did find the entire process to be both enlightening and interesting. I was glad "Z" was on my side. I often wonder what it would be like to face Bill and certainly hope that never happens.

Acquaintances and friends like Bill remain entrenched in your mind even when you are not in active interaction with them. Several years after the REC work, I was involved in the Taiwan project. Everyday when I went in and out of the hotel in Tai Chung, I noticed the statue of a very rotund man that graced the lobby of the hotel. One day I asked one of the bellhops, who I had befriended, who this statue represented. He replied the statue represented the god of riches and pleasures, but he didn't think the god had a name. I immediately responded, "Oh, yes, he does. His name is Bill Zimmerman, and he lives in Kansas City." I proceeded to find and purchase a miniature statue of this god and brought it back to the States to give to "Z." Bill's entire office got a kick out of "his likeness," both in appearance and in representation.

"Z" paid me a number of compliments during the time I worked with him. However, the one that still means the most to me is "Roth, you are so darn honest you are boring!" I don't necessarily try to be boring, but I do hold honesty as a prime characteristic in people. I think one of the most honorable goals in life is for your words and actions to speak so loudly of your indigenous honesty there is never a need for the question, *"Do you solemnly swear to tell the truth?"*

# CHAPTER 24
# Used Cars

I have made a history of buying used cars, trucks, and farm equipment. Cars and pickups do not begin to age until they have at least 250,000 miles. I have driven cars beyond 400,000 miles.

I have two philosophies for doing this. First, the economics of this approach will always work versus buying new or near new. Second and more importantly, if you buy a new car, you are in a class by yourself for perhaps a few minutes. Anyone else with a little money or credit can replace you as soon as you drive out of the dealership by purchasing a car after you. And you can rest assured within a few minutes (or maybe a few hours in small locals) that is exactly what will happen. If, on the other hand, you are able to nurse 400,000 miles out of a car and enjoy it, you are in a class by yourself. You can rest assured no one is going to replace you in the next few minutes. You own a position on the road that no one else can just buy his or her way into. Every mile and minute that passes puts you into an even more elite category!

I think the logic of such an approach is sound and of value. That, however, is not what this chapter is about. It is about from whom you would buy a used car. What type of person, exhibiting what kind of values, would entice you to part with your money?

We have all seen posters or cartoons of "shyster-looking" people with the caption, "Would you purchase a used car from this person?" The answer is always "No!" However, in these cases, it is always "no" based on appearance alone. How can you sort out the good salespersons from the charlatans if appearance alone is not a give-away? There are a number of good "sorting poles" available to identify the really good salespersons. More than just helping us make the best choices from whom to purchase an item, each of us is a salesperson every day for our ideas, our projects, and even ourselves. We would do well to learn some skills from the really good, professional salespersons. In my career, I am sure many times when I was not able to make my point or sell my position, it reflected as much on my inability as a salesman for my position as it did on the inability of the other party to recognize the value of my approach. In many instances, the impact of my selling failure was profound.

The absolute best salesperson I have ever met and who I aspire to be like was Ray Freeman. It so happens that Ray and his wife, Janiece, were the second set of parents to my wife and me and the third set of grandparents to all of our children, particularly Renee and Derek. However, this "non-blood" parental bond has nothing to do with my assessment of Ray's sale's abilities and methods. (Note: Ray passed on to his eternal reward since the original writing of this segment, but his impact and legacy remain.)

The first element of Ray's make up that made him a super salesman was that he was a devout and practicing Christian man. I hope any non-religious types in the audience will stay with me on this and allow me to expand on it. Ray's Christianity manifested itself through his honesty and integrity. While I don't necessarily believe you have to be a Christian to be honest and have high integrity, you cannot be a *true*, practicing Christian *without* those characteristics. A truly superior salesperson must have integrity and be honest.

Perhaps a point of clarification is needed here! When I consider salespersons, I think in terms of on-going activity and relationships. I realize there are a few items that only are purchased once in a person's life (like a prepaid burial plot). However, these are few and far between. While a few salespersons may make a lot of money on one-time sales where less than honest behavior may not get exposed, most salespeople must rely on at least some repeat and reference business to survive. Where references and repeat business are essential, less-than-honest sales behavior must be coupled with on-going and perpetual deceit if the customer is to be kept unsuspecting and unknowing, therefore allowing the salesperson to continue making sales.

The second thing that made Ray so good was that he knew his product. While it should go without saying that a salesperson must know the product, it bemuses me how many times that is not the case. It defies logic how many people think brochures, sale's literature, advertising blitzes, and other people will satisfy the knowledge base. Ray's knowledge of his products *and* his competitors' products put him in more elite territory. Interestingly, while it seems impossible, there are times when we fail to sell *ourselves* because we do not know the product.

An understanding of the customer's business is a natural follow up to the knowledge of one's own product. We hear all the time about the need to understand the customer's needs, but seldom do we attach the requirement to understand the customer's business or operation *in order* to fully understand his needs. That is one of the major areas that won me over to Ray in his early sales calls some thirty years ago. I was in the soybean processing business, and Ray was selling hammer mill screens and hammers. Yet he could speak with me intelligently about the soybean business. While hammer mills are used in many industries, Ray focused on just a few industries with which he could become very familiar.

Ray then began to aggregate the elements of his knowledge. Knowing our operation allowed him to understand our needs. Knowing his product and his competitor's products allowed him to focus on how his product could meet those needs better than his competitors could. Ray then took the necessary steps to see that his product did just that. This may have included changing the product or pricing or delivery or whatever. Ray made sure his product actually did best meet his customers' needs.

At this point, Ray had all the technical requirements handled for effectively selling. He then mixed in the personality characteristics and the person-to-person contact requirements necessary to create the super salesman, which Ray was. My earlier comments on honesty and integrity came into play as this gave us absolute confidence that Ray's product would be what he said and perform as promised, or he would make it right.

Ray also liked his customers as persons. If he didn't like you, he stopped calling on you. Ray's philosophy was that life was too short for unpleasant conditions that could be avoided. If Ray didn't like a particular customer, it was likely because that customer was arrogant, rude, condescending, dishonest, or deceitful. Ray knew you could not build a trusting relationship in that environment, so he would simply move on to more fruitful and pleasant opportunities elsewhere.

For those of us Ray liked, he dedicated himself to helping us improve our operations through his products and our lives through his friendship. It was through both of these efforts that Ray and his company became and remained a most valuable supplier. It was through the second effort that Ray and I became very good friends, and ultimately our families became as close as non-blood relationships could become.

Following Ray, all salespersons who I encounter ultimately get compared to him. Like Joe Culbreath and Eldred Swoboda in Chapter 12, no one else has yet fully measured up to Ray's standard. That notwithstanding, there have been many other salespersons who have also been great teachers.

Mike Dallan is one of those persons. In 1987, when Excel purchased the Beardstown pork facility from the Oscar Mayer Company, we immediately began a major renovation of the project. Since we were on a tight timeline to get the plant turned around and back into operation, the work was essentially all done on a design-build basis. In this system, you design as you go and then build immediately from that design. The Omeco Boss people from Omaha, Nebraska, had the greatest degree of expertise and capability in the fresh-meat business at that time so we contracted with them. At the time, Mike was still employed at National Beef in Liberal, Kansas, and was not a part of the Omeco Boss group.

Over the course of the next six months, we turned the Beardstown facility into the highest capacity and one of the most efficient pork operations in the country. The Omeco people played an important role in that. However, the cost tracking that the Omeco people did was incredibly shoddy. I had instructed them to tell me when we approached $350,000 in spending on certain items. We just kept building with no notification, and when I asked our salesperson, he would say we were still okay and that he would take care of us. Finally, I approached the key bean counters at Omeco and said, "Look, I know we have to be way beyond $350,000. Get your act together, and let me know where we are at!"

Well, where we were at was approaching $800,000 in committed work, as well as another couple of hundred thousand that would be needed to complete the work we had in progress. Without question, the Omeco salesman had taken care of us! He had helped us work our way into a gigantic economic corner versus our budget for this work. Fortunately, we had significantly under spent in some other areas so our total project budget was still intact. Nevertheless, the Omeco fiasco was an embarrassment to all of us, and we had a number of heart-to-heart conversations with them over the ensuing six months. Eventually we settled all of the issues, but our relationship had been strained to near the breaking point.

Enter Mike Dallan. Mike joined the Omeco sales team shortly after this fiasco and was assigned to our territory. Mike called on me at the Beardstown plant to introduce himself. I remember the meeting, but I do not remember the conversation. Mike does remember the conversation and tells me I did all the talking and told him in no uncertain terms where the Omeco organization stood with us. They and he had a huge hole to dig out of. Mike tells me he walked out of my office and said to himself, "Man, I'm not sure I ever want to encounter that character again!"

Many salespeople would have written the account off, but not Mike Dallan. Mike continued to call on us and to specifically make contact with me whenever possible. A year later when we did a similar major expansion at our Ottumwa, Iowa, facility, Mike steered his company to the top of the bidder list, and they were awarded the work. Mike personally handled a good part of the project. That impressed me. Salespersons who made the sale and then disappeared did not find favor. Mike personally saw to it that the Omeco portion of the project proceeded without a hitch.

I was very impressed with Mike's work ethic and follow-through approach. To this day, no salesperson I have met does a better job of following his sale through the total implementation process than Mike does. As we worked together on the Ottumwa project, we both gained an appreciation of each other's knowledge and work ethic. As often happens when two people begin to appreciate each other in a work setting, Mike and I developed a personal friendship. That friendship has continued to this day.

While some people worry that friendships create opportunities for biased interaction on a corporate scale, I argue just the opposite. Mike would never jeopardize our friendship with inferior performance. On the contrary, because Mike likes and appreciates me, he tries all the harder to do a good job on all of the projects he has an opportunity to work on. For my part, I know Mike will treat me better than anyone else will, and anytime we can move work in his company's direction, we will do that.

Mike is also the apotheosis of the concept that you do business with individuals within an organization more so than you do with the organization as a whole. In the late 90s, Mike left the Omeco organization and joined one of their competitors in the Omaha area. Within a time period of only a few months, a substantial amount of Excel's business (not just that over which I had control) had been switched to Mike's new company. At the plant level, it was as though nothing had happened. Mike continued to call regularly, helped us assess our needs, saw that his "new" company performed to the highest standard, and continued his unequaled project follow through. His replacements at the old company did none of the above.

Several years ago there was an advertisement segment for one of the airlines. A gentlemen (a CEO type) carrying a handful of airline tickets entered a boardroom filled with other manager types. The segment started out with this gentleman saying he just had a call from an old friend at a major account who informed him they were dropping their account with them. He went on to say, "We used to know our customers; we discussed things face-to-face. Now it's a PO or memo in the mail, a phone call here, a fax there, and no one ever sees the other person. Well that is going to change! We're going to get to know our customers face-to-face again."

He proceeded to hand out tickets to everyone else in the room with instructions as to where each of the other managers was going. Finally, he had given everyone a ticket, and he had one left in his hand. One of the other managers then asked him, "Where are you going J.B.?"

"I'm going to visit that old friend!" was the reply.

I'm a real connoisseur of advertisements. As I've noted before, the good ones are often the only redeeming quality on TV. That is one of my all-time favorites. I like it not for its entertainment value, but because it is again one of those classic micro-shots of what has really happened in the world. I am a firm believer there is no substitute for face-to-face interaction. I don't care if we have all the teleconferencing and Internet connective communications systems in the world at our fingertips, they do not replace a handshake and looking someone directly in the eye. They also do not replace the message present with each personal visit.

That message is timeless. "I value you and your business so highly that I have taken the *time* to come and see you."

Ray and Mike both met their customers face-to-face, and both lived by the rule that you cannot be an effective salesperson over the telephone. They are (or were) two of the most diligent face-to-face salespersons I have encountered. Certainly their successes have been a direct result of their face-to-face skills.

While perhaps not as natural a salesperson as Ray or Mike, another of the really good face-to-face people is Paul Reinartz. Paul is a salesperson for Walling, a company that specializes in water treatment chemicals. Paul showed up at the Beardstown facility every Wednesday morning whether he was welcome or not. Actually he was welcome, but I will admit there were times when we may have thought he was a burden and took time we may not have thought we had.

Nevertheless, Paul methodically won his way into favor and confidence and even into our hearts. He did this by his dogged persistence and the knowledge of his products and his willingness to go right to the front lines of battle and help solve any problems there. Paul was even persistent in getting us to eat one of the donuts he regularly brought with him to treat anyone who happened to be in the particular office of his call.

Much like Mike Dallan, my first encounter with Paul was less than an embrace. Again, while I do not recall the details, Paul does, and he informs me he certainly saw me as anything but an easy target. Paul continued to come, bringing donuts and water treatment expertise. On those ensuing days I happened to be in Beardstown when Paul called, I continued to be polite, but distant. Eventually Paul's butt-of-the-joke demeanor broke through my barriers, and I actually began to respond to him in some positive ways. I came to look forward to Paul's visits, and even though we pimped him mercilessly, he knew we enjoyed his visits and respected his knowledge.

Paul's face-to-face work cemented his position as a favored supplier on the Excel baseline water treatment business. I'm sure this was the primary objective Paul had at the outset. Interestingly, within a few years we found ourselves using a myriad of Paul's products in applications we didn't even know he had products for. At each visit, Paul would always specifically ask if there was anything we needed or if there was anything that he could help us with. However, he would also get a cup of coffee (we traded one cup of coffee for a dozen donuts) and just listen to what we happened to be discussing when he came in.

On what was a significantly disproportionate amount of the time, he ferreted out of the discussions solutions utilizing the products he possessed. Paul got paid amazingly well for the time he spent in these visits. Telephone calls, faxes, and e-mail messages cannot share donuts and eavesdrop on seemingly mundane daily topics.

I do not mean to suggest there are not places for telephone sales, and God only knows how many goods and services are purchased over the Internet today. However, if you intend to market a value-added product and not just a commodity, you can most effectively do that face-to-face where you have the opportunity to prove both the added value your product brings as well as the added value *you* bring personally.

Few people really recognize they are constantly marketing themselves and their products whether they are in sales or not. I have regularly had to sell my position on any given topic or situation, and as earlier noted, failure to be able to do that effectively often has a big impact. See the "More Stories" section for "Jerry Gets Religion," a unique story of how we were able to sell one of my bosses and in the process make him a future salesman for our positions. Over the years, I have been involved in hundreds of millions of dollars worth of plant expansions, new construction, or new business ventures. Even when the studies of these are commissioned by top management personnel, the final decisions are generally based on the ability of the "researcher or developer" to sell the decision makers on the merits of the work or project.

More than simply ferreting out and detailing facts, one must find the hot buttons of the people to whom one is addressing any request, just like a conventional salesperson. Understanding both the perspectives and the bias of your target audience was never more apparent to me than in 1984. We at Excel were aggressively pursuing an entry into the leather tanning and finishing business. I had been working for several months with the principals of an old-line USA tanner. We were working on a deal that would have had Excel joint venturing with them to build a new leather tanning operation in Texas. This new facility was to be set up to process both sole and upper leathers. The guys with whom I was working were super guys to work with, and I thoroughly enjoyed putting the package together with them. Moreover, I really looked forward to "doing the deal" and eventually managing an operation with them.

I had done a very thorough analysis of the leather business as well as the shoe business, which is the point of final use for most of the leather. I had also dissected the operation owned by these gentlemen. The transparent relationship we had developed made this a relatively easy job. We had a site selected in Texas and had done a significant amount of work on incentives and site requirements. We had held discussions with a number of key customers and had promises of support from several of them. Most persons in the Cargill hierarchy were at least warm to the idea, and it seemed to be a strategic fit.

Pete McVay, one of the top operational officers at Cargill, however, seemed to be seriously in doubt. Pete told us he was not familiar enough with leather operations, and he didn't know if they would fit the commodity mind-set of Cargill. He asked if we could get in to see the best leather operation in the country, wherever that may be. I asked around and was pointed to Phister and Vogel (P&V) in Milwaukee. We proceeded to make contact with P&V, who at the time was a major customer of our beef hides. We didn't tell them directly we were contemplating a competing entry into the business, but we did tell them we wanted to understand more about the opportunities in the industry. They agreed to give a number of us a tour.

We set up a tour of the P&V facility in Milwaukee, followed by a tour of the old-line existing operation of the company with whom we were working. The P&V people gave us an unbelievably comprehensive tour. They showed us every minute detail in their operation. When our group deplaned for the second segment of our tour (the old-line operation), one of the principals was the first to greet me and said, "How did the tour at P&V go?" I told him how thorough and comprehensive of a tour they had given us.

"Then they had no idea Cargill is contemplating a move into the leather business!" he noted with a bit of relief.

"On the contrary," I replied, "they know exactly that we may be contemplating such a move, and they did precisely what they needed to do to squelch any thoughts we had about competing with them."

I had to further explain! If P&V had been at all evasive or secretive, we may have determined the business was easy, anyone could do it, and they (P&V) were determined to protect their knowledge base. Since we could likely convince ourselves P&V had no exceptional technology, no exceptional proprietary processes, and likely no unsinkable customer base, their actions could easily have been taken as fear of competition. We may not have walked away with the belief it was a tough business. We may not have understood that P&V was highly successful because they were highly skilled at executing the minute details of both the leather processes and the customer relationships.

However, by playing to their strengths (and although perhaps not specifically known to them to Pete's primary concern), P&V shut the door tight. Pete was ready and willing to walk away, convinced what P&V had going for themselves was an ability to manage an incredible myriad of specific details and customer needs in a highly successful manner. None of us could dispute that since they were certainly the class of the industry and did do those things very well. Without firing a shot, P & V convinced Pete that going to war with them would result in a lot of casualties on our side. Pete voted NO and that was the vote that really counted.

Much like P&V sold Pete (and thus Cargill) on not pursuing any further plans to enter the leather business, a great many of life's seemingly everyday activities are actually sale's challenges of one kind or another, whether we recognize it at the time or not. And like it or not, we are all salespersons. It is always in our best interest to give a positive sale's impression to others. We can never be sure that others are not looking at us and saying to themselves, *"Would I buy a used car from him or her?"*

# CHAPTER 25
# You *Don't* Get What You Deserve

I once heard it said, "You don't get what you deserve, rather you get what you negotiate!" Perhaps. It can be argued, however, if you are not prepared and therefore get out-negotiated, then, hey, you get what you deserve. However, I am bothered by the concept that fairness is only a matter of negotiation skill. Certainly other things must come into play. Even so, one needs to recognize negotiation is a part of life and to be effective in business or life, one must negotiate.

Experience has taught me there are three critical factors that make one a good negotiator. The first one is integrity. In many circles integrity and negotiation are considered oxymoronic. I think not, rather they are critically related. The second factor is intelligence or more properly, knowledge of the negotiated treatise. The final critical factor is the willingness to walk away from the negotiation or conversely the willingness to raise the ante. Interestingly, if all three of these are effectively used, all parties to the process will generally get what they deserve.

In the late 70s we purchased and installed coal boilers in our corn processing operations in Cedar Rapids, Iowa and Dayton, Ohio. I had primary responsibility for building the coal boiler in Cedar Rapids during the days and being the night superintendent at the Memphis, Tennessee facility in the nights. While that seems logistically impossible it was really only logistically difficult, but that is a different story.

One of the components of the coal boiler was the ash handling system. Three prospective suppliers made it to the short list. I reworked the system specifications and bidding requirements and resubmitted them to each of the three companies with these instructions. "First, review your package and make any adjustments necessary to comply with these requirements. Second, come to the Holiday Inn at the Chicago O'Hare

Airport on Wednesday two weeks hence. Third, bring a decision maker with you."

I then detailed my plan. I would meet individually with each group for one hour in the morning for them to make their presentation on the revised requirements. I would help them understand any requirements in question and answer any other questions. They would then retreat to their own room or the restaurant or wherever and put together their final dollar bid. I told them they could bid it however they chose, but to remember it would be their last chance and they would be evaluated on the basis of that number. "Give me the number you wish to live or die by!" were my instructions.

I would then meet with each of them again individually for a few minutes after lunch to get their final proposal and cost number. I would then take an hour or so to spread everything out and make a final decision, after which I would call them each back in and let them know who was receiving the order. Someone, I promised, would leave Chicago with the order on that day.

Everything proceeded according to plan. Based on that action, Detroit Stoker was selected. They happened to be the second presenter and since each retained his position for each of the encounters, I met with one of the "losers" first. When I informed him his company had not been chosen, he asked if he had lost largely on the money issue. I told him he had and he proceeded to tell me he had another 10 percent reduction in price he could offer. I was flabbergasted!

"Would you have told me about the extra 10% if I had informed you that you were the successful bidder?" I inquired. He just dropped his head. "Why did you not believe me when I told you to give me your live or die number?" I continued. "And how could I trust you to follow any of my continuing requests or instructions if I selected you if you couldn't follow such a simple one in the bidding process?"

Obviously, there was no need for an answer as the damage done had already put any relationship with this company beyond repair. This bidder had nothing further to say. I politely thanked him for his effort and he left. Although chance has not resulted in encountering him or his organization again, I must admit if I would have, he and they would have come right out of the box with *at least* two strikes on them.

Detroit Stoker, the wining bidder, was the second to come back into the room for the third time to receive the good news. Obviously they were elated. They thanked me for the process and the order and promised to maintain that same relationship throughout the installation. And they did.

Interestingly, the last company to return was probably the best all around organization, but had simply left a couple of holes in their proposal. I informed them of my high opinion of them as well as the fact they had been muscled out by Detroit Stoker. They replied they were sorry to have been defeated, but they viewed the entire process as the most honest, refreshing, and high level bidding process they had ever experienced. Class organizations have integrity and honor. They were later selected as the vendor of choice for the Dayton plant. Ultimately, I think everyone got what he deserved in that case.

I have used the same or close variations of that process again and again over the past 25 plus years. While it continues to serve me well, I remain amazed at how often people think *they* know better what you want and what you are saying than do you. That was never more evident than in the bidding process for the hot and cold sides of the production equipment supply to our operation in Taiwan in the early 90s. Mike Dallan, who you have already met, worked for an organization in Omaha that was one of the highly favored vendors to our Pork Division. This was because they (largely as a result of Mike's continuing efforts) had served us well in numerous prior projects.

We were using essentially the same bidding process as developed in the 70s for the ash handling system. In this case Mike's company was on the short list of three we invited to Taiwan for the final round. The instructions given were largely identical to those given the ash handlers in Chicago years earlier. A couple of Mike's company executives accompanied him on the trip. As they prepared for their final presentation, the executives began the process of inflating the final numbers to "have room" for wiggling and negotiation.

Mike was beside himself as he pleaded with them. "I know Jim and I know how he operates, and when he says he wants our final number, he means it," Mike argued to no avail. The others informed him they knew how other people operated and they always liked to have some room to negotiate down. "It makes them look good to be able to knock the price down some," they informed Mike.

"I don't care, that is not how Jim operates," was all Mike could say and he entered the room fearing they were doomed. They were, in fact, doomed! Interestingly, they were bewildered when we informed them they were high on both their hot and cold side proposals and the book was closed with no further discussion.

Fortunately for them, they did luck out on the cold side, since all bidders were over our budget. We were forced to revisit the design of that component and do some value engineering. We then re-invited each of the short list people to reevaluate the new design criteria and resubmit their bid. Mike's guys listened to him this time and while the others could only reduce their price by the new design criteria, Mike's company did the same as well as removed the extra "fluff" they had earlier inserted. As a result, they did win the cold side work in this revised mode. Had they believed in the integrity of the instructions in the first place and/or listened to Mike who did believe in them, they may well have won the work on both the hot and cold sides. As it was, it took a little luck to get anything. Maybe they got more than they deserved.

I do not believe integrity is a simple matter of honesty and believing in what one says. It is also in the approach to the process and how each person in the process is treated. At the young age of 26, I was the plant superintendent of the East Side Soybean Plant in Cedar Rapids (Chapter 15: "The Family"). We usually negotiated the labor agreements annually. If you have read Chapter 12, you could probably surmise Eldred Swoboda and I could have sat down and in a short time negotiated a fair and equitable agreement.

That is often not the way big companies work, however. Important labor lawyers from the ivory towers would come down to meet with the local union bosses to "hammer out" an agreement. Guys like me were allowed to sit in on the negotiations, but we were summarily instructed to keep our mouths shut and just be present. Even when we were not in the joint sessions, some of the big shot lawyers essentially silenced us in the private caucuses as well.

The particular lawyer who handled our plant was particularly adamant about that. He had been given so many cents per hour by senior management and he had his own negotiating plan and he wanted no interference from any of us at the plant level. He was very good at negotiating settlements that had "apparent" economic values a couple of cents per hour less than what senior management had given him. He was a hero! However, in the exchange he would think nothing of shackling us with language and work rule changes that cost many times those few cents per hour and yet benefited no one. Did both company and union get as good a deal as possible? Seldom! The hierarchies perhaps got what they deserved, but the real players; local management and the labor force, usually did not!

A few years later, I found myself working with a different labor lawyer for the operations I managed. Bill Dillon was a breath of fresh air. Bill was a student of knowledge. He not only tolerated our ideas and concerns, he also encouraged them so he could be fully educated in what we needed in order to effectively manage the business and serve our employees. Bill was able to draw his circle around all of Cargill and not just around the specific economic guidelines he had been given. This circle also included the unionized employees who were also a part of Cargill, although that fact often got lost with other negotiators. Bill incorporated both integrity and knowledge (walking away was not his call) and I think all of the agreements we negotiated with his assistance served all parties with equity.

The type of knowledge Bill brought was real. I have also discovered perceived knowledge can be as effective as real knowledge. In 1987 when we purchased the pork processing facility in Beardstown, Illinois, we worked with the Illinois DCCA (Department of Commerce and Community Affairs) to secure a number of incentives to assist us in making the operation viable. The largest opportunity was in job training. We cited a gigantic package the State of Illinois had recently provided for that purpose to induce an automotive concern to locate in the state. The DCCA people gave us a number of songs and dances about why we did not meet the same criteria. Most of their rationale centered on the specific classifications of jobs in our operation. They made frequent reference to the DOT.

Following one of numerous meetings in which we had made little progress, I inquired as to what this reference was to. We were informed the DOT was the *Dictionary of Occupational Titles* and was the critical defining medium for all job classifications. We made several inquiries outside the agency as to how we could secure one of these documents and were finally directed to a government print shop in an obscure location in Chicago. I asked Tom Hayes (one of my assistants at the time who later became one of my bosses - so always treat your assistants well) to find this place and purchase this DOT document for us on his next trip home to Illinois. Tom did, and returned with a gigantic book that had upwards of 1000 pages.

I searched through the DOT book to find the critical information to our case. I then thoroughly educated myself on about *two* pages worth of key information to support our platform. We then returned to Springfield for another meeting. I entered the room with the DOT manual under one arm. As we began our discussion, I called attention to several key DOT definitions and classification issues reciting article number, paragraph number, sub-paragraph number etc. The DCCA folks made virtually no counter arguments and we were ultimately awarded a big chunk of training money. It was obvious we had their "Bible." More importantly, I have no doubt but that the DCCA people were convinced we were far more religious scholars of it than were they.

One of the movies I like is "Born Yesterday". I particularly like the part where a reporter asks Melanie Griffith's character about her favorite part in a specific book. This was a book ostensibly read by all higher society people. Melanie's character must respond she hasn't read it, thereby identifying herself as being "a nobody." Following this encounter and in an attempt to better herself, she reads the book. On her next encounter with the reporter, she responds with a very articulate description of the part she liked the best. She then asks the reporter what *her* favorite part was. The stunned and embarrassed reporter must then admit she had never read the book herself.

This is such a microcosm of life. It is amazing how many times a very little bit of knowledge and sometimes even no real knowledge at all, can be passed off as expert until it is countered with the real stuff. If you can wrap your hands around even a little bit of the real thing, you can disrobe a lot of false "experts."

A second notable and profitable negotiation also occurred as a part of the purchase of the Beardstown, Illinois facility. This one took the combination of all three of the major components of effective negotiation. When we first arrived to do our due diligence work, I had requested copies of the electric power tariff the plant was under, as well as all of the other tariffs the electric power provider had on file with the Illinois

Utility Commission. Our contact person was a super nice guy who delivered all this material to me with the polite remark that if I were looking to see if there were any better rates, I would not find any.

I assured him that was precisely what I intended to do. I further informed him while he was likely correct, I needed to do that for my own satisfaction as well as to do my duty as a good manager. I did not find a better tariff as I expected and as had been predicted by the utility company rep. However, I did find in the small print a rather obscure filing called Rider 13. Rider 13 had been established as a way to bring new industry into the territory. It promised a 50% reduction in demand charges for the 8 non-summer months of the year for a five-year period for new customers of the power company. I ran the numbers and determined application of Rider 13 could save us very close to $1 million over the five year period.

I called my "sales buddy" back out and explained to him what I had found and asked him what I needed to do to get the ball rolling on getting Rider 13 put into force. Joe was very much taken aback. He proceeded to explain he did not think Rider 13 applied to us. Over the next few weeks, I had several meetings explaining in great detail how Excel was a new customer and therefore absolutely fit the "letter of the law" aspect of this filing. More importantly, we were in fact a white knight for purchasing a plant that was being closed down so we also met the "spirit of the law." I argued the preservation of the industrial base certainly had the same effect as losing it and having to create another. It was obvious higher authorities were coaching Joe. All he could ever argue was, "I don't think it was intended for situations like yours."

Finally, unable to get me to move off of my insistence that we "get the ball rolling," Joe arranged a meeting with one of the utility company vice presidents. When the meeting time came, Joe, his boss, and the corporate VP showed up at my office. The utility company executive carried the conversation and was polite, although very emphatic in his discussion this provision was strictly for new operations and not new customers. I carefully went through all of my arguments that I had earlier given. Through regular repetition, I had polished them up quite well. Had this been a high school debate, I am absolutely certain I would have been the hands-down winner. I was arguing from a position of strength and the utility company position was one of weakness.

The only thing they had going for them was they, in effect, held the money. They had to "initiate the action and put the provision into effect." They had learned well he who holds the money holds the power. Finally, exasperated over the inability to get me to back down from my position, the VP told me he would "inform" the greater Company Board of our request for the application of Rider 13. However, he was certain the decision of that Board would be we were not entitled to any of the provisions of Rider 13.

I had approached the negotiation with integrity and I had done my homework. It was obvious these had taken me as far as they were going to take me with the utility hierarchy. I responded to those final remarks by saying I had no control over what decision the Board made internally. However, if they did not grant us Rider 13, our next conversation would be in front of the Illinois Public Utility Board. I was both ready and willing to raise the ante. I have absolutely no military experience, but common sense is all you need in order to recognize there is no better place to wage a battle than from the high ground. If you hold it, why raise the white flag?

The utility company entourage left with polite but rather terse closing handshakes. Several days later, I received a call from our local rep's boss requesting an audience with me. I gave him a mutually acceptable time and he arrived at my office. When he arrived, he informed me that following our conversations, the upper management group had decided we *were* eligible for Rider 13 after all, and they would get all of the necessary paperwork done. I was delighted.

He went on to say he had no real reason to be at the earlier meeting except for one thing. He said he had been in charge of utility construction contracts for many years and had overseen over a quarter of a billion dollars in new construction work. "With all that work and all the associated contracts, I thought I had seen all the good negotiators in the world," he explained. "However, I was told I had yet to see one of the best. I decided to come along that day to see him in action!" I took that as a great compliment, not to me personally, but to my theses and principles of negotiation - integrity, knowledge, and willingness to move to further action.

I was told well more than a decade later, that particular "negotiation" process was still a sore spot with some of the people at the utility.

I assume they must have continued to believe we did not get what we deserved, but rather what we negotiated. On the other hand, I absolutely believe we got what we deserved.

Not all negotiations involve hundreds of thousands of dollars. In 1970, very early in my career and soon after I had taken over as the maintenance foreman in Memphis, an old black gentleman in a beat up truck with a beat up trailer came into the facility and drove over to the maintenance shop. Harold Cook and a couple of the other fellows advised me this was the scrap iron guy. He would pick up all of our old scrap iron and other scrap metal and offer us $5 for it. Harold said it was kind of a game and we would always "bargain him up" to $7.50 or maybe $10 if we had some good stuff.

I remember thinking I should be able to do better than that and after a considerable amount of haggling, the old guy finally agreed to my price of $20. He paid me the 20 bucks and took his load and left. Harold and all the other guys were amazed at my bargaining prowess. Certainly the extra $10 meant nothing to Cargill. I had done it for the satisfaction of "the kill". The old black gentleman on the other hand was doing it for sustenance and my bargaining had likely left nothing in it for profit and perhaps dinner that night.

The fact is the old black gentlemen did not ever return to our plant while I was the maintenance foreman. I had to either stumble over the scrap we generated or find another source of removal. I am sure I got what I deserved!

Certainly, the utility company and the old black gentlemen examples bring forth one of the generally accepted elements of negotiation, the adversarial role of the parties. While this can be and often is the case, when the parties are adversarial, they have failed somewhere at the beginning of the negotiation process. If all relationships can be approached with a win-win mentality, then the negotiation process changes character. It becomes a process of intense requirement definition as well as an exploration exercise in matching requirements with performance capabilities.

When we did refrigeration projects, I did not even get competing bids. I went straight to Jim Salmons and Preston Refrigeration (Chapter 31: "Three Million Dollar Handshake") and began to define and refine our requirements. Jim would also define his requirements, which included things like prerequisite civil and mechanical work, coordination with other trades, etc. When we had fully developed those, Jim could give me the best price and value available in the industry and meet our requirements in their entirety. In turn, I could give Jim work he knew would yield him a fair return. It also gave him a platform from which he could increase his selling power to others. In addition, Jim and I found working together to be a lot of fun.

I work very hard to move all negotiation processes from the modus operandi of the utility company to the Jim Salmons' modus operandi. When that is done, only two of the critical elements are needed: integrity and intelligence. There is never a need to walk away or raise the ante. Walk away only occurs in a friendly environment when both sides determine requirements and capabilities are simply not a match. When negotiation is moved to a relationship-based experience, one can rest assured *what you negotiate will also be what you deserve!*

# CHAPTER 26
# What Size Circle

A picture is worth a thousand words and those who have the skill to sketch can greatly stretch their ability to communicate. I know if I were developing a management curriculum it would include at least a 3 credit hour course in sketching. Yet many of us fail to even attempt drawing because we find straight lines and shapes difficult. Perhaps the most difficult of all is the circle. Getting a smooth arc is not always easy and making the end point match with the originating point is usually a real challenge. We learn early on in life, the smaller the circle we draw, the easier it is and the more likely we are to have it "look good" with the end arriving at our desired destination point.

Difficulty in creation notwithstanding, the circle has been one of the most important geometrical shapes known to man throughout history. From the invention of the wheel to modern times, the circle has stood the test of time. While the functional value of the circle is without question, the circle is just as well known for its symbolic value.

Perhaps the best-known symbolic value is in wedding rings, where the circle represents love that is continuous and has no end. Additionally, the symbolic value of the circle is often used as the representation of closed boundaries, as in a circle of friends or circle of influence, etc. I have always been intrigued by the Olympic symbol of the five circles that are inter-locking and inter-lapping. Their symbolic value is we are all connected in at least some way (inter-locking) and often occupy the same space (inter-lapping). In the Olympic Games, this is through athletic competition and friendship.

I think the business world (as well as our personal worlds) would do very well to take a close look at the Olympic circles. One of the things that creates failure is the inability or unwillingness to look at how actions affect other people and disciplines. If we could better understand that most of our lives and activities are done within an environment shared by others, many times lots of others, we would have far fewer problems and eventual conflicts. We tend to act as though we live in a vacuum and our small circle is the only one in the universe. Accordingly, we take action without regard for, or perhaps consciousness of, how it may affect others.

The business world makes significant use of the symbolism of the circle, both consciously and unconsciously. Certainly one of the business "circles" of great importance and at the same time one of the most pervasive is when we "draw a circle" around a given boundary to measure performance, progress, condition or whatever.

Obviously, the breadth of those boundaries noted (the size of the circle) has a dramatic impact on what those measurements will be and consequently what actions may be taken to influence those measurements. The bigger the circle is drawn, the more likely it is to be performance driven while the smaller the size of the circle, the more likely it is to be personally or politically driven.

You may remember Eldred Swoboda, the union steward in Chapter 12. Most individual union members and most union stewards tend to draw their circle around only one person and circumstance when a labor dispute occurs. Eldred did not stop there. He tested the influence of any potential resolution on all union members both in the present and in the future. He also was cognizant of how it might impact the competitive position of the company from which all member benefits ultimately came. The effect of drawing this larger circle was to assure the overall good of all employees on a long-term basis.

In 1990 we needed to clean the accumulated sludge from the anaerobic lagoons at the Beardstown facility. Cost estimates for doing this were in the $300,000 range. It so happened at that time I attended a pork producer's conference where I made the acquaintance of Gary Chamness. Gary was an entrepreneurial young man who had carved out a small niche pumping out and land injecting manure from farm storage lagoons. As we conversed about his business, I asked him if he felt he could handle much larger lagoons.

After some discussion, Gary was sufficiently interested to schedule a visit to Beardstown to investigate. Following an on-site analysis, Gary was convinced he could clean the lagoons and inject the sludge on our farmland. He gave us a price of $165,000 to do this work. Since this work was significantly larger than the work he had been doing, I asked him again if he was sure he could produce. He was, so we awarded him a contract to do the work.

Gary anxiously began and had operated only a few days when he contacted me and informed me his "lagoon end" equipment did not have the size and muscle to get the job done. I asked Gary what he proposed and he told me it would take a dredge to do the work. He had located a dredge and was willing to invest in it at a cost of $110,000, but his banker was apparently nervous about the whole project and would not loan him the money.

Our choices seemed limited. Under all of our prescribed and standard operating procedures, we would terminate the contract for cause and seek to recover our down payment from Gary. Drawing the circle around these standard operating procedures would have been the safe harbor. However, the larger circle included both Gary's well- being as well as the fact that if we could make Gary successful, we would get the work done for about one half of what it would otherwise cost. It seemed in the best short-term and long-term interest of both Cargill and Gary to find a way to keep Gary on the job.

I asked Gary if he could "survive" the job with cash payments of only $55,000 and title to a dredge. He said he could. I then began the process of slashing red tape, ignoring SOPs, and jumping through a series of hoops to guarantee the purchase of the dredge with Cargill money and then allow Gary to work off the entire cost in the one-time cleaning of our lagoons.

We bought the dredge. Gary used it and at the end of the job it was his, along with the $55,000 in payments. We were still able to get the entire job done for the $165,000 total we had originally contracted for. I was thrilled, although certain elements of the company (who actually knew the arrangements) thought I was crazy for running the risk of owning a dredge and still having to ultimately pay someone else $300,000 to clean the lagoons.

Gary was no more done with the job in Beardstown than the Excel guys in Dodge City were asking how we were able to get our lagoons cleaned so inexpensively. As may be expected, Gary loaded up and went to our plant in Dodge City. Today, Gary Chamness owns a very successful waste stream management business. Cargill is his largest customer and has been receiving value from Gary for well over a decade. All of this because a couple of willing accomplices and I were willing to draw a larger circle based on performance.

Interestingly, over the years, there were few jobs Gary did for Excel Pork where he did not draw his circle all the way back around the Beardstown project in 1990. Gary recognized this was pivotal in the dramatic growth of his company. He did not take lightly the efforts we made on his behalf, even though we may selfishly have profited as well.

Not all circles have as happy an ending as Gary's. For many years, the secretaries and administrative assistants made travel arrangements within Cargill. The arrangements were made through the use of whatever resources they could find. We have been blessed with some superior assistants who could be counted on to make sure our travel would come off efficiently and with minimum hassle.

The corporate hierarchy then acted and determined the company could save money by having all travel coordinated by a third party. Ostensibly, this *independent* organization could consolidate handling costs, spread similar overhead, use their size in the market to secure the best rates, and put their considerable expertise to use in providing superior customer service to all Cargill travelers. It looked really good on paper!

It seemed the only thing missing was the size of the circle was apparently too small to include the traveler. Moreover, as time progressed, there were times when neither the traveler nor Cargill's financial well-being seemed to be included in the circle. The circle seemed to be drawn very narrowly around the best interests of the third party and perhaps sometimes around only the arrangement maker him or herself.

I heard horror stories from all sorts of Cargill travelers about not getting the best rates or about getting thoroughly messed up arrangements. While I may often dismiss some or most of this type of complaint as hearsay, my own experience told me most, if not all, were probably well founded in fact.

Throughout most of the decade of the 90s I traveled extensively to Ottumwa, Iowa and stayed at a Days Inn close to the plant. My cost was $37.40 per night. In 1999, I stopped spending much time in Ottumwa. By late 2000, when I was again assigned a project in Ottumwa, the Days Inn had closed. I called the corporate travel group to get a motel room and was told it would be at the Fairfield Inn. I was told the rate would be about $61 plus tax. Thinking that substantially above what I paid only a couple of years prior, I raised the question as to whether that was the best rate in Ottumwa. I was assured it was about the normal Ottumwa rate and further, all Cargill travelers to Ottumwa stayed at the Fairfield Inn.

I dutifully agreed and proceeded to do my traveling business. The Fairfield Inn was (and is) a very nice hotel and I began staying there. I paid the $68 total bill on departing and winced a little, but went on my way. Then on one trip I failed to meet Mike Dallan, who I was expecting to be at the hotel ahead of me. The next day when we met at the plant, I quizzed him about not getting in the night before. "Oh, I was here," he explained.

During further conversation about why we hadn't met, Mike informed me he always stayed at the Super 8 since it was about $20 per night less expensive! On subsequent trips, I began asking our travel arranger for the Super 8 only to be challenged as to why I would want to stay there. "It's $20 per night cheaper!" I explained. Even then I would have to argue each time. I finally gave up and just called the Super 8 direct, which was a No-No in the overall corporate travel arrangement scheme of things.

While I cringe at the thought of needlessly spending the extra $20 per night, I am even more appalled at the experience of Kelly Young, one of our high performing young supervisors. We scheduled Kelly to attend a seminar in San Diego, California. Since neither Kelly nor her husband had ever been to the West Coast, we suggested she might wish to take an extra day to include a weekend and make a small vacation out of it.

Kelly called the corporate travel people to get airline rates to go to San Diego on the given days. She asked for the best rates for her own personal needs, since she was paying for her husband's ticket, as well as for the company's benefit. Kelly was given a rate of about $550 per person. She then went to an on-line e-travel group and found rates for $236 per person. She booked those rates and saved the company over $300 on her ticket.

Unfortunately, the story didn't end there. The unconscionable part was when Kelly submitted her expense report she did not get an "Atta-

Boy" or rather "Atta-Girl" for saving $300. Instead, she was handed a rather strict dressing down for not using the corporate travel group. She was further informed failure to use this group on future travel could result in failure to be reimbursed.

I would like to believe these are isolated instances, but I think they are not. When engaged in casual conversation with one of Cargill's international travelers, he told me he could get tickets himself for $2000, but when purchasing through the corporate travel group they were over $4000. Perhaps there were (are) rebates to Cargill at the end of the year I am not aware of, but if so, I doubt if they are 50%. Moreover, the overt message that gets sent to travelers throughout the year is cost is not important, only adherence to procedure.

I have to question how the company could have moved so far. I remember the Cargill of 1969 that moved me out of the North Star Inn at $35 per night and into the Curtis at $8.00 per night as soon as I was on the payroll (Chapter 7). Certainly this sent me a very positive cost control message. Is this the same company that has allowed circles to be drawn so narrowly as to "throw away" $20 each night a traveler stays in Ottumwa, Iowa? Moreover, how many times does the $20 loss or the $300 loss or even the $2000 loss get multiplied over and over again with tens of thousands of employees all over the world?

As one looks back over all of the chapters in this book, or even forward to those that remain, it is easy to see virtually all of the examples and anecdotes recounted could be redefined in terms of the size of the circle drawn. Consider Doug Brooks in Chapter 2 and his ability to encircle not only what was being said, but also the perspective from which it was being said and the perspective from which it was being heard. Or, what about the ability of any of the great salespersons of Chapter 24 to encompass the real needs (recognized and unrecognized) of the customer? Certainly the relationship based entities of Chapter 31 and the all-inclusive manner of treating each circumstance as an opportunity to share victory is a prime example of drawing a circle larger than oneself. In many or most other experiences related; the size and inclusiveness of the circles or spheres of impact and stake holding were critical factors in the positive or negative results generated.

As many episodes of narrowly or broadly drawn circles as I have encountered in the past several decades, few stand out so vividly or are so memorable as what I encountered at a chromium symposium I attended in Washington D.C. in the early 80s. At the time, we were involved in the first stage of leather tanning at two of our beef facilities. In this process, hides were taken through the chroming process.

The chrome tanning process involved removing the hair, preparing the hide to "take the tan" and then the actual tan (immobilizing the proteins by tying them up with chromium). The term tanning came from the original process where vegetable extracts were used to immobilize the proteins and this process left the hide tan in color–thus the term tanning. The chrome process turns the hides blue in color and is sometimes referred to as "bluing" or "in the blue." The blue hides were then shipped to tanneries for the intermediate and final steps in converting them to fine leather.

At that time, chromium (chrome) was in the spotlight as a possible carcinogen. Certainly this was a critical issue for us. We did not wish to be handling a product that was carcinogenic. We took a certain sense of relief in the conventional thinking of the time that hexavalent chrome was a likely carcinogen, but trivalent chrome, which was the type we used, was not. When Excel got word a worldwide chromium symposium was being held it was determined I should be in attendance.

I dutifully made my arrangements to go to Washington D.C. and pay the exorbitant local fares attendant there ($68 a night would have been a huge bargain even then). While we certainly had a stakeholder interest, we also wanted to know the facts. If chrome was a problem, we at least wanted to know so we could be properly guided. High costs in Washington D.C. notwithstanding, however, it did not take long for me to decide this was not so much a symposium to find answers as it was a forum on which to promote one's position on the issue. Perhaps it was fitting that the symposium was in Washington D.C., where drawing small circles and "spinning" one's position is always the order of the day.

I sat and listened as researcher after researcher described his or her work with white mice (or maybe they were white rats–a rodent is a rodent). The first would detail how his studies of exposing the rodents to high levels of chromium (in the absence of virtually everything else to conclusively prove any ill effects were the result of the chromium) showed no ill effects on the animals at all therefore proving beyond any reasonable doubt chrome was not carcinogenic. Another researcher who would detail just the opposite results and conclude beyond a shadow of a doubt chrome was carcinogenic to the $n^{th}$ degree would then follow him or her.

This bantering of opposite "science" continued for most of the two-day session. In most of the discussions, it seemed to me the results of the studies were directly related to the interests of the parties funding the studies. Circles were drawn very narrowly to help impact the results in a given direction. Generally I became so disenchanted and bored with the entire process I virtually stopped paying very close attention.

Just as I had given up hope of any real value coming from this journey, a rather common type guy strode to the podium for his presentation. This researcher began by saying the study he would be discussing dealt with real people in a locale with a chrome-roasting (processing of the chromium ore into usable chemicals) factory. His research looked at people who had been residents of the specific area for some 40 years or longer.

This particular study divided the "participants" into four separate categories. Category 1 involved people who had been long time residents of the area and did not work in the chrome factory or smoke. Category 2 people were long time residents who smoked, but did not work in the chrome factory. Category 3 people were similar residents who worked in the chrome factory, but did not smoke. Finally, Category 4 people were those senior residents who smoked and also worked in the chrome factory.

The study then set out to analyze the cancer occurrence rate of each category over the past certain number of years. Category 1 predictably had the lowest rate and this rate was set to zero with all other categories then compared. I do not recall the exact numbers, but I do recall the general relationships. We were told Category 2 people had an incidence rate of 10. We were then informed Category 3 people also had an incidence rate of 10.

As the speaker went on, I'm sure most of us in the crowd were already figuring out the answer to Category 4. I assumed most average thinkers in the crowd were simply adding 10 and 10 together and getting 20 as the most likely answer for the incidence rate in the final category. Of course, I was a much deeper thinker and I had already determined the number would be something less than 20 since some of the smokers in Category 2 and some of the factory workers in Category 3 likely had similar pre-disposition to the cancerous components, and therefore adding the additional risk would not impact them. After all, any one person could only be counted as getting cancer once.

As the speaker started into the discussion of Category 4, I sat with a certain smugness. "The incidence rate then for Category 4 people," the speaker noted, "was 40!!" I sat straight up in my chair. My first reaction was shock that I had been so far off. However, that shock soon gave way to the incredible truth of the entire matter. The health risks of smoking and chrome exposure were synergistic.

That example has stuck with me and has greatly impacted my approach to a number of known health hazards as well as a myriad of things that may or may not be hazards. I do not stand downwind of the nozzle when I am filling my car with gasoline for example. I am much more aware of and concerned about the affects of various chemicals, herbicides, pesticides and the like. I have become aware even minute amounts of certain materials that may be harmless on their own, may create dynamite when combined with others in the larger circle. The scary part is we do not know what most, or hardly any, of the formulations are.

Beyond the practical lesson learned, I remain in awe of the chrome researcher's ability *and willingness* to draw a circle big enough to encompass the real life conditions and let the results be what they would be. Inevitably, that is almost always the challenge; draw the circle big enough to encompass the real life conditions. If we do that, we will affect performance that is optimum under real life conditions.

Unfortunately, just as we draw small circles on paper so we can manage the curvature of the arc and make the end come to our desired point, we often draw our management (as well as our personal) boundary circles small for the same reasons. We are not as interested in performance by encompassing all the real life conditions as we are in being able to "spin" a more limited set of conditions within the circle to our own advantage. More importantly, we want to be sure we can make the end point arrive at our desired destination.

# CHAPTER 27
# Timing

A few years ago there was a Seiko advertisement I think is one of the classics. It began with the steps of a professional man walking briskly down the sidewalk. I do not recall the name given to the man, but let's call him Steve. The narrative began by saying, "This is a key day in the life of Steve. Today he will engage the woman of his dreams."

At this point the scene shifted to the brisk steps of a well-dressed and attractive professional woman. The narrative went on, "This woman is a successful lawyer who will go on to become a well respected judge. She will become Steve's wife and the mother of his three lovely children."

As this narrative goes on, the scene shifts back and forth between the man's steps and the woman's steps as they are obviously headed toward each other on an apparent collision course. Just then the woman passes by and Steve is a couple of steps behind the collision path and the two simply walk on. As the collision is obviously avoided, the narrative continues, "Unfortunately Steve's watch is off by a few seconds and he is running a little late today!!!" The sales line is with a Seiko timepiece, you will always be exactly on time and you will not miss the opportunity of a lifetime as Steve apparently did.

As I have noted in past chapters, I am a bit of a connoisseur of TV commercials. I think the really effective ones are those that entertain, create memory of the product, and apply key life principles and/or situations. I think this one fits all of those categories.

You may recall from Chapter 6: "Heroes," the somewhat chance meeting of my wife and I. As one recalls that story, the most apparent key to our meeting was my car did in fact start on that very cold December day. That notwithstanding, timing likely played as big a part as my car. Had I arrived at the Memorial Union a few minutes or perhaps even a few seconds earlier, the three young ladies may not yet have arrived and created the opportunity for me to fill the fourth seat at their table. Or had I arrived a few moments later, the chance is good the fourth seat would have already been occupied by someone else (male or female). I would have been forced to find a seat somewhere else. In either event, I think it would be highly unlikely I would have engaged my future wife that day.

Steve's experience in the TV advertisement was not an impossible happening. In fact, it happens numerous times daily. It is often said knowledge and action are not as important as timing. Steve found that out. Certainly we all know timing is the critical factor in investing; be it securities, new businesses, new products, plant expansions etc. It is often not as important whether we are ultimately right as whether we are properly timed.

One can be absolutely correct in the *general* direction of a market or a stock, but if there is even a modest reversal of that direction before the predicted major move; disaster can occur. An investor without sufficient staying power can get wiped out before there is a chance to capitalize on the major move. One can be correct and yet broke.

Timing in the management of business and industry is subject to that same set of rules. In the late 60s, Cargill wished to purchase a corn processing facility in Cedar Rapids, Iowa. The owner of this facility was willing to sell, but also owned a soybean processing facility in Cedar Rapids and wanted a package deal. Since Cargill already owned a soybean facility in the same town, they were really only interested in the corn facility.

As the story is told (perhaps with some embellishment), the owner told the Cargill people, "Look, I want to sell both, and here is the combined price. If you wish to buy only the corn processing facility, that is okay, but the price is still the same. So you can pay the price and get only the corn facility or you can pay the same price and get both. You decide."

Well obviously if you are paying for something in the deal, you just as well take possession of it. This is the facility (Cedar Rapids East) that is detailed in Chapter 15: "The Family." Within a few short years of this purchase, the soybean business became very lucrative and the Cedar Rapids East facility paid for itself many times over in the decade of the 70s.

This wasn't even a question of correctly predicting a market. It was an example of great timing, however. Owning this facility during the very good times was an economic boon that began as an unwanted stepchild. The old adage, "You don't have to be good, just lucky!" could be paraphrased, "You don't have to be smart, just timed right!"

In a soybean processing facility, the primary fat product is crude soybean oil. This is the product that was made at the Cedar Rapids East plant at the time of the purchase and on into the early 70s. Many plants took the oil one step further and did the first step in the refining process by degumming the oil. This process removed the phosphatides (gums) and created a more transparent oil. Most of these facilities added the phosphatides back into the meal stream. The exception to this was the Memphis plant that further processed these into lecithin, as described in the Jimmie Williams' story in Chapter 16.

During the mid 70s, the processing capacity for degummed oil became very tight. Margins for degummed oil soared. As Cargill looked around for opportunities to capitalize on this, the Cedar Rapids facility jumped out immediately. We had the second largest capacity to produce soybean oil in the company at over 750,000 pounds per day (second only to Memphis at about a million). Further, we were the only major Cargill plant not currently producing degummed oil.

We were told to secure a no longer used Westphalia centrifuge from the San Francisco Copra (coconut meats) plant and to get a degumming system in ASAP. As I have discussed in earlier chapters, soybean extraction operations use hexane, a gasoline like product that is highly explosive. There are no cutting or welding processes allowed in these areas and even the tools must have special coatings.

We proceeded to complete the entire installation in just a few weeks. Everything had to be measured in the extraction facility, fabricated in the shop, carted to the extraction facility and then bolted in place. Any cutting in the extraction area had to be done with a hand or air operated hacksaw and carefully at that. This was a monumental task that was completed in record time. The millwright foreman on the job even had a broken toe (not injured on the project) he had to contend with along the way.

With the installation complete we had the assignment of getting the Westphalia to operate. This was something neither the Des Moines nor San Francisco plants had been able to achieve. With the able help of

John Kinney who had been chased from Des Moines to San Francisco and now to Cedar Rapids by this machine, we were not only able to get it to operate, but were able to get it beyond its rated capacity and degum our full stream.

While this is a story about an extraordinary effort to get a project completed under very challenging conditions, it is even more a story about timing. We were able to tap into a market with a capacity shortfall. We did this with a very high volume of product and capitalized on that market at its peak. The entire installation paid for itself many times over just in the next few months.

Cargill's history is replete with examples as noted above where great timing, sometimes with extra-ordinary effort and sometimes virtually without any conscious effort, has resulted in a high level of earnings, which has allowed the company to grow and expand. Chapter 21, which is largely a series of stories about Ernie Micek and his ability to cut red tape, could easily be recast as a chapter dealing with timing. This is certainly not coincidental. Red tape is the antithesis of rapid action. Rapid action is usually the precursor to tapping into an opportunity that is time sensitive.

In the early 80s, Estee Lauder introduced a new product on the cosmetics market called Night Repair. This was a little bottle (0.87 ounces) that retailed at that time for $35. Its market claim was it could help reduce dry skin problems. The directions were to put a little on any dry skin spot, like elbows or heels, and then rub a cold cream type material over that. The key ingredient in Night Repair was a product called hyaluronic acid or HA for short. HA has incredible hygroscopic properties and can hold hundreds of times its weight in water. It would hold the moisture and healing ingredients in the cold cream in place all night and in effect "repair the dry skin over night".

Interestingly, the natural supply of HA was very limited. It occurred naturally in recoverable quantities in only three places; umbilical cords, rooster combs, and vitreous humor (eyeball fluid). Most of the commercially available material at the time was recovered from rooster combs. Because of the limited supply and the difficulty of recovery, this product fetched a price in the market in the range of $1000 per gram. That's about a half a million dollars per pound for non-mathematicians.

Some of the people in the Minneapolis Research Department had begun the process of looking for ways to add value to the businesses we were in. As they were made aware of this product they were attracted to its potential for our beef business. After slaughter, cattle heads, including eyes, were rendered for animal protein feeds. Certainly the cattle eyeballs, which contained about 5 milligrams of HA each, had little value in rendering. If we could recover those 5 mg of HA, we could make each eyeball worth about $5.00. Multiplied by two eyeballs per animal and several thousand animals per day, this was a significant opportunity.

So the chemists and technicians in the backroom at The Cargill Central Research Facility put together the chemical process to remove and purify the HA. They then sent this process to us to put together the physical and mechanical systems to effect the chemical process. My staff and I put together these systems along with a very unique device for recovering the vitreous humor from the slaughtered cattle heads. We collected about 70 gallons of the eyeball fluid, rented a pilot plant facility in Lake Mills, Wisconsin, and gathered there with the central research people to conduct the pilot run.

We were able to produce the product at a purity of between 90 and 95 percent, which we knew was not yet good enough. However, we felt we had the necessary knowledge of what it would take to get high purity and we had a good idea of what our production costs would likely be. From the pilot work we projected full scale operating costs in the range of $100 to $125 per gram or about $50,000 per pound. With market prices in the $1000 per gram range, this would still leave a handsome margin.

A couple of the research people, including Carol Pletcher, and I hurried off to Long Island, New York with a sample of our product to meet with the Estee Lauder people. The Estee Lauder people were extremely cordial. They told us our product was obviously not pure enough, but they assumed we knew how to manufacture it in a more pure form. They then hit us with the bombshell. "Take a hard look at what your production costs will be," they entreated. "The biotechnical people are just breaking through with the ability to create this product through biotechnical methods. We believe costs for the biotechnical production will be in the $25 per gram range!"

The limited supply resource was about to go away. Biotechs could make this stuff by the busload. We walked out of the Estee Lauder facility without much hope. We knew that at even $75 or $80 per gram, our most liberal cost projections, we could not compete with the biotech guys. It was great timing for them. For us it was too little, too late. We were correct in that we could make the product and we were correct in that there was a ready market. Timing changed the market economics dramatically, however. Unfortunately it changed them before we could capitalize on our resource!! Fortunately it changed them before we invested millions in a full scale manufacturing facility!!!

As the years went by, Cargill continued to seek opportunities such as HA. Certainly some of these were timed well and resulted in successful ventures. In the late 90s one of the hot products on the market was chondroitin and glucosamine for the treatment of joint problems like arthritis. The chondroitin component of this comes from cartilage type material (chondro means cartilage). Early on, much of this came from shark cartilage. One of the best places to secure a lot of cartilage material is in trachea. The best source of this is beef trachea. Again, if you are processing thousands of cattle per day for meat purposes, a lot of trachea is generated and ultimately handled at low value. As with the eyeballs of the HA example, the beef trachea was primarily rendered.

Suddenly, beef trachea had a value. We were glad for the increased value. Moreover, we were intrigued by the process of creating chondroitin sulfate from the trachea. If others could capitalize on our product, shouldn't we also. Again, the men and women in the backroom at the central research facility began work on this in the early part of 1998. In the summer of that year, Cargill had licensed a processing technology and Bryan Yeh, a bright young production manager from the corn and soybean processing businesses of Cargill was given the assignment of developing the plant facility. In the early autumn of that year I was given the part time assignment of joining Bryan's team as the "meat solutions" expert.

Again, the "young" Ernie Micek modus operandi of *move quickly to action when opportunity approaches or watch it from the rear as it passes* seemed to be applicable. However, the company, now headed by an older Ernie, just couldn't make it happen that fast. Try as we may to move the process along rapidly through some of the bureaucratic quagmires, even with a young aggressive knowledgeable Bryan Yeh, a seasoned veteran Jim Roth, and a few other cast members, we could not move the locomotive forward. In April of 2000, fully two years after the "charge" to go, we started the facility.

Certainly there was (and is) still time to capitalize on the chondroitin market although the initial luster was off. More importantly, with time delay comes decay of the mental sharpness and the absolute can-do approach that is born of rapid and sustained action. Take note of how few baseball games that are played following a rain delay have the same level of intensity and performance as prior to the delay. Missed timing inevitably makes for a steeper mountain to climb.

Not all timing issues have to do with economics and missed markets. In 1987 when we took over the Beardstown operation we were interested in what non-monetary benefits we could provide to the employees. The former owner had "closed the doors" paying production workers in the range of $10.00 to $10.50 per hour. We reopened those doors and as a result of competitive pressures, we were proposing a reduction from those levels of pay. Even so, we expected to rehire many of the same people. Recognizing none of us are very thrilled about taking a cut in pay, we wanted to try to address other employee needs if possible.

One of the things employees told us there was a need for was daycare for their children. Some even went so far as to say a daycare center located on site would be most beneficial. Such a location would make the management of drop off and pick up virtually automatic. These people also noted perhaps they could even eat lunch with their children and that too would be a worthwhile benefit. Since one of the transferring wives, Nancy Imholdt, had little to do immediately after the move; she volunteered to investigate the requirements for a daycare center at the plant site.

After some time and research, Nancy had put together all the necessary information to initiate some form of further action. I took the issue to one of my bosses at the time for discussion and further action. He listened somewhat impatiently to my explanation and request for the needed resources to move to the next step. He then looked at me and spoke in a rather short and measured tone, "What do you think this is anyway Jim . . . a social club?!" On-site daycare centers were obviously not yet recommended in the "Big Black Book at Harvard," and our dreams of a daycare center died on that day in 1987.

Maybe those dreams died in 1987 because my boss did not want us to become a social club. I think we faced an uphill battle even if we could have secured his support. We were ahead of our time. The time had not yet arrived in Cargill (and much of the industrial world) for such forward thinking employee services. Interestingly, by the late 90s, the Beardstown facility was actively looking for a place to provide daycare services for the employees. *Recent* surveys had indicated the employees had that need!!

There were several other instances in the late 80s where the Beardstown management team was ahead of Cargill in a number of pro-active management measures; reduced supervisory and manager levels, management/employee interaction, highly restricted smoking areas, alcohol restrictions at company functions and production/maintenance operational interaction to name a few. Interestingly, at the time we were held in a certain degree of contempt for many of these, yet only a decade later most all had become the company standard.

Perhaps in this case we were just running too far ahead of schedule. Our watch was not slow, but rather too fast and we passed the point of collision long before the rest of the company arrived there. On my twenty-fifth anniversary with Cargill in 1994, I received a SEIKO watch. I wonder if they were sending me a message!!

# Chapter 28
# Short Skirts and High Heels

I have never been much of a reader, but when I began traveling to Taiwan and Europe in the early 90s I discovered reading was a superb way to pass the time during 3, 6, and in particular 12 hour flights. Although I often secured reading material before the flights, I sometimes relied on the bookstores in the airports through which I passed. I was particularly fond of one of the bookstores in the San Francisco airport.

During the San Francisco stop on one of my journeys to Taiwan, I was browsing through this bookstore when a particular title caught my eye, *Boobs, Boys, and High Heels* by Dianne Brill. Being somewhat amused by the title and curious about the content, I picked up the book and thumbed through it. Although I did not buy it, I found myself reading enough of it in the bookstore I probably should have at least paid rent to the bookstore or royalty to Ms. Brill.

As one could guess from the title, this was a book written for women about how to attract men (boys) using body parts (boobs et al) and attire (high heels et al). Many people have written about the physical nature of sexuality in men versus the more mental nature in women, so I did not find the general thesis of this book out of step with common knowledge. What I did find interesting, at least in those parts I read, was the manner in which the author instructed women in the particulars of sending messages to men using the above referenced tools at their disposal, namely physical parts and attire. The instructions included the specific management of these things. I had to admit many of the things she instructed had exactly the desired effect on me she predicted.

A few years ago, I heard a woman caller to a self-help talk show voice concern that her 4-year-old son was infatuated with her breasts. The talk show host politely reported that such an infatuation put the boy in the same category with about 98 percent of all the other males in the world and there was likely nothing too much to worry about. Years earlier, one of my college friends commenting on girls (my wife included) who he had seen me date, remarked I always seemed to come up with girls who were "well endowed." My wife in particular will tell you another of her physical attributes I have always been infatuated with (and still am) are her nice legs. In view of that, I have always liked short skirts that show off those legs and high heels that add a certain swagger to the walk and extra femininity and sexiness. I am fairly certain most of these things keep me in that 98 percent category as well.

As I mentioned in Chapter 6, my wife, Chris, has always done an excellent job of increasing her attractiveness by focusing on those things I find alluring. Although with age she has become much more reluctant to wear short skirts, she has found skirts with judiciously placed slits or buttons (rather unbuttons) are quite good substitutes. I am also fond of her wearing high heels and although age has lowered the "high" a little, they still wear very well on her. Whenever Chris is attired in this way, she sends two messages to me.

The first message is she is an alluring and sensuous woman. It is a rare occasion when I do not receive this message. Not surprisingly, that message may also accrue to anyone else who may view her whether Chris intends that or not. Remember the Chapter 6 episode at the Left Guard restaurant in Minneapolis. This message sent is generally universal with most women and the message received is also fairly universal with most men. Only the intensity or amplitude of the message changes with the person.

The second message Chris sends is one that says, "I care enough for you that I choose to dress in this way to please you." I am afraid I often do not receive that message with the proper recognition of effort such action requires. Certainly, walking around in high heels requires a lot more "comfort" sacrifice than I tend to acknowledge. Maybe I should take my thesis in Chapter 2 literally and walk around for a day or so in high heels so I can fully appreciate Chris's second message. However, I fear doing that in public may cause *me* to send a very unintended message.

Certainly, unintended message sending as well as intended message sending happens on a daily basis in all environments including the business and industrial settings. These messages may be implicit or explicit. Unfortunately, whether explicit or implicit, intended or unintended, the messages are often received without regard for the manner in which they are sent.

When I was managing the production function in the corn processing facilities (first Cedar Rapids and then Memphis) in the late 70s, margins were good, but not so good that we did not maintain a focus on generating as good a yield as possible on each of the various products we derived from a kernel of corn. The product with the highest per unit value was the germ even though it made up only about 6 percent of the total mix. We knew failure to capture the maximum amount of germ would result in revenue loss as it would then wind up in the fiber, the product with the lowest per unit value. To do this maximization, we had to optimize the germ recovery components of the milling system.

As the years passed, corn-processing margins became and remained very good. So good in fact, the more production that could be pushed through a facility, with little regard for efficiency, the more profit could be recognized on the bottom line. The explicit message sent to all parts of the production operation was to maximize the total volume of raw material put through the facility. The implicit message was yields and efficiencies were of secondary importance.

Although never intended, over the course of a couple of decades the message on germ yields became one of indifference. While the germ had to be separated to make the rest of the system work, volume was so critical that maximization of yields was not much of an issue. Operating people became extremely good at driving volume to the maximum. Without specifically trying, yield-achieving expertise slipped away.

In the mid to late 90s, the market demand neared maturation and margins began to shrink. Maximization of yields suddenly became more important and ultimately became critical. Our son, Derek, worked for the Cargill Corn Processing group as an intern in the summer of 1998. Of particular interest to me was his involvement with the "Germ Team." This was a group assembled to "re-understand" the germ recovery maximization process. It seemed so many generations of operating people had come and gone since there had last been a focus on yield maximization that as a company we had lost our understanding of how to do it effectively. We now had to go through a re-learning and re-education process.

As in the above example, unintended messages are received and processed and the results are often not what we desired. Obviously, it is always best when the message sent and received is common and also is the one specifically desired. You may recall the discussion of the Processing Division equal employment seminar in the mid 70s from Chapter 20. The group conducting this seminar attempted to bring us up to speed on the legal requirements of the equal employment opportunity laws as well as to "heighten" our awareness of the diversity of the workforce and how to capitalize on that diversity.

To this end, one of their theses was that it was necessary to create an atmosphere for the various diverse groups within which they could have a high comfort level. This included the dress codes as noted in Chapter 20 as well as a number of other areas. One of these areas dealt with the spoken word and, in particular, profane and vulgar language. We were informed of a popular vulgar expression "of the Black community" and told we both needed to get used to that term and accept it as a normal part of corporate speech.

First of all, I am continually amazed at what we call and fail to call prejudice. Here were so-called sensitivity teachers of anti-bias (a black man among them) trying to point out how racially prejudiced we all were whether we realized it or not. Yet, the very example they were using suggested a racially biased tone of their own. To suggest a given vulgar term is indigenous to the Black community should be abhorrent to all Blacks. Certainly I had heard, and continue to this day to hear, this expression countless times from the lips of non-Blacks. The suggestion Blacks "exclusively own" this term is a slap in the face of every Black person.

My own thinking notwithstanding, the seminar leaders began our indoctrination of the popular acceptance of this term by using it in common speech and then informing us they would be continuing to use it liberally during the seminar to "heighten" our sensitivity. At this point Jerry Mitchell, one of the processing division executives, stepped forward and set the record straight.

"Look, I don't care what native street language may be common with any particular group of people," he began. "We do not now condone profane, abusive, or vulgar language in any of our operations and we are not about to adopt that as any part of sensitivity or anything else. Further, if you wish to continue to teach and train us in this seminar you will refrain from the use of any of that type of speech as well! We do not believe that position is in conflict with any laws and if it is, we'll take our chance on defending ourselves!"

Jerry sent a very explicit and intended message to the seminar leaders as well as to each of us as participants and also as local managers. I gratefully received that message. We all eventually returned to our local facilities with a clear understanding of what did *not* pass the "sensitivity" test. I credit Jerry with heading off what could have been a very disastrous approach to "diversity" management. Interestingly it was only a few years later we were in "sexual harassment" training recognizing profane and vulgar talk was not only improper, it could be illegal. Jerry's message was a textbook example of a message properly delivered and received.

Jerry Mitchell's highly effective message of the mid 70s was singular, clear in its intent, and delivered one time. Often, messages are not so clear and in fact it is the cumulative effect of mini-messages that create the lasting effect. Employee safety has been preached as a key concern of Cargill's as long as I can remember. Since I have always placed a high value on protecting my co-workers as well as me, I have been a ready receiver of this message. As we continued to strive to improve both our performance and our record, special emphasis had been placed on effectively managing employee safety.

Beginning in the early 70s and on a continuing basis thereafter, we had been through a series of safety training programs, exercises, and processes all designed to deliver the messages of "the what" and "the how" of safety management. To emphasize safety's key importance, incentive programs were to be managed in such a way as to reward good safety results and penalize poor safety performance. How else to better send a message than through one's pocketbook. Ostensibly safety would be on a par with production and profit.

As we assembled the management group at one of our new facilities, people from other plants were brought on board at various times throughout the year. We had worked hard at the safety effort and our performance ranked us in the top third of the facilities. However, start up costs and market conditions had left our business in the red.

At bonus time, all the checks were sent to me for distribution to those among our management team who were fortunate enough to receive one. Only a few of the people who had been on the team for the entire year received a bonus. The fattest bonuses went to those people who had transferred in late in the year and had most of their performance based on the operation from whence they came. What struck me that year was one of the largest bonus checks I handed out went to a recent transfer from one of the other plants that had produced well, but had a very poor safety performance.

I'm sure the message to this person and others who were treated similarly was production was still more financially beneficial than safety. Unfortunately, word also gets around! Sadly, over the next few years that message continued to get reinforced, both implicitly and explicitly. Within a short time, this operation had improved in some of the production measurements, but had become one of the poorest safety performers in the company. Only when the reward mechanism matched the verbal proclamation did the message become clear that safety was indeed a top priority and performance began to improve.

Positive and negative examples of message sending that have direct and significant impact on the business as just noted abound. In addition, there are lots of examples of message sending that are unique, interesting, and even non verbal. Many of these have absolutely no impact on the business. Often these are the most fun to observe as nothing is really "riding" on them. One of my favorites involves Phyllis Wolfe, one of the most efficient administrative managers (secretaries) I have had the pleasure of working with. See "Phyllis and the Candy Dish" in the "More Stories" section for this story.

Messages are also a great teaching and behavioral adjustment device. Certainly no chapter titled such as this one would be complete without a story involving attractive women. As luck has it, just such a story exists and is a prime example of behavioral adjustment. The Beardstown environmental management team throughout the end of the 90s and into the early 2000s was made up principally of five people; me, Mike Richtig and Bill Leischner, both of whom you have already met, and the two attractive young women just noted, Kelly Young, who you have also met, and Julia Leischner.

Each of us brought separate and unique talents and knowledge to the mix. While we did not necessarily attempt to conduct all activities in a "democratic" manner, that is usually the way it worked out simply because each of us had something to offer and we each recognized that in the others. External persons committed to "finding" the decision maker in the team and focusing efforts on that person were doomed to failure.

In the summer of 2000 we were completing the compost system equipment procurement process and had come down to a final product screener. This was an investment in the $100,000 plus range. We asked Kelly to collect data on a number of potential vendors and various unit models. Kelly went to work and secured the information requested. Paul, a sales representative from one of the vendors, asked Kelly who the decision maker was and essentially what *man* he could speak to about his system. Kelly politely told him it would be a team decision. Paul then asked her who the *key man* on the team was. Kelly reluctantly told him that was likely me and then promptly reported the conversation to me.

Now I firmly believe men and women are different. I am further quite glad of that and happy with the arrangement. Nonetheless, nothing in that belief suggests men are better decision makers or even better mechanics than women. Few things infuriate me more than someone, man or woman, who refuses to acknowledge equality of mental ability.

Bill, Mike and I were ready for Paul. Each time he would call one of us to discuss the qualities of his screening system, we would acknowledge our participation in the team, but then dramatically emphasize Kelly was the ultimate decision maker on this system. While this may seem to be a small lie, Kelly was gathering the information and since it was the information on which we would all rely to make the decision, it was not much of a stretch to call Kelly the ultimate decision maker in this exercise. To further reinforce the equality of the sexes theme, we would also point out Julia's key impact on the process as well.

We sent this message so uniformly and so persistently, Paul finally came to the realization he had to deal with Kelly and women were going to be involved in the decision whether he liked it or not. Even though his prejudices coming in may have been that they didn't have all the required credentials to make the final judgment, his ability to make a sale was going to depend on his ability to sell them, and Kelly in particular. We even had Kelly set up to meet Paul at a site where one of his screeners was in service to evaluate it. We were determined Paul was going to *get* the message.

Prior to Kelly's trip to inspect one of Paul's machines, Mike and I went with Kelly to inspect a competitor's machine so we could coach Kelly on what to look for when she visited Paul. This is not to suggest Kelly had inferior skills, Mike and I simply had the benefit of much more prior experience in machine and process inspections, so such coaching was only natural. Interestingly, Scott, the salesperson for this competitor of Paul's, was as attentive to Kelly as to Mike and I. Ultimately we purchased the unit from Scott's organization and Kelly was the main point person in working with them. Even though Paul didn't make the sale, we remain confident he eventually got the message and we would be surprised if he continued looking past any woman to find a man.

Man or woman, message sending and receiving happens!! It can be rewarding or damaging. It can be profitable or disastrous. It can be intended or unintended. It can be used or abused. Managing body parts and attire as instructed in *Boobs, Boys, and High Heels,* can be lovingly provocative. It can also be seductively corrupting. Which one it is usually depends not on the message, but rather on the messenger!

# CHAPTER 29
# Turn Me Loose

Although I am not much of a movie buff, I do have three favorite movies that I watch over and over: *Hoosiers, Down Periscope, and Dave.* Certainly all of these movies have a certain amount of "feel good" in them and the central characters achieve victory. I do prefer movies with these characteristics, but that is not what makes them special to me.

Interestingly, on the surface they would not seem to have any other common thread. *Hoosiers* is a basketball drama set in the early fifties in a small town in Indiana where a new coach, Norman Dale, played by Gene Hackman, one of my favorite actors, attempts to put together a winning program. *Down Periscope* is a comedy set in modern time about a submarine war game in which an outdated diesel sub captained by a somewhat maverick Navel officer, John Dodge, played by Kelsey Grammer, simulates an attack on the USA eastern sea coast as may be perpetrated by a rouge nation (a movie that takes on some new meaning following September 11, 2001). Finally, *Dave* is a comedy-drama in which a USA presidential look-alike, Dave Kovick, played by Kevin Klein, is utilized as a one night double for the president and is then sequestered into an extended charade when the real president suffers a debilitating stroke.

So what then is the common thread that so endears these three movies to me? In each movie, the main characters are "turned loose" to make good on an opportunity that seems to be out of reach. In each movie, the main characters are able to capitalize on that opportunity. What is even more fascinating is they often accomplish this by using non-conventional methods and by utilizing non-conventional people.

In *Hoosiers*, Coach Dale, a successful college basketball coach, is given a second opportunity to coach (this time with a small town high school team) after being banned from the college ranks for an earlier incident. He accepts this challenge and brings his own brand of discipline and coaching prowess to the small Indiana town of Hickory. His methods are at odds with the general wisdom of the natives, but he stays his course. Utilizing a cast that includes some non-conventional players and assistant coaches, he takes the small town team all the way to the Indiana state championship. It is a heart-warming adventure based on a true story.

In *Down Periscope,* Captain Dodge is given the virtually impossible war game task of penetrating USA high tech defenses and nuclear submarines with an old World War II vintage diesel sub. Captain Dodge is assigned this task by a three star general who is worried that old Russian subs being sold off to rouge nations could pose a threat to USA security. Ostensibly, Dodge is selected for this project because of his past record that includes maverick and non-conventional behavior as well as a rather unusual tattoo. To further complicate his efforts, Dodge is given a crew of apparent rejects. Undaunted, Captain Dodge proceeds to turn his dilapidated vessel and motley crew into a cohesive fighting unit that compliments his own non-conventional naval maneuvers to accomplish the objective.

Finally, in *Dave,* Dave Kovick is pressed into a presidential charade not of his own doing as a result of the debilitating stoke to President Bob Mitchell, also played by Kevin Klein. Expecting he will act as a puppet-figure head, top-level staffers plan to utilize him as a cover to make their own moves to secure the presidency. However, Dave soon sees the "real charade" that is going on with these staffers and within the government and begins to seize the opportunity to make course corrections. Again utilizing some non-conventional methods and non-conventional people like his friend Murray, the First Lady, and secret service agent Duane, Dave is able to make positive things happen for the country.

A final common thread in all three of these movies is that while each of the main characters is doing the *right* thing, each must constantly swim upstream against counter efforts directed against them. These counter efforts are borne primarily of personal gain on the part of the "counter characters" and not generally initiated for the public good.

I am drawn to these movies because the main characters were turned loose to accomplish a task even though the odds were often stacked against them. Once turned loose, they responded not by trying to protect some personal agenda, but by utilizing all the weapons in their arsenal and all the people under their command and within their sphere of influence. What a wonderful parallel to the real world.

Most of us simply want a chance. We just want to be turned loose to utilize our native skills even though they may be somewhat non-conventional and the odds may at times seem to be stacked against us. While we do not expect we will always be flying in the face of counter forces, many of us do in fact remain undaunted by these counter forces and the odds that may be stacked against us both intentionally and unintentionally.

Throughout my career, I have been fascinated by the people who have blossomed when they were given a chance to perform. It is like a flower that is suddenly exposed to the sun's rays and bursts into full bloom. The best corporate example of this was the Cedar Rapids East Soybean plant crew. As you may recall from Chapter 15: "The Family," they had been shackled for years under a very autocratic regime. Much of the success I was credited with at this facility was simply a result of our unshackling them, turning them loose, and giving them a chance to utilize their skills and abilities. Once empowered, they responded with superior performance.

In the early 70s with the expansion of the CRE plant above noted, we needed to add an additional supervisor to handle the logistics function of managing the incoming raw materials and the outgoing finished product. We made our request through the Minneapolis general operations office and were offered Virgil Tharp, a supervisor in his early fifties from another Cargill facility. I had been advised that Virgil was not a particularly strong manager type and the other facility would likely be happy to pawn him off on us.

Being a young manager and assuming I had no choice, I simply accepted Virgil's transfer to our operation. Soon after he had arrived, he stepped into my office one day and asked if it would be okay to purchase a push broom for the grain elevator operation.

"Why are you asking me?" I inquired.

"Well," Virgil stuttered, " You're the boss and I kind of thought we needed a broom and it would be helpful in cleaning the cars. But we can do without!" he quickly added.

"No, no, I'm not opposed," I replied. "I simply don't understand why you think you need to ask me to purchase a $5 item for your department. I expect and want you to manage the department. You control a half a million dollars worth of raw materials and finished product every day. I trust you with that responsibility. Don't you think I would also trust you to manage at least the basic tools to accomplish what I hold you accountable for?"

Virgil was somewhat stunned. "Well, where I came from you weren't allowed to make any of those kinds of decisions!"

"Well where you are now, you are not only allowed, you are expected to make them." I commented in a very positive tone. That simple conversation empowered Virgil to step forward and manage his operation. He was just looking for the chance to perform. Virgil became and remained a solid performer and a key manager for many years. A person who was viewed as marginal by one operation became a stellar performer in another simply by being turned loose to perform.

Ron Dirks who you have met in a number of previous chapters was another prime example. You may recall Ron was the hippy appearing, restless, and sometimes impulsive young man who had just returned from Viet Nam and had become our plant clerk in the early 70s. Ron had a number of strikes against him coming in. I gave him the chance to be the plant clerk. Ron struggled with this position and I fired him or he quit a number of times and then I would rehire him on his promise to improve. In my mind, I was continually giving Ron chances, but I had apparently not really turned him loose to perform to his potential.

Ron's problem was the simple plant clerk position was not challenging enough for his capabilities. My problem was I did not recognize this and while I can credit myself with seeing enough of his ability to continually rehire him, I must accept some responsibility for having to continually go through that exercise. Fortunately, Ron eventually recognized the problem himself and took steps to create his own chance to succeed.

As I noted in an earlier chapter, Ron was the best judge of applicants for employment of anyone with whom I have been acquainted. In Ron's job as the plant clerk, he was in charge of no more than handing the prospective employee a blank application. Ron took it upon himself, however, to conduct his own simple interview and then further took it upon himself to inform me, the ultimate decision maker, of his appraisal. I soon found out he was far better than I and he became the primary decision maker with both my support and endorsement. We could also now see that Ron had far more potential and we began to expand his roles. We turned him loose and he grew, blossomed, became, and has remained a solid plant operations level manager for well over 25 years.

Women often have steep uphill climbs in the business and industrial environment. While the plight of women has improved, it was often particularly pervasive in earlier decades. In 1981 as I had completed the assembling of the engineering and purchasing team at Excel, I determined our department needed a secretary. I had a couple of candidates in mind, both attractive young women with what appeared to be a good work ethic. I approached the Human Resource Department (HRD) leader with my request.

He was a seasoned veteran and agreed that a secretary was needed in our department, but balked at my choices. "I have just the person for you," he explained. "Her name is Linda Sokolosky. She is currently in the HRD department on 21$^{st}$ street. I will set her up for an interview with you." I agreed to the interview knowing it would be no more than a charade as the decision had already been made and any further input from me would be valueless.

Linda was an attractive and very pleasant, but somewhat reserved young woman in her early 30s at the time. The interview went well and I felt at least we would be getting a lady and a decent worker. I was later informed Linda had expressed a serious desire to move out of the HRD department she was in. The engineering department's needs afforded an easy opportunity for HRD to make that happen.

Linda's story is similar to Ron's in that she was far overqualified for a secretarial position. Nevertheless, she performed all the secretarial functions cheerfully and flawlessly. A few months after her arrival we were charged with putting together a $30 million capital proposal for our Dodge City facility. The internal "selling tool" for the fund's request for this was a 30-page report with tables, charts, text etc. Linda was responsible for assembling this report from the various collections of information we supplied.

Once the document was completed, the proofing process began. I refer not to the grammatical proofing, Linda had handled that, but rather to the information proofing. As we continued to find "holes" in the information we had supplied, we re-fed the missing information to Linda. It was Linda's job to work that into the report. Today that is a simple task with word processors; just add the information and it changes all the subsequent pages automatically. Print out the result and go home! However, in 1981 we did not have word processors. Linda demonstrated an incredible ability to compress and condense and mix and match words so that as we changed information she needed only change one or two pages and not retype every subsequent page in the document.

As we watched Linda's performance we recognized it took way more than secretarial skills to do what she was doing. She had to have grasped the general business concepts and nature. She had to have language and vocabulary skills well beyond simple secretarial grammar knowledge. In addition she had to have some very good organizational skills to craft and re-craft the entire report. Finally, she had a certain spunk about her that made her extremely effective in getting us to get our information together, complete and right the first time and without question the second time!

As we endorsed her work on this project, we also recognized her vast abilities and began to tap into her talents. She became the most valuable player in the department. Any one or all of the rest of us manager types could be gone and the department continued to function normally as long as Linda was there. However, whenever Linda was gone, things slowed to a crawl. She so efficiently managed all of us that we almost lost the ability to manage ourselves in her absence.

Wrapped up inside of what was ostensibly viewed as a secretary was a dynamic administrative manager who simply needed to be brought out and empowered. Interestingly as time went on I was made aware that it was the "spunk" in her that had been squelched in some of her previous assignments. More than anything, we had created the environment and opportunity for that "spunk" to resurface and that is one of the qualities that allowed her to be so effective.

As job changes moved Linda and me in opposite directions, I continued to watch her career. Whenever she had the opportunity to work for people who allowed that spunk to flourish, Linda was happy and successful. However, she also found herself working for people who again squelched or tried to squelch it and as a result Linda eventually left the company. I for one counted that as both a loss and a Company human issue failure.

In the early 90s, I was assigned the project of adding another ham boning line to the operation in Beardstown. Most ham today gets consumed as boneless. In this process, the skin, bones, sinew, membranes, and fat are removed and the muscles are then "put back together" and processed much as the old bone-in hams were. Now, however, the product is much more consumer friendly. The industry movement from bone-in to boneless increased dramatically in the 80s and early 90s. Removing the bones and other materials noted above could most efficiently be done at the packing plant. As a result, packers moved rapidly to increase their capacities for boning.

The most efficient method of boning was to have each worker on the line do one small job, but do it hundreds of times per day. The problem with this was that the repetitious nature of this often resulted in cumulative trauma type injuries. Was there perhaps a better way or at least a way to make the system better? With this question in mind, we secured approval to attempt to design a more operator friendly ham boning line.

We began by assembling a team of "experts" on the subject. This team included boning line operators and laborers, union stewards, supervisors, nurses, ergonomics professionals, equipment manufacturers, equipment designers, and general management personnel. We then removed all the obstacles. We asked for every idea anyone could think of that would improve the safety of the line. We turned loose all the innovative juices in that entire team. The initial result was a multi-page listing of ideas. The team then modeled every idea and included all those that seemed to work in a design specification.

The equipment designers and manufacturers then built a small prototype unit that was further modeled by the team. Additional designs were made on the basis of this work and the final product was an "operator friendly" ham boning line.

The creative result of turning all of these people loose was an ergonomics success and was described by one of Cargill's primary ergonomics consultants as "unique in American industry."

We later used this same design in the facility in Taiwan and over the years used components of it in countless ways. In addition, in the decade plus since, the operator friendly line continued to be used as a springboard to other worthwhile ergonomic tools and processes. It was certainly a success story in tapping the human intelligence resource and empowering employees.

Interestingly, my favorite example of employee empowerment involves simplicity and is also the very first extended supervision encounter I had. That is probably an indictment of how we continue to over-supervise as the years go by. Other than my brief experience in the lecithin operation with Jimmie Williams (Chapter 16: "Team"), the first employee who I was given to manage on my own was a young man in the late autumn of 1969.

I had been assigned the position of construction ramrod for the process of relocating, upgrading, and rebuilding the old Redfield, Iowa soybean facility to the Memphis, Tennessee complex. The entire lot of electrical switchgear and controls that we transferred was covered with "crud" and in poor condition. One of my responsibilities was to get this equipment cleaned up and in good operating order.

Harold Cook set up a tent for me as a sort of work area to accomplish this task. All of the electrical equipment was piled in the center of this tent. I then set up a small manual cleaning area on one end and a repair/re-wiring area on the other. My plan was to have someone hand clean the equipment and then transfer it to the repair area where I would do the repair and rewiring. Harvey Marxhausen and Fred Brosius, both of whom you have met earlier, liked my plan and Fred hired Eddie Johnson to work for me.

Eddie was a young modestly educated black man in his late 20s so he was a little older than me. Fred simply turned Eddie over to me along with one tool for Eddie to use. That was a standard issue hand-held wire brush, the same as can be purchased in any hardware store today. Being new to supervising people I did not yet realize all the things the Big Black Book says you need to do so I just handed Eddie the wire brush, took him to the little workstation (a small table), and said "Pick a piece of equipment, clean all the crud off of it, bring it over to my repair station, and put it on a pile here, then repeat the process." I essentially just turned Eddie loose to do the job.

I then went about the rest of my ramrod duties and whenever I had a little spare time, as well as a couple of hours after work each day,

I would go to my repair station and repair equipment from the "clean" pile. There was always a pile of clean equipment so I didn't concern myself much with whether Eddie was staying busy or not. I had enough other duties that I did little more than exchange good mornings with Eddie and thank him for keeping clean equipment ahead of me at the repair station. Eddie just always seemed to be at the workstation working.

About two weeks after we had started this process, Eddie came to me one day and asked if I thought it would be possible to get him a new wire brush. As he made the request, he handed me the original brush he had been given. The wire bristles were worn down to just over ¼ inch—from a starting point of about 1½ inches. Now most of us have at least some experience with hand wire brushes and yet I would venture to say few if any of us have ever seen one *wore* out. We see them broken or with the bristles bent and skewed and so forth, but never with 80 percent of the original bristle length wore down.

I immediately secured a new brush for Eddie along with the comment I would gladly replace it long before the bristles wore down to ¼ inch. I then took the old brush and showed it to Harold and Fred who could not believe it. We actually mounted the old brush in a frame with a red velvet backing and hung it in the production office as a reminder to all of us as to how to get value out of our tools.

I'm sure that brush is long since history and does not exist today. However, if perchance it does happen to still exist somewhere, I can assure anyone who happens to know of its whereabouts that they could extract a fairly sizable sum of money from me for its return. I would hang it in my office as it hung in the Memphis soybean office during the early 70s. I would *not* hang it there as a reminder of getting value out of tools, however. *I would hang it there as a reminder of how to get value out of people.*

# CHAPTER 30
# Souls for Sale

There was a popular song recorded several years ago by the Charlie Daniels Band, "The Devil Went Down to Georgia." I have always liked that song even though I have been somewhat at odds with its message.

This song is about Johnny, a young man in Georgia, who was ostensibly the best fiddle player in the world. He certainly was in his own opinion. Johnny makes the statement in the song, "I'm the best that's ever been!" As the song details; the Devil is behind in his quota of souls, so he goes down to Georgia to see if he can steal one. In Georgia, the Devil encounters Johnny and challenges him to a "fiddle playing" contest. The stakes are the Devil's golden fiddle if Johnny wins against Johnny's soul if the Devil wins.

As the story unfolds, among some unique fiddle playing music, Johnny does in fact win and in doing so gets the golden fiddle and preserves his soul. While I recognize this is just a song, I still marvel that Johnny is willing to risk the afterlife for a mere golden fiddle. Being a religious person and accepting heaven as a place of eternal bliss and fearing hell as a place of eternal punishment, I don't think I would be willing to take the same risk Johnny took in the song!

That notwithstanding, I must admit, people "play with, risk, and ultimately sell" their souls on a routine basis daily. While people certainly do this with their *eternal* souls, although perhaps not as graphic as did Johnny in the song, they also do it with their *earthly* souls. While we generally think of our soul as that part of us that transcends our earthly existence, there is also a second type of soul, an earthly soul if you will.

Webster defines this type of soul as "the immaterial essence, the animating principle or actuating cause of an individual life." It is that fundamental make-up of our moral and emotional nature. It is those qualities that go to the very core of our being. This "soul" is what we stand upon and what gives meaning and purpose to our lives. It is what motivates us to action. Unfortunately, *this* soul is also routinely sold to the highest bidder in today's business and personal environment.

For me, the makeup of my "soul on earth" is fairly simple. In addition to being a Christian, I am devoted to my family and they come first. I believe God gave all of us one unit of worth and we are expected and commanded to honor that in each other. God is the Perfect Creator and accordingly we are to honor His creations (which includes people) in such a way that we preserve God's intended nature. I seek to be fair in all things, even when the laws and rules of man do not demand it. Ultimately, integrity and fairness are my first and final guides.

It is these things and principles that give meaning to my life and direct my actions. When I am in tune with them, I find I am inevitably happy and content. When I am troubled or perplexed, I can usually find somewhere I have deviated from this "essence of my being." That deviation causes emotional pain and I must take steps to get back to my "base."

There are many people who seem to have lost their soul and have no base. There is no immaterial essence of their being. These people often drop out of the mainstream of everyday life, leaving family and friends in the lurch, to go off to "find themselves." I am always amused, but saddened that the very thing they are looking for does not exist in the places they are looking.

These people try to get as far away from moral fiber, family, and history as possible as they tend to view these as the millstones around their neck. They are out looking for persons, positions, performance, or material things that will bring them the happiness they have not been experiencing. Unfortunately, the sad fact is they are out looking for something (their soul - the *immaterial* essence of their life) in a place where it cannot be found (the *material* world).

My heart goes out to these people. I do not think they have much chance of ever achieving long lasting happiness. Their inner being simply has no foundation. There is no "home" for their soul. Consequently, they have no reference point, no internal compass, and no place to come back to when they are lost.

Other people do have a definable soul. They are animated by certain principles and/or actuating causes. The fundamental inner core make-ups of these people are certainly different from one to another.

This is to be expected since much of our background (Chapters 2 through 6) is shaped by our heredity and environment.

Some of these persons are or have been willing to compromise their inner core make-up (sell their soul). On the other hand, some steadfastly work to maintain the integrity of their soul. I think it is again worth noting that our soul deals with the *immaterial* essence of our lives. Selling one's soul may very well serve the *material* essence of one's life and that is precisely where the rub lies. However, the material benefits can only bring apparent or at best, temporary happiness.

One of my very good friends had a make-up similar to mine. One of his operating tenets, like mine, was you should treat people with ultimate fairness and compassion whether the laws of man demand it or not. He wanted to succeed in industry and achieve at least a vice-president position in his career. He recognized he had to be viewed favorably by his superiors in order to continue to advance and achieve his goals.

The problem for both of us came in that at one particular point in time, the business unit we found ourselves in and the business leaders for whom we worked did not necessarily share the same interpretation of "fairness" as did we. There was no "apparent" compelling reason why one had to go beyond the simple laws of man in the treatment of people or any other element such as the environment in the business and industrial setting. Indeed, one cannot offer any legal argument to do so. My friend saw fairness in a more compassionate light and he struggled endlessly with these issues.

He attempted to find that "middle ground" whereby you walk the fine line between your internal compass and the external direction given. Unfortunately, this inevitably results in at least a little bit of your soul being chipped away (even when that is not your intent). Usually that results in all parties being left unsatisfied. That is virtually always what happened. The business leaders remained dissatisfied with his approach and he remained perplexed and troubled as his soul was not at peace.

Interestingly, there are times when selling one's soul even backfires in the material sense. The nature of one of our facility's operating regimes had begun to create some environmental problems. In an effort to correct these and short circuit future difficulties, the engineering people at both the local plant and the corporate level evaluated the problems and proposed a sizable capital expenditure. By virtue of their signatures on the official capital fund's request document, this capital project was ostensibly supported by a number of the division business leaders.

One of the people in the hierarchy, who I believe actually supported the proposal, apparently determined it was best to first test the waters before affixing his signature. He may even have begun to argue in favor of the proposal, but was apparently brought to an understanding by higher elements of the decision making group they would not be in favor of spending those capital dollars. Since he had not affixed his signature to the capital documents beforehand, he withheld that signature and thus was willing to "take the credit" for stopping the project at his level. Even if he believed in it, he was unwilling to maintain his position and preserve his integrity. He may even have been applauded for that posture at the time.

Ironically, a few years later, action was brought against this facility by the state environmental regulatory body for non-compliance with permit conditions. The cry went up in the ivory towers as to why this had been allowed to happen. It was quickly brought to everyone's attention a capital proposal had in fact been brought forward a couple of years prior, but had not been approved. Sure enough, on inspection of the archived document the first signature missing was that of the official above noted. All of the decision makers above were "off the hook." It certainly appeared the document had never reached them since it was essentially "killed" by the absence of a forwarding signature. As one may predict, memories were short about any water testing. According to the archived document, it had never moved "off of the desk" of the one particular officer. Obviously, that officer then became subject to *material* heat as well.

Certainly, corporations and other collective bodies have souls just as individuals do. You may recall in Chapter 1 how impressed I was with the Cargill organization during my college interview trip. It had appeared to me in that short day in Minneapolis the soul of Cargill was very much in concert with my own. For many years, I found that to be largely the case. We were judged above the bottom line as well as by that line. Experience proved Cargill was interested in the spirit of the law as well as the letter of the law. Most importantly, demonstrated action proved we were all respected for the individuals we were.

For 12 years I progressed rapidly through the Cargill organization, first in the soybean operations and then in the corn operations. I let my soul guide my management style and there was harmony between my inner self and my outer person.

In 1980 I transferred to the meat business (later named Excel) Cargill had just purchased. I was a vice president and for several years took on a variety of assignments. Several of these assignments involved employee safety, environmental sanctity, and purchasing integrity as well as plant construction and engineering operations. Most of these platforms allowed me to maintain my soul's integrity and also to make it a full partner in my management mode. Bill Fielding, my boss and then president of Excel, commented several times he thought one of my greatest contributions to Excel was as an ambassador/teacher of the "Cargill way" (Cargill soul). I took that as a great compliment.

The meat facilities had historically invested only minimum capital dollars in employee welfare facilities such as cafeterias and locker rooms. This instinctively bothered me as I thought it not only unfair, but further sent a message to our people at least I didn't want to send. In the early 80s during a major construction project at our beef facility in Dodge City, Kansas, I instructed Jerry Blackerby, the project manager, to "dress up" the welfare facilities. "We need quarry tile floors, high quality booths in the cafeterias, excellent lighting in all areas, bright colors, tile ceilings etc.," I told Jerry.

Jerry responded while that would be nice, it added a lot of cost and hadn't been done before. "Don't we have enough money in the budget and aren't you the project manager and I the project executive supervisor?" I asked.

Jerry smiled and said, "Yes, I guess we can just do it then, huh!"

We did it with Jerry adding a few extra touches of his own. The plant production people were delighted. We really didn't even have to take much heat for how we had spent capital dollars, as the results sold themselves and it was not hard for other managers to quickly see the value. After the management teams at the other plants saw its impact on the people, they began to clamor for similar actions in their own plants. Within a few years all of the welfare facilities were equal to or even better than Dodge City. Those kinds of results may not materially impact one, and indeed time dulls most memories of even who the champions of the cause were, but they sure make your soul feel good.

In 1985 and 1986, I focused much of my attention on analyzing the pork business. Excel was involved only in beef at that time and we investigated various potential entry points into pork processing. In January of 1987, agreement was reached with Oscar Mayer to purchase their Beardstown pork processing facility and that became our port of entry into the pork business. I was selected to head up the organization of the operation at Beardstown as well as the reconstruction of the plant. As that work drew to a close, I was selected as the general manager of the Beardstown facility.

I had a long history of personnel, safety, environmental, and general operational integrity. This was my own belief as well as the stated policy of Cargill and what I had generally found to be the practice of Cargill as well. Meat industry facilities with 500 to 2000 employees are much more difficult to manage with close personal touch and yet I set out to do just that. I purposely kept layers of management to a minimum and sought to involve and empower employees at all levels. I was determined to be compassionate, fair, and equitable in all our dealings and treat all of our resources with the highest level of integrity.

We operated the plant under these principles for several months during which we struggled financially. This was due to both start up challenges and our inability to sell our production on a par with the industry, neither of which are particularly unusual when wading into a new industry. In spite of the financial difficulties, I was determined to stay the operational course we had charted. I "knew" it was the right course to follow from both integrity as well as long-term economic perspectives. As time progressed, others in the organization did not share my opinion. They determined the only way to work ourselves into a profitable position was to increase our production by several thousand animals per day so that we could spread our indirect and fixed costs over a greater number.

I was both an engineer and a manager and I had a number of other engineers and technical people on my staff. We did detailed analyzes of the operational and personnel needs for increasing production and reported a number of capital expenditures must be made to the refrigeration system, waste water treatment system, rendering system, and general employee line positions to safely and properly handle additional volume. We were informed no additional capital money was available to be spent, and further, adding to fixed capital costs would defeat the purpose. We needed to increase the production with the existing resources to get to a profitable position. I was ultimately instructed to increase the daily production rate in spite of the facility limitations.

My team raised the rate from the 11,000 head per day we had planned and forecast in the purchase and renovation work to about 12,500. We had determined this was the level of increase we could accomplish while still maintaining integrity of operations. That was not enough I was told. A production rate of 13,500 per day was the minimum to get per unit operating costs down to the range they needed to be. My own experience and analysis, as well as the input of key staff members, told me at such a level we would over run our ability to refrigerate, treat wastewater, manage by-products, and maintain the level of personnel safety we desired. I explained and argued my points profusely, but I was unable to convince my superiors. I was not able to "make the sale" of my position and sell my own analyses and expertise as you may remember from Chapter 24. Ultimately, I had no choice but to refuse to raise the production volume to the levels requested for the reasons noted above. I was confident there would be adverse consequences to the environment and the people if I raised the rate. I also realized there could be adverse consequences to me personally if I didn't. However, I was not willing to "sell my soul" on this issue and I held the rate where it was.

Within a few weeks, I was removed as manager of the Beardstown operation and was replaced by someone who was willing to take the daily production rate first to 13,500 and later to 14,500 and above. To this day, I do not doubt most of the people making those decisions actually believed they were doing the proper and necessary thing to create "material" success in the business. As noted, I had not been able to sell others on my position and I believe they thought my analyses were flawed, my warnings were without substance, and few adverse consequences would occur. Nevertheless, as time progressed, it became increasingly obvious there were several and serious adverse consequences to the action that had been taken.

Both my soul and my integrity had been fully preserved. Time and history proved that my evaluation had been sound and my predictions had been right. Even had I been wrong, however, and raising the production rate had not resulted in those operational, environmental, and safety compromises, I would have still made the right decision for my soul. My decision was made on the basis of my knowledge and analysis and I had every reason to believe it to be sound and correct. To have acquiesced, even in the face of higher authority, would have sacrificed my integrity (and my soul) since I had good reason to believe such action would put elements of God's creation at risk.

Ultimately, the fact I had not sacrificed my soul cost me dearly in terms of job position, pay, and promotional opportunity. Understandably, it is often difficult to distinguish between actions taken to preserve integrity and insubordination. Being right in the end often (perhaps usually) doesn't result in restoration of one's material well-being. However, material well-being can never overcome the sense of loss in selling one's soul. Moreover, there is a silver lining in most clouds as you will see in Chapter 33.

As I noted earlier, organizations have souls as well. These souls generally begin as virtual copies of the souls of the owners. As the business grows, it is often this soul that guides growth. I believe this was certainly the case in Cargill for many decades from its inception in 1865.

There are many examples in the history of Cargill (and I am sure in other organizations of high integrity as well) where corporate soul stands firm. Just as is the case in one's personal life, preservation of corporate soul also frequently results in adverse material well-being. I know of many examples where Cargill did in fact act on the basis of immaterial value to the detriment of material value.

However, as organizations get larger, it becomes increasingly difficult for the owners to "clearly see" activities at lower levels. This was dealt with in greater detail in Chapter 18: "Stained Glass Windows." The sad thing is the "corporate soul" often gets trampled or at least stepped on in the process. Managers begin to reward themselves and their units, often without regard for the corporate soul. These actions can go unnoticed at the higher levels.

When the "soul" decisions get made at lower levels, corporate soul may get subordinated to personal gain. The pressures for success (individually and corporately) become too great for some to handle. The temptations are just too great and the personal career rewards (or potential rewards) for pawning a portion of one's soul makes the reward versus risk ratio look too good to pass up.

It is on this point that managers within corporations are very much like Johnny in our song. Johnny gambled with his soul. He had no intention of losing it and in fact, in this first encounter with the Devil, he was able to leverage it to secure a fiddle made of gold.

What we also know about gamblers though, is they return to the table time and again to attempt to multiply their winnings. We have every reason to believe the Devil could come up with another fiddle made of gold. Moreover, the Devil has access to a whole range of other enticing rewards. What we do not know about Johnny is whether he accepted any return challenges from the Devil and if so how he fared on those. *We may have to wait until we get to Heaven and see if Johnny is there!!*

# CHAPTER 31
# Three Million Dollar Handshake

On Super Bowl Sunday of 1997, the Excel processing plant in Ottumwa, Iowa experienced a major explosion and fire. This occurred at about 7:30 P.M., just around halftime of the game between the Green Bay Packers and the New England Patriots. We were at our daughter and son-in-law's home for supper and to watch the game with them. When we returned to our home at about 9:00 P.M. there were two messages on our answering machine for me. The first was from Mike Richtig in Ottumwa, and it was a very brief description of the circumstance there. The second was from my boss in Wichita, requesting I call him.

Following a discussion with my boss regarding various alternatives, I hung up the phone, packed my suitcase, got in my car, and left for Ottumwa. I arrived in Ottumwa about 5:00 A.M., checked into the Days Inn—my home away from home anyway as we were in the middle of a major expansion at the plant at the time—and then headed out to the plant. The local police had the plant barricaded off, but when I explained I was an Excel official from Wichita, they passed me through.

After checking in at the office with the plant management team, one of the engineering managers came around to escort me back to the scene of the explosion. No one had been killed or even injured in the blast as very few people were in the plant on Sunday night. Other than that bright spot, it was like a war picture. I remember having two distinct thoughts. First, "I can't believe this has happened and I am here viewing it, I'll wake up soon!" And second, "How will we ever get from here back to an operating plant again?"

Briefly, what had happened was an ammonia refrigeration valve had failed, spilling large amounts of liquid ammonia into the product storage area. Ammonia forms an explosive mixture with air if it is present in very large concentrations. Apparently that concentration was reached and there were ample sources of ignition in the lights, fans, and electric operators. The result was an explosion that ripped the roof off of the storage area, collapsed and blew out surrounding walls, and ripped piping and equipment to twisted rubble. After the explosion came a fire. Although the fire was not large, it was virtually impossible to arrest as it got into the wall and roof insulation and worked its way back through the plant. In spite of sub-zero temperatures, the engineering and production managers at the Ottumwa plant, along with fire department personnel, had done a super job of containing the fire.

The next seven days were pure hell as we fought continuing sub-freezing temperatures to contain the fire, remove the remaining ammonia from the plant, control access, prevent further collapse, assess damages, and begin demolition and reconstruction. On March 24, we started the plant back into operation on a limited basis and within a few more weeks we were essentially back to normal operation. A prodigious number of people, companies, and contractors contributed to that phenomenal recovery process. While that is a story in itself, it is only a contributing part to my thesis and the point of my discussion about this occurrence.

As I noted, we were in the midst of a major expansion on the other end of the Ottumwa facility at the time of the explosion. As a result, we had on site and under contract a number of construction companies and an engineering firm. Four of the entities already on site were Story Construction, Knickerbocker Construction, Preston Refrigeration and Structural Engineers. Over the years these organizations had developed strong relationships with Excel Pork. Beyond those business relationships, a number of principals of these organizations were close personal friends of mine. These included Larry Sperlich of Story, Bob Knickerbocker (Nick) of Knickerbocker Construction, Jim Salmons of Preston, and Larry Olson of Structural Engineers. You have already met some of these people.

Each was there or made contact on Monday morning to see what they could do to help. By Tuesday morning, all were involved in some form of damage control, demolition, or reconstruction. In the ensuing days, the activity of these people with regard to the recovery process grew exponentially. At this time, all work was being done on the basis of word of mouth and good faith.

A few days after the explosion, the Excel management group had enlisted the assistance of a company out of New York to help in the management of the insurance loss. Their work was to help us identify and document all of the losses and costs of recovery. Their work was very arduous and while I had some difference of opinion with some of their methods, I came to very much appreciate their work ethic and their organizational abilities.

At the time the New York Group mobilized and arrived on the scene, we had already done a huge amount of work. The refrigeration work we had begun was one of the most visual. We already had pads and stands poured and large vessels set on them. We had shunted some of the equipment and vessels from the expansion project to the recovery project and reordered for the expansion. Most impressively, we had already installed and partially welded several thousand feet of ammonia piping from a 20-inch diameter down to four inches. While I say we, this was mostly Preston with civil work assistance from Story and Structural. The New Yorkers were amazed at the progress we had already made.

Moreover, they were absolutely dumbfounded by the fact this work was essentially all going on based only on good faith and without anything yet reduced to writing. One of the principals of the New York group commented on this phenomenon. "In New York, you don't do three dollars worth of work without reductions to writing and assurances that all t(s) are crossed and all i(s) are dotted. Here, Jim Roth and Jim Salmons cut a three million dollar deal on a handshake!" Actually it was a three and a half million-dollar deal!

That brings me to the focal point of this chapter, *relationships* and their impact. Relationships do not simply happen; they are built on integrity, fairness and character. Accordingly, if you allow me to choose one strength in a manager or any professional person, I will always pick the ability to establish and maintain *long-term* relationships.

Getting back to my story—It was not an accident that Jim Salmons and Jim Roth either did or could cut that three million dollar deal on a handshake. I first met Jim Salmons in 1982 when he was involved in a construction project with me at our beef facility in Dodge City, Kansas. We had some infrequent contact for the next few years. However, Jim had changed companies and I was not as involved in construction projects, so we essentially lost touch. Then in 1989, Excel had a major expansion project in Ottumwa that Preston Refrigeration was involved in. I was the project manager for Excel and Jim Salmons was the construction manager for Preston. We worked closely on that project and both began to experience what the other was all about.

Both Jim and I are honest and straightforward. We do not put on an air for anyone. Obviously, we both appreciated that in each other. We knew what we said was what we meant. There was not any need to try to interpret what the other *meant.* I could see Jim fully understood refrigeration and his business. He could see I understood my business and could effectively manage projects. We both had a high work ethic to go along with our professional ethic.

With this appreciation for each other in the industrial work environment, Jim and I began to move parts of our discussions outside of this venue. We found that each of us is also a farmer and livestock person. Jim was predominantly in cows and calves at that time and I was predominantly in hogs and fat cattle. We found a tremendous commonality and quickly became close personal friends.

As I have noted before, much of today's conventional wisdom would say in the business environment it was no longer proper or prudent to have Jim Roth and Jim Salmons working together. We were too good of friends. To hold to this thesis, one must also hold to the thesis that life is a zero sum game and for every winner there is an equal loser. Given that thesis, one must always work to win at the expense of the other. If you are good friends, you lose your killer instinct with that person and will not work to insure he loses.

I do *not* believe life is a zero sum game. In fact, I know life is not a zero sum game. Life is an exercise in win-win opportunities. If you hold to this thesis, you immediately move to the point where you are working to assure a win for the other party as well as for yourself. The value of friendship then becomes apparent. You will work much harder to assure the other party's success along with yours because you like him or her. In like manner, he or she will work that much harder to assure your success for the same reason.

One of my operating principles is "Lasting and worthwhile relationships occur when each party is as interested in the well-being of the other party as they are in their own." This is not an altruistic approach. Neither party is of more or less value than the other. Neither is sacrificed for the other. Both are equally important and the needs of both are considered. Try to name one marriage that thrives outside of this attitude.

Try to name one parent-child relationship that thrives outside of this mode of operation. Try to name one teacher-student relationship that thrives outside of this principle. Why should one think the business and industrial environment would be any different?

Following the 1989 Ottumwa work, Jim Salmons and Preston Refrigeration continued to do millions of dollars worth of work for Excel Pork and Jim Roth. This included work in Taiwan as well as work in the Excel plants here in the States. The more we worked together, the more we understood each other's needs and the better able to serve those needs we became. I learned that Jim always gave us more effective tonnage than any other supplier and he always gave us a complete job. He accepted our challenge to do the job from A to Z. He did not come back looking for more money when he missed something, which he seldom did.

Jim learned we were exceptionally good project managers and coordinators and we would always assure any pre-requisite work was done before he arrived at the point of need so he didn't have to plan for mini or maxi demobilizations and remobilizations. He also learned we were fair in the language when we did finally reduce our agreements to writing. Further, Jim knew we would take on our own lawyers when needed to assure fairness.

What we both received from the other was value. Jim was able to give us a better system for less cost because we were able to meet his needs. He could predict very low risk in working for us. As noted, he could effectively schedule his work and maximize his own crew's efficiency. He did not have to worry about payments and if there happened to be delays, he knew we would go to bat for him internally and get it handled. He could confidently predict we would not unfairly hassle him on legal issues and if there were unforeseen problems not of his making, we would help him on the money side. What all of this meant to Jim was he could give us more system for less money. What it meant for us was we could get more system for less money and still know Jim would be in business tomorrow, willing and able to assist us with any system problems. We both knew the other would deliver!

So on January 28, 1997, Jim Salmons and Jim Roth could concentrate on what was needed to put the Ottumwa plant back into operation and how that could be most effectively and expeditiously managed. Once that was developed, it was full speed ahead. Three and one half million dollars, over five miles of pipe, and a collection of vessels, valves, compressors, and other refrigeration equipment later, the system was back in operation. Jim Salmons and Jim Roth were (and are) still the best of friends.

I have always been intrigued by how ineffective we often seem to be at building relationships on the sales side of a business. Several years ago we went through a strategic planning exercise. One of the key components of the strategy was to increase the percentage of relationship-based customers. All of the studies from the sales gurus indicated margins were best from relationship-based sales. From our discussion above, I could understand why. However, I remain amazed at how so many sales people expect to go about making this happen and the apparent lack of understanding of where relationship-based customers come from. They seem to think you "identify" them from some list, "Oh yeah, this company is a relationship-based company and this one is a price buyer." Once identified, all you need to do is start selling to the relationship-based guy and not to the price buyer.

The proof many of them do not understand relationships are built, not downloaded from a list, continues to come from the way they sell. There seems to be a dearth of face-to-face sales. Likewise, little sales time is devoted to going out to learn the customer's business and needs. Finally, while there is understanding in putting value in our own product, there seems to be little understanding of the development of mutual value, that point where value can be added and shared from buyer to seller and vice versa.

I find it difficult to understand how anyone in any walk of life cannot understand the value of relationships and what they are built around. There are so many perfect examples in our daily lives it boggles the mind to imagine how one can continue to be blind to their origination, cultivation, importance, and relevance.

As alluded to earlier in this chapter, one of the most obvious and apparent personal examples is the marriage relationship. Imagine one partner is a "price buyer." This person will always be looking for the quickest and easiest method of personal satisfaction without any regard for its impact on the other partner. That partner exists only for the "price buyer's" benefit. The partner is disposable if a better or cheaper product comes along. This marriage has a very short half-life and its survival rate is just about zero. Unfortunately, just as many customers fall in the "price-buyer" category and sales are consummated on that basis, a very large number of marriage participants also fall in this category. It is not surprising the divorce rate is so high. Unfortunately, the stakes in changing products are much higher in the marriage relationship than in the business relationship.

Both partners in a marriage must be as committed to the well-being of the other as they are to their own well-being. Only in this manner can each be completely fulfilled and happy. While one may view this as lofty and romantic, it holds true even from the most basic pragmatic approach. I challenge any husband to show me how his life can be filled with happiness if his wife is not also happy. Spouses have a way of making each other miserable when they are unhappy themselves.

Again, getting back to business relationships, it is interesting to me while relationships germinate, grow, and survive in the climate of everyday activity, they come to full bloom in times of trial. The example of the explosion in Ottumwa is a prime example. Another example also occurred in Ottumwa. This time the date was October of 1998.

A part of the roof system of a waste treatment process we had installed and commissioned a year and a half earlier unexpectedly collapsed early one Saturday morning. Calls were immediately made to Story Construction, Structural Engineers, and IPC, informing them of our problem. All moved to action immediately. By Monday morning all were on site and had cranes, lifts, shoring, and other supplies and equipment moving in our direction.

During the next two weeks, everyone worked together to get the system back into operation. In tandem with this effort, everyone participated in the process of determining if any of the other parts of the system were similarly subject to failure. Finally, everyone analyzed the occurrence in full transparency to determine the cause of failure and take the necessary steps to prevent any future failures. At no time in this process did anyone ask for, much less demand, any purchase orders or contracts or confirmations they would get paid for the work they were doing. Similarly, at no time did anyone ever raise a question about where culpability for the failure rested nor did anyone attempt to manipulate any efforts to shift possible scrutiny away from them.

When the process was fully complete, all the parties came together for a discussion of what would be a fair distribution of cost sharing in the reconstruction. We had determined the failure occurred because all generally accepted engineering and construction tolerances had accumulated in the same direction. With a couple of hours of discussion, we all agreed on a cost distribution with Cargill paying just over 50 percent and the contractor and engineering group paying the remainder. We all shook hands on the deal and life went on.

Lawyers for Cargill may have argued we should not have had to pay anything since it was not a result of our doing. Lawyers for the contractors and engineers may have argued they owed nothing since the materials and workmanship warranty extended for a period of only 12 months and had long since expired. Lawyer costs would likely have exceeded the total costs of the reconstruction process and, other than the lawyers, everyone would have wound up losing. As it was, relationships were neither severed nor strained. In fact, the entire process strengthened them.

I do not think it is possible to pick and choose when and with whom to build relationships. Granted, there are people with whom we must deal who themselves are not relationship oriented, and we need to gear our action accordingly. However, I believe in most instances people and businesses can be found where valuable and mutually profitable relationships can be built.

Relationship based operation, whether in business or in life, is in fact a *modus operandi.* It is not a part of the way we operate, it IS the way we operate. There are so many elements of building solid relationships that must be a part of a person's general make-up. Without honesty and integrity, transparent communications are difficult. Without a spirit of fairness, win-win conditions are more difficult to foster.

It is easy to see when we wish to limit relationships to those circumstances that most benefit us, we are indigenously violating many of the tenets of relationship building. Jim Salmons and Jim Roth could not have cut a three million dollar deal on a handshake if either had to worry if this was an instance where the other was willing to sacrifice their relationship to his current advantage. On the contrary, Jim and Jim continue to have more confidence in the other's outstretched hand than in all the documents a ship full of lawyers can generate.

# CHAPTER 32
# The Face in the Mirror

Although I am not a big movie buff and am often at odds with the themes in many movies, I will admit there are sometimes simple and profound messages to be found. One of those occurs near the end of *Cool Runnings,* a movie about the Jamaican bobsled team. On the night before the big race the bobsled driver is discussing his desire to win with the team coach, played by John Candy. He raises the question with the coach as to why after winning two gold medals he (the coach) had felt the need to continue winning so much that he "cheated!" The coach acknowledges it is a flawed self-esteem and goes on to say, "If you're not enough without it (the gold medal), you'll never be enough with it!" It is the culmination of the coach's efforts throughout the entire training process to build up each member of the Jamaican team. Ultimately, it is not in winning the gold that the team members find personal satisfaction.

The coach's statement reflects my own feelings and philosophy. No matter what you accomplish, if you are not at peace with yourself and your efforts, your accomplishments will be hollow. Beyond that, if you achieve those accomplishments by moving in a direction that results in the loss of peace within yourself, those accomplishments are not only hollow, the process will eat away at you so much that you will eventually fail to even recognize the accomplishments.

Unfortunately, many people do not recognize these end results and move through the process of life seeking only the gold. They seek only these accomplishments and they are even willing to sacrifice pieces of themselves to achieve their goals. The discussions to follow are in many ways extensions or perhaps forerunners to the things that happen in Chapter 30: "Souls for Sale."

I have long believed the only mortal person you need to satisfy in life is the person whose face you see in the mirror each morning when you shave or put on make-up. It surprises me how people can be so enamored with looking good to others, who may be in their presence for only a few moments at a time, and yet fail to satisfy the person they must live with for 24 hours of each and every day.

I do not wish to suggest that I hold to a self-satisfaction based on indifference, isolationism, or arrogance, although there are those for whom self-satisfaction comes from those or similar self-centered characteristics. Rather I believe if you can look at yourself and say honestly and with a humble nature, "Well done," you will also have satisfied all others who are also filled with integrity of purpose. Throughout much of my life, I have thanked God that He created in me a high level of what I have held to be honest self-esteem. I have never felt the need to acquiesce to someone else's idea of who I need to be or what I need to represent. Please take note at the end of the chapter, I now thank God for a different pattern.

I have always found it interesting and instructive to observe how others view themselves. Early in my career, I encountered one of the premier line operators in the company. This gentleman had hoped for a supervisory position. As such, he did not like me, or any of the other young engineers coming into the operations where he worked. Ostensibly, we presented a threat to his objective. In earlier years, he had held a position in a company where certain legal improprieties had occurred. I am told he was set up as the fall guy and was convicted of wrong doing and thus inherited a "record."

Whether viewed from a distance or up close, this guy looked like (and was) a model citizen. However, his record prevented him from being bondable and that kept him from being considered for a supervisory position. It was easy for me to understand how he could carry a chip on his shoulder and I fully understood his feelings toward me. Even knowing how he felt about me, I remained impressed with his knowledge, dedication, and work ethic. If he had ever lost his personal integrity, he had certainly regained it. I was (and remain) fully convinced that he went home every night with the full knowledge he had given the company the fullest measure of value in his power. It always impressed me that he had to gain and maintain his strength of character by "knowing" who he was and what he stood for, even if others denied that, and life seemed anything but fair.

When it came time for me to train in his area, I specifically asked to be placed on his shift to train with him. Although he approached his teaching assignment with some apprehension, and I suppose some reluctance, he took it on. I was put through the paces every night. I'm sure a part of it was to test my ability and perseverance, and I'm sure a part of it was to put me through the mill and perhaps suffer a bit. At the end of the two-week period, I had made him a new friend and he had made me a solid operator.

He continued to do his job as an exceptional operator and I soon became a shift supervisor, which was the normal path for a young engineer. He accepted my new position with enthusiasm and whenever he and I happened to be on the same shift I spent as much time with him as I could. I would schedule my break time to correspond to his and we would share together. Knowing the pain he felt at not even being able to compete for the job he wanted, let alone win it, I continued to marvel at how he was able to push that back and do the remarkable job of operating he did day after day.

I had discussed his plight with my superiors on several occasions. Wasn't there something we could do to at least get this very deserving man's name thrown in the mix for the next supervisory opening? My bosses shared my concern, as did many others on the team. When the next opening came, I again went to my bosses with my concern. They agreed it was time to take a stand in his defense. The next thing I knew, he was awarded the supervisor's position. I have no idea what had to be done to make that happen, I just know it did.

As one might predict, he did a very good job as a supervisor. He and I continued our friendship even as I advanced to higher management positions. Eventually I lost track of him. Nonetheless, I often think about how he must have felt as he stood before the mirror the morning after winning his supervisory position. For years he had looked at a man who would apparently never have an opportunity to achieve his career goals. Even in the midst of this, he maintained his personal integrity. Now suddenly, he was looking at a man who had both his career goal and his personal integrity. I'm sure the two men were smiling at each other.

If my earlier friend had to live in the present with an eye glued to his past, a later friend lived in the present with an eye glued to the future. I first met him in the early 80s when I was the Excel Engineering VP and he was one of the department managers. Although we did not have any significant contact with each other for several years, he always struck me as a likable guy with good knowledge of what he was doing.

When I was selected as the general manager for one of our operations, he was offered to me as the assistant general manager. I was happy with that and he and I quickly became friends as well as associates. He brought industry knowledge to my engineering and problem-solving skills. We were both people focused and had similar approaches to the human side of management. Unfortunately for me, within a few short months we also secured a second operation and he was off to be the general manager at that facility.

In the next few months we often found ourselves in the same predicament. We were both trying to keep the focus on long-term people-centered and fairness driven operating methodologies in the face of short-term red ink. Our bosses were continually putting the pressure on us to turn around the P&L performance immediately. Of course in their defense, their bosses were doing the same thing to them. My friend and I both firmly believed the best short and long-term course of action involved compassionate and involved management. These were the preferred courses of action and I still believe the desired *modus operandi* of Cargill in general. Yet, the default condition during times of stress was (and often today still is) to revert to traditional hardball and hard-nosed management techniques, decision making from the top down, and a focus on short-term profitability with too little regard for collateral damage.

We took somewhat different approaches to this predicament. I had already achieved officer status in the company although I would soon lose it. To be sure, officer status was not something I had particularly aspired to. He on the other hand, had been working his entire life to get to that point. Achieving officer status was an important milestone to him.

I worked hard to try to convince our bosses to stay the course, particularly in those areas where changed positions would put people, systems, or the environment at risk. When I failed to sell my position to my superiors, I took a resistant approach, especially in those areas of risk. In the face of higher management instruction to do otherwise, I stayed the course and eventually paid the price personally.

On the other hand, my friend was far more reluctant, as are most people, to resist higher management instruction. When he could not sell his position either, he was forced to follow higher management instructions. He tried to assure our bosses that their demands of a more autocratic approach would be put in place. Yet this was so out of character that he could not make it happen. I know he struggled with the face he saw in the mirror daily. He saw a face that knew what was right and yet a face that could not dismiss the risks of apparent insubordination. I could see and sense this struggle daily. His soul was not at peace. The irony is we both fell from favor with our superiors in about equal proportion.

We had become close friends through these battles. We shared both a common approach to managing resources as well as a comradeship in trial. We were soon again thrown together in the construction and operation of another facility. He was the general operating manager at this facility and I was the manager in charge of construction and commissioning. Interestingly, we continued to face some of the same challenges with many of the same results.

He was later offered a key management position with a different company. He struggled with the decision for a time. It was the age-old question of security versus potential opportunity. Is the devil you know better than the devil you do not know? Then I believe he clearly saw the face of his soul in the mirror. He recognized while the new company may or may not be the long-term economic opportunity it seemed, it was an organization whose soul more closely matched his own. He accepted the position with the new company.

Unfortunately, with the change in position, we have little opportunity to see each other. We remain close friends and still maintain contact with each other. He is very successful with the new company and it is interesting and most satisfying for me to see and feel the serenity in his demeanor today, which obviously goes well beyond economic and status success. It is obvious he is now fully satisfied with the face he sees in the mirror. While he is an executive with the new organization, I truly believe that he would now consider "executive status" as only a side benefit.

Some people find peace within themselves in the midst of daily conflict, others seek out that environment where that conflict no longer exists, and yet others must find that peace amidst a conflict over which they have no control. The journeys are different, but the destinations are the same, they achieve peace within.

It has also been my experience that some people, including me, sometimes look in the mirror to find temporary satisfaction by seeing a given type of person based on a more self-centered desire. Generally this look is no more than a snapshot in time. I still maintain that for long lasting satisfaction there must be more substance to what one is seeking to see. See "Leveling the Playing Field" in the "More Stories" section for just such a story.

Short term (snapshots in time) self satisfaction as just noted actually gives us a good clue to what makes us content in the long-term; in a sense, what makes us "enough" without the gold. If you read "Leveling the Playing Field," you will have noted I had leveled the playing field with a top officer. At that point in time, he was still "higher ranking" than me, but he was not "superior" to me. He could still own the gold, but I had the self-assurance I could compete.

As I noted earlier, ultimate contentment with the face you see in the mirror is a direct result of a person's own self-assurance, self-esteem, and self-worth. Although my father always struggled with his own self-esteem, I owe a huge debt to him for the part he played in establishing my own self-esteem. Unfortunately, I do not think I recognized what he was doing and what life long impact it would have.

It took the Chinese to teach me that. One thing that is very important to the Chinese culture is to save face, particularly the one in the mirror. Accordingly, the Chinese are very slow to either admit a mistake or "charge" a co-worker with a mistake. An outgrowth of this is a reluctance to even admit to a lack of knowledge of any type.

For a number of years, I found this to be highly irritating. It either reduced the speed with which decisions could be made or it caused failure of the decision-making process altogether. Yet, I continued to fail to see the lesson to be learned. The Chinese had learned better than we the importance of maintaining a person's self-esteem. In the name of speed, accuracy, and efficiency, we were and generally are content to devalue a person. Even though our intent is not a specific devaluation of the person, it is often how the subject person sees it.

In the mid 70s, while I was the production manager at the Cedar Rapids corn processing facility, I chanced to work with several persons of high capability and one in particular. John was a big strapping guy with a high capacity to work. John was a guy, however, who had to be properly challenged and motivated (probably not much different than any of us). John had just accepted a job transfer to Feedhouse helper and was learning that job. One of the key jobs in the Feedhouse was the operation of the gluten filters.

It was in the summertime and one of our shift supervisors was on vacation. As was the normal practice, whoever was on weekend maintenance crew management duty came in at 3:00 A.M. on Saturday morning to spell the shift supervisor for the last 4 hours of the Friday night graveyard shift. This duty was rotated between the plant engineer, the maintenance superintendent, and me, and on this night I was handling it myself. John was training on this shift and as I made my rounds I stopped in the Feedhouse operator's control room as I always did. John was in the room along with Don and Bob who were the normal operator and helper.

I quizzed John as to how the training was going. John told me it was going ok and then quickly pointed out that at 7:00 A.M. he would be on vacation and getting ready to go to the river to spend his vacation time fishing. "Hey," I suggested, "While you're in the boat waiting for a bite, how about reviewing the operation of the gluten filters in your mind!"

John looked at me with a certain amount of indignant bewilderment, "I am certainly not going to think about work when I am out on the river fishing!" he commented.

"Why not?" I shot back, "You think about fishing while you're in the plant working, don't you?" Don and Bob roared with laughter and John was shocked into silence. I walked out of the control room with a small smile on my face and headed off to my next stop.

Interestingly, try as I might as the years went by, I could never get John to open up to me nor could I ever get him to optimize his vast potential. I didn't ever give my comment that night much further thought, but it is possible how it was received that night by John (particularly in the face of his peers) was an unforgivable sin in his mind. While I made the comment with a certain amount of fun intended, it was also geared to hit home, which it did. Unfortunately, it was not going to influence or coerce John into thinking about the gluten filters while fishing, so I was playing a game in which I could only lose.

Now after all these years, I think I finally got it! Contentment with who we are is not usually of our own doing. Others have built us up. In the example above, I had not built John up and in fact I likely knocked a few bricks down. Rick Nielson of Blueprint for Life appropriately calls the people who build others up "builders." In this instance for sure, I had not been a builder.

I now understand that I am happy with the face I see in the mirror, not simply because of some God-given self-assurance, but rather because my father, my mother, Miss Leichty, Lyle Bowers, Dr. Charity, Harvey Marxhausen and dozens of other people throughout my life have worked hard to build me up. Without my knowing, they "saved my face" many times when there was opportunity to devalue it. I now thank God for them. Because of them, I do not feel a need to win the gold. I am enough without it.

Aristotle said, "Dignity consists not in possessing honors, but in the consciousness that we deserve them!" Those of us who have been fortunate enough to have "builders" around us have both the knowledge and the required self-esteem to have that consciousness.

Accordingly, we need to recognize our own good fortune and look beyond our own face in the mirror. We need to find the face of another person for whom we can be a "builder!" The true measure of how satisfied we should be with our own reflection should be whether we have helped cause another to be satisfied with his (or her) reflection.

# CHAPTER 33
# The Same Day

In the movie *City Slickers*, three "big city" residents, Mitch Robbins, Phil Berquist, and Ed Furillo (played respectively by Billy Crystal, Daniel Stern, and Bruno Kirby), are spending their vacations on a working ranch, driving cattle from New Mexico to Colorado. As the three urban cowboys are riding along the trail, they begin a discussion of the best and worst days they have ever had. After Mitch and Phil talk about their best and worst days, they try to get Ed to relate his best and worst days. Ed suddenly turns somber and says he doesn't want to play anymore. After some prodding from Mitch and Phil and a period of silence, Ed suddenly begins to speak.

He recounts a day when his mother and father were fighting because she had caught him with another woman—again. Ed then continues. He realized his father was cheating on the entire family, not just Ed's mother. So he told his father they didn't love him or need him. Ed then says his father left and didn't ever bother them again, and he took care of his mother and sister from that day on. He abruptly ends by saying that was his best day.

When Ed is done, he simply rides on. A somewhat bewildered Phil then speaks up. "That was your best day!!! What was your worst?" he inquires in way that seems to ask how things could get any worse.

With no expression change, Ed responds coolly, "The same day."

A number of years ago I was in a meeting where a high-performing manager was asked what quality, other than value characteristics such as honesty or integrity, he thought had most fueled his successes.

"I am an independent thinker who moves rapidly to action, and I can make things happen," was his response. He was then asked what qualities about himself were most limiting and resulted in the most roadblocks being put in his way to success.

"The same thing!" he quickly replied.

It may seem strange to some people to have phenomena such as these, where the best and worst are the very same thing, where success and failure rest on the same issue, and where North indeed meets South at the same place. However, as I have moved through life, I have found a significant number of instances where those very phenomena exist. North and South do in fact often meet at the same place in everyday life. Best and worst times often do occupy the same time and space.

Ever since my late teens, I have been plagued with spinal problems. It seems I have an extremely narrow spinal canal, and that is coupled with a tendency for calcium to be deposited on the inside of the vertebrae until there is no longer room for the spinal cord to move freely. I am told the calcium depositing is fairly common in older folks and narrow spinal cords are not uncommon in the general populous. However, my doctors told me the combination virtually never happens in young people.

Yet there I was in 1982, at The University of Iowa Hospital in Iowa City, Iowa, digesting this diagnosis. I was in my 30s and had two earlier surgeries. Yet I was facing eventual paralysis if Dr. Lehman and the team of orthopedic surgeons could not undo what nature had apparently done.

On August 10, 1982, my physical body went through the worst day of my life. I underwent a six-hour surgery to attempt to correct the spinal condition. When they rolled me back to my room from the recovery process, my wife looked at me and later said she felt I looked as close to death as one can without actually visiting death itself. It was well into the evening when I regained enough of a conscious nature to be aware of my surroundings.

My body had undergone almost extreme conditions for 12 hours—from the morning until evening. In that period of time, however, I was essentially oblivious to the pounding my body had taken. Then in mid-evening when my full senses returned, I began another 12-hour period. This one was of pure misery. I hurt everywhere, and I could not move any part of my body without generating even more excruciating pain. As I struggled through an essentially sleepless night, I vowed I would never subject myself to such treatment again.

But indeed, North did meet South for me on that August day in 1982. Dr. Lehman and The University of Iowa Hospital orthopedic team had miraculously given me back most of my life. Within a few short days, I was walking without numbness, burning, and pain. I was standing erect without most of my lower extremities going to sleep. For well over 20 years now, I have been able to do everything that I need to do of a physical nature and most of the things I want to do. Certainly, I must exercise a degree of caution, but I know the feeling of being restored to wholeness in the face of uncertainly and fear. For all the pain and intense misery, August 10, 1982, had been the best day of my life in returning my body to near physical wholeness.

You have been introduced to Beardstown, Illinois, a number of times in this book. This small city at the confluence of the Sangamon and Illinois Rivers had been a bustling community from the early 1800s. Then in the mid-1980s, the wheels seemed to come off. The hospital shut down and several industries, including major players like the Burlington Northern Railroad and Bohn Aluminum, shut down or moved out. It was not a time to invest in a motel business there, and yet that is exactly what Butch and Patti Seaborn did. They purchased a unique mom-and-pop, 20-room motel from Patti's parents.

When it seemed everything that could go south economically had done so, the largest employer, Oscar Mayer, announced they would be closing down their pork processing facility in town. Patti did not see how the motel could survive, but they plugged along. At the beginning of 1987, Excel purchased the Oscar Mayer facility. When we scheduled our first inspection visit in February of that year to meet with the plant people and also with the town's people, I was told to make all the needed arrangements.

I worked with my counterpart at Oscar Mayer and asked about motel accommodations. Bernie suggested several national motel chains in a neighboring town. "Are there no motels in Beardstown?" I asked.

He replied there was one mom-and-pop operation that he thought was okay, but the corporate Oscar Mayer people usually didn't stay there. I told him we wanted to be a part of the community and if there was a motel in Beardstown to get us rooms there.

Patti later told me when Bernie called her to make those six room reservations, one for himself and five for us (Excel executives), she was petrified. The Mascouten Motel was neat and clean, but that was about as far as it went. There were no phones in the rooms. There were no guest spas or pools, no exercise rooms, no restaurants or lounges, and no

American Express cards were accepted. Patti was certain that after one stay we would not make the Mascouten the motel of choice for future Excel travelers. That was not her *main* concern, however. She was most concerned that we might think that Beardstown was a backward city, and as a result, opt out on the purchase of the plant.

Patti was certain things were going as badly as she feared when all five of us crowded into the small office/front desk area and put our American Express cards on the counter. "I'm sorry," she said apologetically, "but we do not take American Express." I was the only person in the group who could produce another type of card. As she marked up all five rooms to my VISA card, she cringed a little more. It was perhaps the most fearful and possibly the worst day of her career as a motel owner.

The next week when several of us returned to Beardstown, we again stayed at the Mascouten Motel—much to Patti's surprise. We have continued staying at the Mascouten Motel for more than a decade and a half. We don't stay because of the lounges or the spas or the exercise rooms. There aren't any. (Although there were soon phones in the rooms, and they do now take American Express.) We stay because Patti and Butch Seaborn are the neatest people and the absolute best motel hosts in the world. I have been drinking Diet Pepsis and tomato juice, and I have been eating meals in their dining room, kitchen, deck, and even garage longer and more often than in the restaurants in all the other motels and hotels where I have stayed put together. And I have yet to be charged for any of those drinks or meals!

The Mascouten Motel has one of the highest occupancy rates I know of for a modest-sized town. Certainly Excel/Cargill people and associated industries fill a significant number of those rooms on many nights. I know Patti Seaborn has had a number of great days as the host/owner of the motel. Yet I would wager a guess that if she were asked to name her best days, very high up in the running would be a day back in February of 1987 when several Excel executives stepped up to the front desk of the Mascouten Motel.

In the 1950s, because of the nature of the solvent extraction process and the critical characteristics of the solvent (hexane) itself, Cargill had established a "Vessel Entry" permit system to insure the safety of people and property. Because of the critical nature of the environment inside of vessels in the extraction process, an involved safety procedure had to be followed before we could enter the vessels for any purpose. The culmination of this procedure was to secure an okay from a top management person in Cargill before entry. To be sure all this was followed, a permit procedure had been established, and this was enumerated on a special card that was filled out and posted at the vessel site each time an entry was to be made.

In the mid 70s, while switching rail cars for the starch load out at the corn processing plant in Cedar Rapids, Iowa, the railroad switch crew accidentally struck a fire hydrant, breaking it off. Water began flooding the starch load out area. Virgil Holub and Mike Eddy (both of whom you met in Chapter 9) and I were summoned to the area. Knowing the main shutoff valves were located at the bottom of a 12-foot deep manhole just outside of the refinery, we hurried off to that location and lifted the lid off the manhole.

Virgil was a little quicker than Mike or me, and he immediately slid himself through the opening and down the ladder to the valves at the bottom. Mike and I watched from the top. Suddenly about halfway through closing the valve, Virgil stopped and began climbing back out of the hole. Mike and I were somewhat bewildered as we watched Virgil climb up the ladder. Virgil's head and shoulders emerged, and he pulled his hands out and placed them at the side of the manhole in preparation for using them to propel himself out. Just then his arms began quivering. Mike and I each instinctively reached out to assist him. Mike grabbed under one arm, and I reached under the other.

Mike and I had no more than grabbed hold of him when Virgil lost consciousness. All of a sudden, Mike and I were holding on to a 200-plus-pound "dead weight" hanging over a 12-foot deep pit. Try as we might, we did not have the leverage to move Virgil up and out so we just hung on. After a few moments, which seemed like an hour, Roger Fickbohm, our office manager, happened to walk out of the office and cast an eye our way.

Without any knowledge of what had occurred, but seeing our struggle, Roger ran over, dropped to the ground in his dress slacks and tie, and wrapped his arms around Virgil's shoulder just above where Mike and I were hanging on for dear life (literally). Roger then did a sort of Greco-Roman wrestling-style maneuver as he rolled backward on the ground. Roger's move, coupled with Mike's and my lifting action, allowed us to pull Virgil out of the hole.

Virgil soon regained consciousness, and we all just sat there in a stunned and unbelievably thankful state. As we recognized what had occurred, we became even more shocked and thankful. The pit was outside of the refinery door where we occasionally had syrup spills. The syrup or "corn sugar" could find its way into the manhole through cracks around the manhole lid. Once in the manhole, it would run down to the bottom and begin the fermentation process. The fermentation process gobbled up the available oxygen and left the manhole in an oxygen-starved position.

Once Virgil had reached the bottom, he ran out of oxygen. As he was shutting the valve, he began to get light-headed. Had he stayed for only a few more seconds, it is unlikely he would have made it up to where Mike and I could grab him. Moreover, if Virgil would have collapsed at the bottom or fell back in, Mike and I would most certainly have immediately gone down to his assistance. It is quite likely we would all have perished that day. It was the most frightening and yet most thankful day of my Cargill career.

As we later contemplated what had happened, we suggested to the Cargill top operational managers that we should enlarge the permit system to include an "Enclosed or Confined Space" permit. This would recognize that many other atmospheric hazards could be present in vessels, pits, or other enclosed space. Everyone agreed, and the Cargill "Confined Space" permit was born. Today OSHA (the government safety authority) also has confined space safety requirements. I am told these are patterned off the Cargill confined space requirements—those same requirements that were born in Cedar Rapids on that day in the mid 70s. Perhaps Cargill's program was OSHA's pattern and perhaps not. Irrespective, Virgil, Mike, and I all lived to see another day. Equally important, a learning experience also grew out of that day, which quite likely allows other people to see tomorrows that they might otherwise never see.

That worst day/best day experience ultimately had a dramatic effect on a wide range of people. However, another one that had the most profound effect on me personally occurred on a mid-January, Thursday, in 1989. I had been summoned to the St. Louis Airport Marriott Hotel to meet with one of the senior Excel officers. I was the general manager at the facility in Beardstown at that time. I got up early in the morning, as it was the day I held my weekly safety meeting with the management group. We held it at 5:30 that morning so I could get away and to St. Louis by midmorning for the meeting there.

I arrived at the hotel a few minutes early and took a seat in the lobby and began to do some catch-up paperwork. The officer arrived a short time later and suggested we go into the restaurant for a cup of coffee. We did; he ordered a cup of coffee, and I asked for a glass of orange juice.

He then began. "Well, Jim, I'll give you the bad news first. We are removing you from the position of general manager at Beardstown." I knew some of the top brass had some differences of opinion with my leadership style and more specifically with my operational insistence on production limits. Nonetheless, this pronouncement still came as a shock to me. I had seen people fall or be pushed "off of the wagon" before. Most conventional wisdom seemed to be that even if you could run fast enough to catch back up with the wagon that it was unlikely anyone would extend a hand to help you get back inside.

Following this initial "bad news" pronouncement and a few other follow up comments, we reviewed some of my options and then we both left. He departed for a flight to another meeting, and I departed to return to Beardstown.

As I contemplated the impact of this action, I was horrified, angry, and hurt. Certainly my rapid financial growth with the company would come to an end, which it did. My status as an officer was likely to end, which it ultimately did as well. My ability to contribute as I thought I could was likely to end, which it did in that *sense!* An entire range of perks and prestige would likely end, which they did. It was without question the worst "career" day in my history *with* Cargill.

As I looked at the damage that had just been done to my future career, I also began to look back and observe past damage that had occurred *as a result* of my career. I had missed numerous anniversaries and birthdays. My son, Derek, played baseball, and I had missed an entire summer of watching him play. I had missed the opportunity to coach any of Derek's baseball teams in any of the years he played. I had certain new health issues that had arisen. I observed an entire array of things that were anything but worth saving.

I vowed to continue to contribute to the best of my ability to the well-being of Cargill as a company. However, I vowed to focus at least equal attention to the process of contributing to a life rather than simply a living.

Interesting things began to happen. My blood pressure started down and didn't stop until it was to a point where the medical people *asked* me how to do it! I have been able to coach every year of Ryan's and Brandon's baseball careers from T-ball through little league. I fully expect to have similar interactive participation with my grandchildren in their athletic endeavors. I have missed precious few games, plays, concerts, birthdays, anniversaries, or other special family events. I have built a family farming operation that consists of a broad range of livestock and grain farming activities.

I had the opportunity to build a world-class pork processing facility in Taiwan, and in the process, I experienced life in several entirely different cultures. I took the lead in resolving a broad range of the company's environmental issues in this country. I have built relationships and close personal friendships with a whole host of persons. The positive impacts many of these people have had on my life have been related in other stories in this book. Without a career "track" change, I would have encountered few, if any, of these persons, many of whom I now count among my dearest friends.

I was put in a position to be able to contribute to the welfare of the company in an entirely different way. I was now able to do this from the perspective of overall societal well-being rather than simply for company profit or welfare. In the process, I was able to provide innovative solutions to a number of environmental, safety, and economic problems that serve others in an equal proportion to Cargill.

That January day in 1989 cost me dearly in lost earning opportunities as well as position and prestige. Yet it was the best day in my tenure at Cargill.

Most Americans will remember September 11, 2001, in the same manner as December 7, 1941. The terrorist bombing of the World Trade Center Twin Towers in New York was one of the most hideous acts of inhumanity most of us have ever experienced. Yet in the face of death and destruction, the people of New York City, the USA, and the world rallied to show their true character, compassion, and resolve.

In an interview with The Fox News Channel people in December of 2001, near the end of his tenure as mayor of New York City, Rudy Giuliani was asked to review his time as the mayor. "Certainly September 11 had to be the worst day of your career," one of the reporters commented. "What was your best?"

Without hesitation, Mayor Giuliani responded, **"The same day!"**

# CHAPTER 34
# Sunsets

Although I am a native of Iowa, I have adopted Kansas as my home and as the home of my family. There are a number of things about the Kansas climate and Kansas landscape I truly appreciate and love. The sunsets in Kansas are principal in that number. I believe each evening God puts His signature on His environment with the Kansas sunset.

Make no mistake; I have observed lovely sunsets in other parts of the country and world as well. However, the climate, the landscape, and the terrain of Kansas lend themselves to the spectacular nature of beautiful sunsets. In addition, the relative lack of atmospheric pollution in the state should not be overlooked as a key contributor to this beauty.

While I find beauty in all sunsets, those that are the most spectacular stretch across the entire western sky and have multi-colors that include all shades of red, orange, yellow, blue, and purple. What I find truly fascinating are the atmospheric conditions that lead to these particular sunsets. These vast multicolored murals occur when there are a significant number of high, relatively thin clouds across the western sky.

While the sun setting against a clear, blue-sky backdrop is certainly beautiful, the colors are much more concentrated in the oranges and reds, and the intensity is much more concentrated directly around the sun itself. However, with the presence of high thin clouds, the entire western sky from the southern horizon to the northern horizon is ablaze and alive with a broad array of blues and purples as well as the shades of red and orange. It is as if the sun is able to multiply its beauty thousands of times by reflecting off the clouds that stretch from horizon to horizon.

What an incredible message these sunsets say about our lives. It is possible to shine brightly and beautifully ourselves, and there are times when that is necessary and appropriate. However, it is only when we are fully surrounded by others who are not there to obscure our light, but rather to reflect it that we can affect the ultimate fire and light and beauty. Conversely, there are countless times when we have the opportunity to reflect the light of others, thereby increasing their beauty.

As I hope you have been able to observe in reading this book, there are scores of people in my life who have acted as high clouds in extending my fire and reflecting my light. There are also scores of people for whom I was able to be the high cloud and reflect their light and beauty. . Unfortunately, there are those people who acted not as high thin clouds but rather as dense clouds and thereby obscured the entire sky, eliminating my ability to shine individually as well as to reflect light and beauty off them. Sadly, there are also those people for whom I acted as those dense clouds that obscured their skies. To that last group of people, I apologize and ask for their forgiveness.

To those people who allowed me to create beauty in life with me, through me, via me, and sometimes in spite of me, I say thank you. As I reread the various chapters, I am struck by not only the stories and the people about whom I have written, but also the many other people who have surrounded me for these past 50 years or so, yet whose names have not even made it into print, much less been the subject of a story. People like:

- Flight examiner Handly who I encountered for only a two-hour period of interaction in my entire life as he conducted my private pilot check-ride. He did give me a passing grade and thus my license, but more importantly, he gave me one of the best pieces of advice for both flying and life. As we finished the check-ride he admonished me, "The easiest maneuver to make mechanically is the most difficult maneuver psychologically, and that is the 180 degree turn. Do not be afraid to make it in an airplane or in life!"
- Jack Burkhalter was my comrade and recruiting partner for several years, the guy who I had perhaps more fun with than any other person in the organization, and the person who had perhaps the greatest appreciation in the company for my personality. To Jack's friendly chiding about one of my flamboyant suits not exactly being standard fare for Cargill head office attire, I commented, "Hey, you have to stand out in a crowd, Jack."

"Oh," Jack replied, "You do Jim. Believe me, you DO!"

- Jean Williams is a receptionist extraordinaire who operates on the premise that "even if someone doesn't *need* a hug, they can still *use* one." Jean lives her life according to this simple principle both figuratively and literally.

- Jim Greinert made my experience in Taiwan possible with his behind the scenes work in training here at home in the USA and who remains one of the most dedicated trainers and developers of young persons I know. Jim does not get anywhere near the credit he deserves for that skill and dedication.

- Edwin Blosser helped me understand some of the mysteries of God's environment and created in me an appreciation for more critical care and management of the natural elements of God's Creation.

- Shane Sandersfeld is my one and only nephew. I do not see Shane often enough, which is unfortunate since he has absolutely the greatest gift of making people laugh of anyone I know.

The listing could go on of persons with names from Anderson to Zorn. However, even with these and the aforementioned listing of persons, I will still have omitted the names of many others who deserve to be acknowledged and still others whose contributions were made in complete anonymity.

Certainly, the fact is that countless people in our lives teach and encourage us without acknowledgment or even the expectation of acknowledgment. Often it is done without the knowledge that a teaching or encouraging experience has occurred. That we do the same for others should be a humbling and sobering fact. We do not know when or how our actions may impact another at any given time or in any given place. Accordingly, we cannot afford the luxury of disinterested or even casual interaction with other people.

Life is God's greatest gift. However, I do not believe simple physiological existence constitutes "life" as God intended. Real life lifts others up and sustains their spirits as well as their bodies. It acknowledges their inner beings and not simply their human beings.

Just as God puts His signature on His environment with each and every Kansas sunset, He commissions us to "put our signature" on each

and every person we are privileged to touch. If we do so, we will create our own beautiful multicolor mural that will span across the entire
horizon of our lives.

# EPILOGUE

As each of us moves about in our own everyday environment—our own Candor U campus—we encounter countless persons who "invite" us to learn from their experiences. To fail to stop, observe, and take advantage of these learning experiences (simple as they may seem) is to pass up education at its finest. Simple learning experiences are often like prerequisite course work; we learn first the more simple concepts so we can master the more difficult.

Understanding the simple "English" language differences between the Midwest and the Deep South back in the late 60s (as detailed in Chapter 7: "Can You Speak the Language") made work and living more enjoyable and rewarding for me at that time and in that environment. More importantly, it set a stage for being able to better understand the much more complex set of language differences encountered between The United States and The Republic of China decades later.

We do well to accept the challenge to take on each and every learning experience, even those that seem on the surface to be "course work" that we have already completed. The lesson *actually* learned is often not the lesson we *expected* to learn. That it took me decades (and several teachers) to learn the reality of what makes one satisfied with oneself (Chapter 32: "The Face in the Mirror") is testament to this fact.

The entire series of stories in Chapter 33: "The Same Day" demonstrate that the *actual* can often be a full 180 degrees out of phase with the *expected.* Moreover, many of these "same day" experiences, which seem to portray a devastating impact, are really "wake-up" calls to us. If we do in fact "wake up" and seek to find the silver lining in these apparent clouds of darkness, we will often discover that a supremely positive impact can result. Of more significance, this positive impact can often only happen following the initial painful experience.

Perhaps the most humbling consideration, as you encounter each day's activities and experiences and in effect "stroll around your own Candor U campus" is that you will often be that person from whom others can learn. To fail to accept your role as the teacher will most certainly deny others the rewards of learning and could in fact dramatically impact the quality of another person's life or even life itself. Had Harvey Marxhausen not been a teacher of integrity and honesty (Chapter

17: "Bedrock"), he would have denied me (and others) a large measure in our efforts to build our own foundations on these characteristics. Had Dr. Leon Charity not taken me under his wing as a freshman-engineering student in 1966 (Chapter 4: "Miss Leichty et al"), I would never have been put in position to meet my wife. Consequently, the children and grandchildren I so dearly love today would not have been!

Important as each element of learning and teaching is, nothing is as critical for real happiness and satisfaction in life as when the immaterial essence of one's life is based on integrity and one remains true to that "soul" (Chapter 30: "Souls for Sale"). The stories in *Candor U, Class in Session,* and the stories you have and will encounter in your own life experiences, hold up the value of integrity, and they prove genuine integrity is, in fact, the stuff of which real success is made.

I am a Christian, but these stories have largely been encountered in a secular environment and retold in a typical, secular sense. One does not have to be a Christian or hold to a religion of any type to be principled and to possess the characteristics of integrity, honesty, fairness, compassion, and honor. Similarly, one can be supportive and build others up without reference to or reliance on God.

All of that having been said, to not have a role model as Jesus Christ, to not have an assurance of a life after death, and to not have a God upon whom you may call in times of crises, makes living a life based on integrity, honesty, fairness, compassion, and honor a very difficult task. The weights and pressures of the world to abandon these in favor of more self-serving interests for even micro bursts of time will put one to the ultimate test. To have a Perfect Role Model to follow, as well as a God with whom to lighten the load and ease the pressure, is the surest way to "pass the test."

Candor U is not associated with any religious organization. It is by all measures a public institution. However, Christianity offers some very attractive scholarships!

# "MORE STORIES"

Jimmy Dean Roth

# "Goodpliers"
# Remembered

On Tuesday morning January 26, those of us in the Zimmerdale community lost a dear friend and neighbor. At precisely the same time, the community of Heaven gained a new singer, mechanic, teacher, sailor, handyman, preacher, woodworker, writer, repairman, and barbecue cook. Joe "Goodpliers" Kauffman ended his journey on earth and entered into his eternal reward.

I have always marveled at the particular gifts that God gave to Joe. I have never met a person with larger hands than Joe had. It is not surprising to me that Joe used the gift of his hands to such a large measure. There was such a wide array and distribution of things that Joe could do with his hands. Although a lot of Joe's livelihood depended on the use of his hands, much of the time those hands were serving the needs of other people, including me. With only a couple of exceptions, the skills noted in the list above are very much hand dependent. If God needed another "good hands" person in Heaven, he certainly got one when Joe arrived. It is also comforting to know that in like manner, Joe is also now in very "Good Hands."

Another gift God bestowed on Joe was his voice. Anything on the above list that is not hand dependent is voice dependent. Joe had a beautiful singing voice. Moreover, Joe loved to sing (particularly in groups and choirs). The Bible assures us that there is a heavenly choir for Joe to be a part of. Beyond using his voice in song, Joe was also a great talker and he loved to engage people in conversation. Just hearing his joyful greeting on the telephone, "Goodpliers here," always lifted my spirits.

God certainly gave Joe many other gifts besides his hands and his voice. I do not ever recall seeing Joe angry with anyone or anything. God gave him such a love for others and a disposition of peace and servility. Of all God's gifts to Joe, however, the one that I have always thought set him apart from most all of the rest of us was how God gave Joe the ability to keep life in perspective. For most of us, it takes some significant happening (a birth, a critical life event, a death etc.) to put the real meaning of life back into perspective.

Unlike many of us, Joe didn't have to put life back in perspective;

he didn't allow life to get out of perspective in the first place. Joe must surely have had God's help to do this. In His Sermon on the Mount (Matthew 6:25) Jesus commanded us, *"Do not be anxious for your life, as to what you shall eat, or what you shall drink; nor for your body, what you shall put on. . . ."* Joe was not rich in material things, but he did not worry about that. He had confidence that God would provide. Joe had health difficulties for decades that most of us were not even aware of. He took these in stride, made the necessary adjustments, and went on with living his life. I have often perplexed at how God seems to provide for some people on a just-in-time basis. While for so many others of us, He allows us to gather up a big inventory ahead of our needs.

Perhaps the answer to this is also in Jesus' teaching; He didn't stop with the command noted above. He went on with an admonition (Matthew 6:26, 28–29). *"Look at the birds in the air, that they do not sow, neither do they reap, and yet your Heavenly Father feeds them. . . . . . . . . . . . . . . Observe how the lilies of the field grow, they do not toil nor do they spin, yet I say to you that even Solomon in all his glory was not arrayed as one of these."*

As I have reflected on Joe's life, I am convinced that Joe took this admonition very seriously. Joe was always in touch with nature and God's creations. Look back over the things that Joe wrote about in his articles for the *Hesston Record.* When Joe wrote about conditions in Zimmerdale, a part was virtually always something about the beauty of God's natural creations—how He had arrayed the world around Joe (flowers that were in bloom, crop colors that were particularly beautiful, breathtaking Kansas sunsets, etc.).

I am now convinced that Joe was able to look out on these things on a daily basis, recognize the hand of God in their beauty, and get his reassurance that God would provide for him just as He had "fed the birds in the skies and arrayed the lilies of the fields" around him. If we can learn one lesson from Joe, it has to be that it is a far greater gift from God to be able to live in the joy that comes from trusting Him unconditionally than it is to have Him bless us with circumstances and things that make our lives more comfortable.

Joe recognized that comfort and joy are two very different things. That Joe named the boat he worked so hard on for the past couple of years "Joy" is no surprise. Joy was what Joe Kauffman's life was about.

We can know that Joe's joy is indeed now complete, and I'm sure that if we could dial up Heaven, we would hear again that joyful and friendly, "Goodpliers here."

# Jerry Gets Religion

Many times "religion" comes from the North/South collision. Jerry Schneiders was the head of operations in the Excel pork business for several years. In fact, Jerry was my boss longer than any other person in my Cargill career. Moreover, he was (and likely still is) without question one of the foremost operations experts in pork processing in the USA. Certainly, Jerry and I did not always agree, but I always appreciated him, and I felt that he was a strong supporter of mine.

Since I was in charge of engineering when I worked for Jerry, project costs fell in my area. Jerry always felt that I overestimated costs and felt further that new construction always seemed to cost too much (precisely how I had estimated it). In the mid 90s, we were thinking about locating a satellite ham-boning operation in Iowa City, Iowa. Jerry had estimated the cost of this operation at something under $200,000 in his capital request worksheet. I reviewed the worksheet and told him that he was way under in his cost estimate and that I would work him up a good number.

"You use all new stuff, and your work always costs too much. I'll call my old buddy, Knick (Bob Knickerbocker who you have met earlier), and get him to price it out to me. He'll get it done for a couple hundred thousand!" Jerry confidently predicted. Then thinking more about the process, he instructed me not to talk to Knick and not to let Dave Kindt (the engineering manager at the Ottumwa, Iowa, facility) talk to him either.

As the weeks went by, Knick left several messages for me. I did not return any of them. He did finally catch me on the phone. "Hey, Schneiders has me working on this Iowa City deal, and I need to talk to you," Nick said.

"I'm sorry," I replied. "Jerry has a gag order on Kindt and me, and we can't talk to you. Jerry wants to be sure that we do not influence you in any way! Much as I enjoy talking to you Knick, I've got nothing to say on this issue." And I exited the conversation.

Knick continued trying to call me and trying to get me to talk to him. Finally he and I both happened to be in the Beardstown plant the same day and Knick caught up to me. "Look, you rascal," he demanded with a smile but dead seriously, "you have *got* to talk to me about this Iowa City deal. I've got to get a number to Schneiders, *or* he'll kill me. I need to know what your number is!"

I started through the gag order dissertation again before Knick stopped me. "Hey, I need to know whether my number is in the ball park or not. You need to help me out here, friend! What is your number?"

I finally agreed to share my number with Knick, but only if we both wrote our numbers down on a piece of paper and simultaneously handed them to each other with the promise that Knick would not change his after seeing mine. We did so, and with a great sigh of relief, Knick opened my paper and read $650,000. His number was $675,000, and he knew that Jerry was expecting something only a fraction of that.

Knick proceeded to get his quotation to Jerry a few days later, and true to his expectations, Jerry exploded with indignation. The capital cost projection was sending this project south on him. Knick carefully went through each component of his quotation. After Knick assured Jerry that he had not spoken with me until after the development of his final number, Jerry commented that he was going to get me in and see what I thought it would cost. I was summoned to Jerry's office, where I shared my number with him.

The Iowa City project had turned out to be too costly, and we didn't proceed with it. However, Jerry got capital-cost religion that day. I think Jerry was genuinely relieved that he had not started in on the project based on his beginning expectations. Following that episode, he didn't ever challenge one of my capital cost numbers again. In fact, he became the most vociferous defender of them in the division.

Actually, Jerry became my project sales rep. Beyond defending my numbers, when Jerry was in a meeting where I was absent and someone would throw out a ballpark capital cost number on a given project, Jerry would think it through in the sense of the Iowa City project. If the number was out of line, he would either challenge the number or insist that I be brought into the equation before going too far down the road with a wrong number. North had indeed met South for Jerry.

# LEVELING THE PLAYING FIELD

Throughout a part of my career, I had a chance to work with one of the Cargill senior officers. I always found this gentleman to be a very talented manager who had a keen ability to cut directly to the chase in a given issue. Although one would often find oneself on the hot seat in discussions with him, I admired his skill, generally liked the guy, and usually found him to be quite supportive. However, two of his management methods that I did not always appreciate were his tendency to "pile on" a cornered opponent and his intimidating nature, which was made more imposing by his tall stature.

As a Cargill executive, he worked at the Lake Office in Minneapolis. This was an old, Swiss chalet mansion, which I think was purchased by Cargill sometime in the 30s or 40s and turned into a swank executive office facility. One of the time-honored perks associated with being in the Lake Office was access to the dining room where you could purchase a variety of food items at below cost prices. I have never fully understood why the highly paid people populating the Lake Office needed subsidized lunches, but that was the case. It was common knowledge that the officers (and other Lake Office employees) ate better and more inexpensively than any (or certainly most) of the rest of us.

Soon after we had renovated and re-started one of our processing facilities, our plant was selected as one of the sites for the annual Cargill Management Committee facility tours. A group of the highest-ranking officials in Cargill, including the gentleman above noted, came to visit. After a gathering in the conference room for the usual "dog and pony show" followed by a question and answer session, we set out to tour the plant.

You may recall from earlier chapters my fetish for dressing up lunchrooms and locker rooms. When we took over this particular facility, we were presented with a wonderful lunchroom opportunity. The lunchroom was on the second floor with windows looking out over the countryside all along one wall. We proceeded to replace the old tables with nice booths, repainted all walls, put down quarry tile floors, and added a few other simple amenities to make the employees' break time as bright and comfortable as possible. A third party operated the lunchroom, and when approached with what percentage of cut we wanted, I told the operator that we wanted no cut. We simply wanted him to provide as good of food service as possible at as low of a cost as possible for the benefit of our people. Of course, we were very proud of our lunchroom and what it represented.

As the manager, I often gave tours to customers. I always started out in the lunchroom, as I wanted them to recognize how we treated our employees. On this day I was touring the Cargill top brass around, and I started out in the same way. As I displayed the lunchroom amenities and told of all that we had done and why, my officer "friend" began to quiz me. "Do you subsidize the meals for your employees?" he asked.

"No," I replied.

"Oh," he continued, "then your third-party operator pays you rent for the kitchen and lunchroom facilities!"

"No," I replied. "We provide that to the operator."

"Well," he continued, "then the operator does all the lunchroom cleaning and janitorial work I assume."

Having had lots of past experience with this guy, I now knew exactly where he was heading with his line of questioning. He thought he had me cornered, and he was ready to pour it on. The face he was seeing in the mirror was one of an overpowering and skillful debater, and he was loving it. "No, we provide the janitorial services," I calmly replied.

"I suppose that the operator then pays you for the utilities that he uses in the kitchen and the lunchroom," he pressed on. At this time I could see that several of the other officers were beginning to squirm a little. Their body language was saying, "Come on, give Jim a break. We all know that you can bury him!"

"No, we handle all of the utilities for the food service area," I acknowledged.

He was now ready to go for the jugular. "So then you really do subsidize the meals for your employees!" he shot back. Most of the other brass winched in pain. Could this guy not give up? Even they were beginning to become embarrassed.

"Oh," I replied looking my assailant straight in the eyes, "yeah, in that sense, I guess you're right. We are subsidizing the meals for our employees. I'm sorry. I thought you meant, are we subsidizing our meals like yours are subsidized in the Lake Office?"

All of the other officers threw back their heads in riotous laughter. The officer who had been interrogating me looked straight at me. His stone-cold eyes met mine. The twinkle in my eyes and my wry grin said, "Look, you arrogant and insensitive rascal, I gave you every opportunity to back off. You forced me to put you in your place in front of all your peers, and I have thoroughly enjoyed it! Moreover, I didn't do it just for me. I did it for all the "little guys" like me that you have done it to in the past few decades."

He knew that I had won that battle big time. His eyes only acknowledged defeat in the sense that they said, "I won't ever forget this and another day will come." Even though I fully expected that day would come, it had not changed my approach. You see, as he began his interrogation, the face that I immediately saw in the mirror at that particular instance in time was that of an equalizer—sort of a David standing over Goliath, a guy who was about to have an opportunity to level a playing field normally tilted severely the other way. Obviously, I am no more perfect than the general populous is and there are "snapshots in time" when I seek or promote a given face that suits my own immediate and perhaps selfish needs and desires.

# Dick Robinson and the Taiwan Mafia

As you may recall from Chapter 8, Dick Robinson was one of the Americans sent over to Taiwan to assist us in the start up of our pork processing facility there. Dick was a master mechanic and engineering manager. Our challenge in Taiwan was to keep Dick using his hands and not his size 14 feet.

While in Taiwan, we stayed at the Hotel National in TaiChung. This hotel was a very nice, Western-type hotel. For transportation, we were supplied with some older Felung automobiles (Chinese brand probably equivalent to a bottom-of-the-line Ford). Most of the other cars in the hotel parking lot were of the Mercedes, BMW, or Jaguar persuasion. We were told that the Jaguars were the cars of choice for the Taiwan Mafia so we had made it a practice of giving them as wide a berth as possible.

Dick is so work brittle that each day he would also insist on driving the car the 60 kilometers from the hotel in TaiChung to the plant at DaCheng. This was okay with the rest of us as we were content to ride and sleep. As we returned to the parking lot one evening, there were any number of parking places available. However, Dick had to pick one small spot between two fancy cars; the one on the left (the driver's side) was a new shinny black Jaguar that the driver was still sitting in.

Unwilling to heed my pleas to pick another spot, Dick eased into that particular spot. As he stopped the car and prepared to disembark, I reminded him of the likely affiliation of the driver in the Jaguar. "Now for Pete sake, Dick," I admonished, "open your door easy so you don't ding the Jag. We don't need a Mafia bomb put in our car overnight!"

The words were barely out of my mouth, and I had just stepped out of the passenger side, when I heard a loud smash and our little car just shook. I looked over, and to my horror, Dick and the driver's side door were laying up against the shinny black Jag. Dick was using his hands and aggressively making some apologetic hand signals to the Jag driver. In trying to get out, Dick had caught his big foot in the door, lost his balance, and his 240-pound frame fell into the door, which slammed into the Jag.

The next morning instead of all of us trekking around to the back lot to the car, we sent Dick to get the car and the rest of us half jokingly and half seriously waited at the front of the hotel. Our reasoning was that there was no use in all of us being blown up, especially since they were likely only after Dick anyway. Apparently, we got lucky. Either Dick's imposing size or the skillful use of his hands in his apologetic hand signals had again crossed the language barrier. If there was a bomb in the car, it failed to go off!

Obviously, we went through that whole exercise with a good bit of humor and generally good spirit. Suggesting that Dick "talked" his way out of a Mafia confrontation with hand signals (good as he is with his hands) is probably a little farfetched. We assumed that even if this were a Mafia car, they would likely not risk an international scene but rather simply extort a little more from some unsuspecting Taiwan businessman to cover any costs of repairing the Jaguar. In any event, we were all at least a little bit relieved that the Jaguar driver (or his bosses) did not choose to extract any reparation from us.

# PHYLLIS AND THE CANDY DISH

Phyllis Wolfe is one of those people who keep departments together. I had the good fortune to work with Phyllis for over a decade. I often describe her as the secretary for whom I worked. People *not in the know* often get a chuckle out of that "reverse" of who works for whom. People *in the know* realize, while I may have a bit of tongue in cheek in that statement, there is more truth than fiction to it.

Phyllis' office cubical was located centrally among the seven or eight of us managers who she kept in tow and on track. Always a person devoted to superb service, she kept a small candy dish on her desk. Various culinary delights would show up in this dish. Peppermint candies would last about a week. Animal cookies would make it for a few days. Jelly-beans were usually gone in a day. Hershey kisses lasted a few hours. Peanut M&Ms lasted no more than five minutes!

I have often used peanut M&Ms as a premier example of synergism. (Chocolate chip cookies are in the same category, but that is a whole other story.) Peanuts and plain M&Ms go well when consumed together, but peanut M&Ms raise that combination to new heights. I have often maintained even the sound of peanut M&Ms falling into a dish generate saliva and the desire to consume.

Phyllis would open a large bag of peanut M&Ms and dump them in the candy dish on her desk. I have been as far away as 150 feet in the opposite corner of the office and heard that distinct sound. Of course, everyone else within that envelope also heard the same sound. The message was clear. Peanut M&Ms are now in the candy dish; get there within the next five minutes if you want some. It was an unmistakable sound and an unmistakable message!

Contact Jimmy Dean Roth
jimroth@cox.net
or order more copies of this book at

TATE PUBLISHING, LLC

127 East Trade Center Terrace
Mustang, Oklahoma 73064

(888) 361 - 9473

Tate Publishing, LLC


www.tatepublishing.com